N. a. Kirkpatrick
Edinburgh.

7th Dec. 1956.

from Alex.

REMINISCENCES OF SCOTTISH LIFE AND CHARACTER

THE KIRK COLLECTION

REMINISCENCES OF
SCOTTISH LIFE & CHARACTER

by

DEAN RAMSAY

WITH ILLUSTRATIONS IN COLOUR
BY HENRY W. KERR, R.S.A., R.S.W.

SCOTTISH CLASSICS
No. 2

EDINBURGH
ROBERT GRANT & SON, LTD.
126 PRINCES STREET
1947

*

This Edition of "DEAN RAMSAY'S
REMINISCENCES OF SCOTTISH LIFE
AND CHARACTER" *is a reprint of the*
TWENTY-SECOND *Edition. It was the
last edition of which the Dean saw
proof sheets. The Preface is that to the
Fourteenth Edition with the omission of
the footnotes duplicated in the text.*

ACKNOWLEDGMENT   IS   MADE   TO
MESSRS M'LAGAN AND CUMMING, LTD.,
FOR THE USE OF THE COLOUR BLOCKS

PRINTED IN GREAT BRITAIN BY
H. & J. PILLANS & WILSON, 20 BERNARD TERRACE, EDINBURGH

CONTENTS

LIST OF ILLUSTRATIONS

From Paintings by
HENRY W. KERR, R.S.A., R.S.W.

PREFACE

SOME years have now elapsed since I commenced recording REMINISCENCES OF SCOTTISH LIFE AND CHARACTER. The first edition of the work was published in 1857, and consisted entirely of *personal* recollections. Since then it has been gradually increasing, and I now write a preface for the fourteenth edition. Ever since the work passed the ninth edition, I had been most anxious to put it into the hands of a larger class of readers, to whom hitherto the price had offered an obstacle in their possessing it. I was quite aware that many of the most racy anecdotes of the collection came from the Scottish peasantry, and that the peculiar features of that humour which it is the purpose of the book to illustrate still linger in various parts of the country amongst the older occupants of Scotland's lowly dwellings. I was desirous, therefore, before I finally closed my connection with the work, to bring out what might fairly be called a PEOPLE'S EDITION—an edition which, from its price, might be within reach of all classes of my countrymen, and which might form a standing portion of every Scottish cottar's simple library. In this design I have been most kindly and cordially seconded by my valued friends the Publishers, who brought out in a cheap form the tenth, eleventh, twelfth, and thirteenth editions of the work.

One most agreeable circumstance connected with this publication I have already referred to in the introductory chapter, and that is the general and sympathetic communications I have received from Scotchmen, I may literally say, *in all quarters of the world*, sometimes communicating very good examples of Scottish humour, and always expressing their great pleasure in reading, when in distant lands and foreign scenes, anecdotes which reminded them of Scotland and of their ain days of "auld lang syne."

I am, on continued observation, only the more fully persuaded that the characteristic peculiarities of our Scottish people are indicated in a very marked manner by our Scottish anecdotes. I have been anxious that specimens of them should be preserved at this time, as it seems evident that, except they are so preserved, in a few years' time they will have become obsolete. It is to anecdotes which bear upon this question, therefore, that I have directed my attention, and for many such stories I am indebted to the kind interest of correspondents. Several stories which have been sent I have been obliged to omit. They were very pointed and very characteristic, but were not suitable for publication, although in many cases I believe the offence was more in the expression than the sentiment. I might from such communications have greatly increased the size of the volume, but I preferred making a selection of those that were truly characteristic and most direct to the point. And of these I have some more recent communications which, without disturbing the order of the text, I would now preserve by recording them in this preface. For instance, I think our national jealousy of Ritualism furnishes a very characteristic anecdote: A worthy U.P. minister, having received a present of a preaching-gown, considered himself bound to make use of it in divine service, although it was a novelty in the congregation. An old-fashioned lady, who looked with suspicion on this innovation, began to catechise the minister upon his proceedings, and opened the question cautiously. " Weel, sir, ye hae preached in a gown ; div ye ken if Paul ever preached in a gown ? " " 'Deed, Janet," the minister replied, " I wad ask, do *ye* ken gin Paul preached in his breeks ? " She was taken aback, and acknowledged " She could not say." " Weel, I suppose ye wadna hae me to preach without my breeks."

I have heard of a very matter-of-fact view of a remarkable contingency as it had been proposed to one of the older race of Forfarshire matrons. Her nephew had been annoyed by the readiness with which the old lady had always admitted strangers into her pew at church, and broke out petulantly with the exclamation, " Indeed, aunt, I think you would let the devil into your pew if he were to offer himself ! " " And what for no'," was the quiet answer, " gin only *he'd behave himsel'*."

There is a quiet mode of turning the tables upon an inquirer or complainant which I have noticed as characteristic of our countrymen which it is impossible to illustrate except by example. Take this account, which I have received of a well-authenticated case very much in point : A gentleman had sent for the village barber, in extremely hot weather, that he might be shaved by him. He soon perceived that the man was much the worse of drink, as he had, in fact, cut the skin two or three times during the tonsorial operation. He desired to notice this in as delicate a manner as possible, and suggested to the operator, " I think, my friend, the hot weather has made your hand unsteady." He very quietly replied, " Na, sir ; it's no' that sae muckle as that the heat has made *your skin some tender*."

The matter-of-fact reception of a sarcastic injunction given by the lady of the house to a servant-girl in the same family is quite delightful. She had a very delicate and favourite piece of china which she put into the girl's hands to be washed, adding bitterly, as a *sure* mode of impressing the necessity of carefulness, " And when you wash it, be sure to break it all in pieces." The girl accordingly brought back the china, and produced it triumphantly, washed and broken, with the address, " I washt the cheena, mem, but I dinna ken whether the pieces are sma' eneuch."

An old servant's reproach of his *horses*, as joining in the accusations of his enemies against him, was very rich and naïve. I had the story from persons who knew the family in which the complainant was. The two Misses —— kept a carriage, of which they kindly allowed friends to have the use. Charges had lately been carried to his mistresses militating against the sobriety of their old servant, and it was especially insinuated that one public-house *he never passed without a glass*, all which he specially denied. The Misses —— had sent the carriage to fetch some friends who, in coming to the house, had to pass the public-house in question. Unfortunately, instead of driving straight past, the horses quietly, and in spite of Donald's remonstrances, drew up to the door as if too well accustomed to the process. Donald urged them on the way with whip and voice, bitterly accusing the poor animals of betraying him, " Get on, ye *leein'* beasts."

The incongruous application of the term " honest " to a woman convicted of theft, mentioned at page 197, is far surpassed by an application of the term, as told me by a Roman Catholic clergyman. Conversation turning upon the excuses of Satanic influence often

x

CHAPTER I

INTRODUCTORY

I wish my readers always to bear in mind that these Reminiscences are meant to bear upon the changes which would include just such a revolution as that referred to at page 15 in the bonnet practice of Laurence-kirk. There is no pretension to any researches of *antiquarian* character; they are in fact Reminiscences which come almost within personal recognition. A kind friend gave me anecdotes of the past in her hundredth year. In early life I was myself consigned to the care of my granduncle, Sir Alexander Ramsay, residing in Yorkshire, and he was born in 1715; so that I can go pretty far back on my own experience, and have thus become cognisant of many changes which might be expected as a consequence of such experience.

I cannot imagine a better illustration of the sort of change in the domestic relations of life that has taken place in something like the time we speak of, than is shown in the following anecdote, which was kindly communicated to me by Professor MacGregor of the Free Church. I have pleasure in giving it in the Professor's own words :—" I happened one day to be at Panmure Castle when Lord Panmure (now Dalhousie) was giving a treat to a school, and was presented by the Monikie Free Church Deacons' Court with a Bible on occasion of his having cleared them finally of debt on their buildings. Afterwards his Lordship took me into the library, where, among other treasures, we found a handsome folio *Prayer Book* presented to his ancestor Mr Maule of Kelly by the Episcopalian

minister of the district, on occasion of his having, by
Mr Maule's help, been brought out of jail. The coincidence and contrast were curiously interesting."

For persons to take at various intervals a retrospec-
tive view of life, and of the characters they have met
with, seems to be a natural feeling of human nature;
and every one is disposed at times to recall to memory
many circumstances and many individuals which
suggest abundant subjects for reflection. We thus
find recollections of scenes in which we have been
joyous and happy. We think of others with which
we only associate thoughts of sorrow and of sadness.
Amongst these varied emotions we find subjects for
reminiscences, of which we would bury the feelings in
our own hearts as being too sacred for communication
with others. Then, again, there are many things of
the past concerning which we delight to take counsel
with friends and contemporaries. Some persons are
disposed to go beyond these personal communications
with friends, and having through life been accustomed
to write down memoranda of their own feelings, have
published them to the world. Many interesting works
have thus been contributed to our literature by writers
who have sent forth volumes in the form of *Memoirs
of their Own Times*, *Personal Recollections*, *Remarks upon
Past Scenes*, etc., etc. It is not within the scope of this
work to examine these, nor can I specify the many
communications I have from different persons, both at
home and in our colonial possessions; in fact, the
references in many cases have been lost or mislaid.
But I must acknowledge, however briefly, my obliga-
tions to Dr Carruthers, Inverness, and to Dr Cook,
Haddington, who have favoured me with valuable
contributions.

Now, when we come to examine the general question

2

of memoirs connected with contemporary history, no work is better known in connection with this department of Scottish literature than the *History of his Own Times*, by my distinguished relative, Dr Gilbert Burnett, Bishop of Salisbury. Bishop Burnett's father, Lord Crimond, was third son of my father's family, the Burnetts of Leys, in Kincardineshire. There is now at Crathes Castle, the family seat, a magnificent full-length portrait of the Bishop in his robes, as Prelate of the Garter, by Sir Godfrey Kneller. It was presented by himself to the head of his family. But, as one great object of the Bishop's history was to laud and magnify the personal character and public acts of William of Orange, his friend and patron, and as William was held in special abhorrence by the Jacobite party in Scotland, the Bishop holds a prominent, and, with many, a very odious position in Scottish Reminiscences; in fact, he drew upon himself and upon his memory the determined hatred and unrelenting hostility of adherents to the Stuart cause. They never failed to abuse him on all occasions, and I recollect old ladies in Montrose, devoted to the exiled Prince, with whom the epithet usually applied to the Prelate was that of "Leein' Gibby." [1]

Such language has happily become a "Reminiscence." Few would be found now to apply such an epithet to the author of the *History of his Own Times*, and certainly it would not be applied on the ground of the Jacobite principles to which he was opposed. But a curious additional proof of this hostility of Scottish Jacobites to the memory of Burnett has lately come to light. In a box of political papers lately found at Brechin Castle, belonging to the Panmure branch of the family, who, in '15, were forfeited on the ground

[1] Lying Gilbert.

3

of their Jacobite opinions and adherence to the cause of Charles Edward, there has been found a severe and bitter supposed *epitaph* for Bishop Burnett. By the kindness of the Earl of Dalhousie I was permitted to see this epitaph, and, if I chose, to print it in this edition. I am, however, unwilling to stain my pages with such an ungenerous and, indeed, I may say, so scurrilous a representation of the character of one who, in the just opinion of our Lyon King-at-Arms, himself a Burnett of the Kemnay branch, has characterised the Bishop of Salisbury as " true and honest, and far beyond the standard of his times as a Clergyman and as a Bishop." But the epitaph found in these Panmure papers shows clearly the prejudices of the age in which it was written, and in fact only embodies something of that spirit and of those opinions which we have known as still lingering in our own Reminiscences.

If it were not on my part a degree of presumption, I might be inclined to consider myself in this volume a fellow-labourer with the late accomplished and able Mr Robert Chambers. In a very limited sphere it takes a portion of the same field of illustration. I should consider myself to have done well if I shall direct any of my readers to his able volumes. Whosoever wishes to know what this country really was in times past, and to learn, with a precision beyond what is supplied by the narratives of history, the details of the ordinary current of our social, civil, and national life, must carefully study the *Domestic Annals of Scotland*. Never before were a nation's domestic features so thoroughly portrayed. Of those features the specimens of quaint Scottish humour still remembered are unlike anything else, but they are fast becoming obsolete, and my motive for this publication has been an endeavour to preserve marks of the past which would of themselves

4

soon become obliterated, and to supply the rising generation with pictures of social life, faded and indistinct to their eyes, but the strong lines of which an older race still remember. By thus coming forward at a favourable moment, no doubt many beautiful specimens of SCOTTISH MINSTRELSY have in this manner been preserved from oblivion by the timely exertions of Bishop Percy, Ritson, Walter Scott, and others. Lord Macaulay, in his preface to *The Lays of Ancient Rome*, shows very powerfully the tendency in all that lingers in the memory to become obsolete, and he does not hesitate to say that " Sir Walter Scott was but *just in time* to save the precious relics of the minstrelsy of the Border."

It is quite evident that those who have in Scotland come to an advanced age, must have found some things to have been really changed about them, and that on them great alterations have already taken place. There are some, however, which yet may be in a transition state; and others in which, although changes are threatened, still it cannot be said that the changes are begun. I have been led to a consideration of impending alterations as likely to take place, by the recent appearance of two very remarkable and very interesting papers on subjects closely connected with great social Scottish questions, where a revolution of opinion may be expected. These are two articles in *Recess Studies* (1870), a volume edited by our distinguished Principal, Sir Alexander Grant. One essay is by Sir Alexander himself, upon the " Endowed Hospitals of Scotland"; the other by the Rev. Dr Wallace of the Greyfriars, upon " Church Tendencies in Scotland." It would be quite irrelevant for me to enlarge here upon the merits of those articles. No one could study them attentively without being impressed

5

with the ability and power displayed in them by the authors, their grasp of the subjects, and their fair impartial judgment upon the various questions which come under their notice.

From these able disquisitions, and from other prognostics, it is quite evident that sounder principles of political economy and accurate experience of human life show that much of the old Scottish hospital system was quite wrong and must be changed. Changes are certainly going on, which seem to indicate that the very hard Presbyterian views of some points connected with Church matters are in transition. I have elsewhere spoken of a past sabbatarian strictness, and I have lately received an account of a strictness in observing the national fast-day, or day appointed for preparation in celebrating Holy Communion, which has in some measure passed away. The anecdote adduced the example of two drovers who were going on very quietly together. They had to pass through a district whereof one was a parishioner, and during their progress through it the one whistled with all his might, the other screwed up his mouth without emitting a single sound. When they came to a burn, the silent one, on then crossing the stream, gave a skip, and began whistling with all his might, exclaiming with great triumph to his companion, " I'm beyond the parish of Forfar now, and I'll whistle as muckle as I like." It happened to be the Forfar parish fast-day. But a still stricter observance was shown by a native of Kirkcaldy, who, when asked by his companion drover in the south of Scotland " why he didna whistle," quietly answered, " I canna, man; it's our fast-day in Kirkcaldy." I have an instance of a very grim assertion of extreme sabbatarian zeal. A maid-servant had come to a new place, and on her

6

mistress quietly asking her on Sunday evening to wash up some dishes, she indignantly replied, " Mem, I hae dune mony sins, and hae mony sins to answer for; but, thank God, I hae never been sae far left to mysell as to wash up dishes on the Sabbath day."

I hope it will not for a moment be supposed we would willingly throw any ridicule or discouragement on the Scottish national tendencies on the subject, or that we are not proud of Scotland's example of a sacred observance of the fourth commandment in the letter and the spirit. We refer now to injudicious extremes, such, indeed, as our Lord condemned, and which seem a fair subject for notice amongst Scottish peculiarities. But the philosophy of the question is curious. Scotland has ever made her boast of the simplest form of worship, and a worship free from ceremonial, more even than the Church of England, which is received as, in doctrine and ritual, the Church of the Reformation. In some respects, therefore, may you truly say the only standing recognised observance in the ceremonial part of Presbyterian worship is the Sabbath day—an observance which has been pushed in times past even beyond the extreme of a spirit of Judaism, as if the sabbatical ceremonial were made a substitute for all other ceremony. In this, as well as in other matters which we have pointed out, what changes have taken place, what changes are going on! It may be difficult to assign precise causes for such changes having taken place among us, and that during the life-time of individuals now living to remember them. It has been a period for many changes in manners, habits, and forms of language, such as we have endeavoured to mark in this volume. The fact of such changes is indisputable, and sometimes it is difficult not only to assign the causes for them, but

7

even to describe in what the changes themselves consist. They are gradual, and almost imperceptible. Scottish people lose their Scotchness; they leave home, and return without those expressions and intonations, and even peculiarity of voice and manner, which used to distinguish us from Southern neighbours. In all this, I fear, we lose our originality. It has not passed away, but with every generation becomes less like the real type.

I would introduce here a specimen of the precise sort of changes to which I would refer, as an example of the reminiscences intended to be introduced into these pages. We have in earlier editions given an account of the pains taken by Lord Gardenstone to extend and improve his rising village of Laurencekirk; amongst other devices he had brought down, as settlers, a variety of artificers and workmen from England. With these he had introduced a *hatter* from Newcastle; but on taking him to church next day after his arrival, the poor man saw that he might decamp without loss of time, as he could not expect much success in his calling at Laurencekirk; in fact, he found Lord Gardenstone's and his own the only hats in the kirk—the men all wore then the flat Lowland bonnet. But how quickly times change! My excellent friend, Mr Gibbon of Johnstone, Lord Gardenstone's own place, which is near Laurencekirk, tells me that at the present time *one* solitary Lowland bonnet lingers in the parish.

Hats are said to have been first brought into Inverness by Duncan Forbes of Culloden, the Lord President, who died in 1747. Forbes is reported to have presented the provost and bailies with cocked hats, which they wore only on Sundays and council days. About 1760 a certain Deacon Young began

8

daily to wear a hat, and the country people crowding round him, the Deacon used humorously to say, " What do you see about me, sirs ? Am I not a mortal man like yourselves ? " The broad blue bonnets I speak of long continued to be worn in the Highland capital, and are still occasionally to be seen there, though generally superseded by the Glengarry bonnet and ordinary hat. It is a minor change, but a very decided one.

The changes which have taken place, and which give rise to such " Reminiscences," are very numerous, and meet us at every turn in society. Take, for example, the case of our Highland chieftains. We may still retain the appellation, and talk of the chiefs of Clanranald, of Glengarry, etc. But how different is a chieftain of the present day, even from some of those of whom Sir Walter Scott wrote as existing so late as 1715 or 1745 ! Dr Gregory (of immortal *mixture* memory) used to tell a story of an old Highland chieftain, intended to show how such Celtic potentates were, even in his day, still inclined to hold themselves superior to all the usual considerations which affected ordinary mortals. The doctor, after due examination, had, in his usual decided and blunt manner, pronounced the liver of a Highlander to be at fault, and to be the cause of his ill-health. His patient, who could not but consider this as taking a great liberty with a Highland chieftain, roared out : " And what the devil is it to you whether I have a liver or not ? " But there is the case of dignity in Lowland Lairds as well as clan-headship in Highland Chiefs. In proof of this, I need only point to a practice still lingering amongst us of calling landed proprietors, not as Mr So-and-so, but by the names of their estates. I recollect, in my early days, a number of our proprietors were always so designated. Thus, it was not as Mr Carnegie, Mr Douglas, Mr Irvine, etc., but as Craigo, Tillwhilly, Drum, etc.

An amusing application of such a territorial denominative system to the locality of London was narrated to me by a friend who witnessed it. A Scottish gentleman, who had never been in the metropolis, arrived fresh from the Highlands, and met a small party at the house of a London friend. A person was present of most agreeable manners, who delighted the Scotsman exceedingly. He heard the company frequently referring to this gentleman's residence in Piccadilly, to his house in Piccadilly, and so on. When addressed by the gentleman, he commenced his reply, anxious to pay him all due respect : " Indeed, Piccadilly," etc. He supposed Piccadilly must be his own territorial locality. Another instance of mistake, arising out of Scottish ignorance of London ways, was made by a North Briton on his first visit to the great city. He arrived at a hotel in Fleet Street, where many of the country coaches then put up. On the following morning he supposed that such a crowd as he encountered could only proceed from some " occasion," and must pass off in due time. Accordingly, a friend from Scotland found him standing in a doorway, as if waiting for some one. His countryman asked him what made him stand there. To which he answered : " Ou, I was just stan'ing till the kirk had scaled." The ordinary appearance of his native borough made the crowd of Fleet Street suggest to him the idea of a church crowd passing out to their several homes, called in Scotland a " kirk scaling." A London street object called forth a . similar simple remark from a Scotsman. He had come to London on his way to India, and for a few days had time to amuse himself by sightseeing before his departure. He had been much struck with the appearance of the mounted sentinels at the Horse Guards, Whitehall, and bore them in remembrance during his Eastern sojourn. On his return, after a period of thirty years, on passing the Horse Guards, he looked up to one, and seeing him, as he thought, unchanged as to horse, position, and accoutrements, he exclaimed: "Od, freend, ye hae had a lang spell on't sin' I left," supposing him to be the identical sentinel he had seen before he sailed.

It is interesting to preserve national peculiarities which are thus passing away from us. One great pleasure I have had in their collection, and that is the numerous and sympathetic communications I have received from Scotsmen, I may literally say from Scotsmen *in all quarters of the world*; sometimes communicating very good examples of Scottish humour, and always expressing their great pleasure in reading, when in distant lands and foreign scenes, anecdotes which reminded them of Scotland, and of their ain days of "auld lang syne."

There is no mistaking the national attachment so strong in the Scottish character. Men return after long absence, in this respect, unchanged; whilst absent, Scotsmen *never* forget their Scottish home. In all varieties of lands and climates their hearts ever turn towards the "land o' cakes and brither Scots." Scottish festivals are kept with Scottish feeling on "Greenland's icy mountains" or "India's coral strand." I received an amusing account of an ebullition of this patriotic feeling from my late noble friend the Marquis of Lothian, who met with it when travelling in India. He happened to arrive at a station upon the eve of St Andrew's Day, and received an invitation to join a Scottish dinner party in commemoration of old Scotland. There was a great deal of Scottish enthusiasm. There were *seven* sheep-heads (singed) down the table; and Lord Lothian told me that after dinner he sang with great applause " The Laird o' Cockpen."

Another anecdote arising out of Scotsmen meeting in distant lands, is rather of a more serious character, and used to be told with exquisite humour by the late lamented Dr Norman Macleod. A settler in Australia, who for a long time had heard nothing of his Scottish kith and kin, was delighted at the arrival of a country-man direct from his own part of the country. When he met with him, the following conversation took place between them:—*Q.* " Ye ken my fouk, friend; can ye tell me gin my faather's alive?" *A.*—" Hout, na; he's deed." *Q.*—" Deed! What did he dee o'? Was it fever?" *A.*—" Na, it wasna fever." *Q.*—" Was it cholera?" *A.*—" Na." The question being pressed, the stranger drily said, " Sheep," and then he accompanied the ominous word by delicately and significantly pointing to the jugular under his ear. The man had been hanged for sheep-stealing!

It must always be amusing for Scotsmen to meet in distant lands, and there to play off on each other the same dry, quaint humour which delighted them in their native land, and in their early days at home. An illustration of this remark has been communicated by a kind correspondent at Glasgow. Mrs Hume, a true Scot, sends me the following dialogue, accompanied by a very clever etching of the parties, from the Melbourne *Punch*, August 17, 1871, headed " Too Poor—*Night of Waverley Concert.*"

Southron.—You here, Mac! you ought to have been at the concert, you know. Aren't you one of the ' Scots wha hae?'

Mac.—Indeed no. I'm ane o' the Scots wha hae na,
or I wadna be here the nicht.

He would not have stayed at home if he had been
one of the " Scots wha hae."

I am assured that the genuineness of the following
anecdote is unquestionable, as my informant received
it from the person to whom it occurred. A popular
Anglican Nonconformist minister was residing with
a family in Glasgow while on a visit to that city,
whither he had gone on a deputation from the Wes-
leyan Missionary Society. After dinner, in reply to
an invitation to partake of some fine fruit, he mentioned to the family a curious circumstance concerning
himself, viz., that he had never in his life tasted an
apple, pear, grape, or indeed any kind of green fruit.
This fact seemed to evoke considerable surprise from
the company, but a cautious Scotsman, of a practical,
matter-of-fact turn of mind, who had listened with
much unconcern, drily remarked, " It's a peety but
ye had been in Paradise, and there micht na hae been
ony faa." I have spoken elsewhere of the cool matter-
of-fact manner in which the awful questions connected
with the funerals of friends are often approached by
Scottish people, without the least intention or purpose
of being irreverent or unfeeling. By the kindness of
Mr Lyon, I am enabled to give an authentic anecdote
of a curious character, illustrative of this habit of mind,
and I cannot do better than give it in his own words :—
" An old tenant of my late father, George Lyon of
Wester Ogil, many years ago, when on his deathbed,
and his end near at hand, his wife thus addressed him :
' Willie, Willie, as lang as ye can speak, tell us are ye
for your burial-baps round or *square* ? ' Willie having
responded to this inquiry, was next asked if the *murners*
were to have *glooes* (gloves) or mittens, the former

being articles with fingers, the latter having only a thumbpiece; and Willie, having also answered this question, was allowed to depart in peace."

There could not be a better example of this familiar handling, without meaning offence, than one which has just been sent to me by a kind correspondent. I give her own words. " Happening to call on a poor neighbour, I asked after the children of a person who lived close by. She replied, " They're no hame yet; gaed awa to the English kirk to get *a clap o' the heid.*" It was the day of *confirmation* for St Paul's. This definition of the ' outward and visible sign ' would look rather odd in the catechism. But the poor woman said it from no disrespect; it was merely her way of answering my question." But remarks on serious subjects often go to deeper views of religious matters than might be expected from the position of the parties and the terms made use of.

Of the wise and shrewd judgment of the Scottish character, as bearing upon religious pretensions, I have an apt example from my friend Dr Norman Macleod. During one of the late revivals in Scotland, a small farmer went about preaching with much fluency and zeal the doctrine of a " full assurance " of faith, and expressed his belief of it for himself in such extravagant terms as few men would venture upon who were humble and cautious against presumption. The " preacher," being personally rather remarkable as a man of greedy and selfish views in life, excited some suspicion in the breast of an old sagacious countryman, a neighbour of Dr Macleod, who asked him what *he* thought of John as a preacher, and of his doctrine. Scratching his head, as if in some doubt, he replied, " I'm no verra sure o' Jock. I never ken't a man *sae sure o' Heaven, and sae sweert to be gaing tae't.*"

He showed his sagacity, for John was soon after in prison for theft.

Another story gives a good idea of the Scottish matter-of-fact view of things being brought to bear upon a religious question without meaning to be profane or irreverent. Dr Macleod was on a Highland loch when a storm came on which threatened serious consequences. The doctor, a large powerful man, was accompanied by a clerical friend of diminutive size and small appearance, who began to speak seriously to the boatmen of their danger, and proposed that all present should join in prayer. " Na, na," said the chief boatman; " let the *little* ane gang to pray, but first the big ane maun tak an oar." Illustrative of the same spirit was the reply of a Scotsman of the genuine old school, " Boatie " of Deeside, of whom I have more to say, to a relative of mine. He had been nearly lost in a squall, and saved after great exertion, and was told by my aunt that he should be grateful to providence for his safety. The man, not meaning to be at all ungrateful, but viewing his preservation in the purely hard matter-of-fact light, quietly answered, " Weel, weel, Mrs Russell; Providence here or Providence there, an I hadna worked sair mysell I had been drouned."

Old Mr Downie, the parish minister of Banchory, was noted, in my earliest days, for his quiet pithy remarks on men and things, as they came before him. His reply to his son, of whose social position he had no very exalted opinion, was of this class. Young Downie had come to visit his father from the West Indies, and told him that on his return he was to be married to a lady whose high qualities and position he spoke of in extravagant terms. He assured his father that she was " quite young, was very rich, and very beautiful." "Aweel, Jemmy," said the old man, very quietly and very slily, "I'm thinking there maun be some *faut.*" Of the dry sarcasm we have a good example in the quiet utterance of a good Scottish phrase by an elder of a Free Kirk lately formed. The minister was an eloquent man, and had attracted one of the town-council, who, it was known, hardly ever entered the door of a church, and now came on motives of curiosity. He was talking very grand to some of the congregation : "Upon my word, your minister is a very eloquent man. Indeed, he will quite convert me." One of the elders, taking the word in a higher sense than the speaker intended, quietly replied, "Indeed, Bailie, there's *muckle need.*"

A kind correspondent sends me an illustration of this quaint matter-of-fact view of a question as affecting the sentiments or the feelings. He tells me he knew an old lady who was a stout large woman, and who with this state of body had many ailments, which she bore cheerfully and patiently. When asked one day by a friend, "How she was keeping," she replied, "Ou, just middling; there's *ower muckle o' me* to be a' weel at ae time." No Engishwoman would have given such an answer. The same class of character is very strongly marked in a story which was told by Mr Thomas Constable, who has a keen appreciation of a good Scottish story, and tells it inimitably. He used to visit an old lady who was much attenuated by long illness, and on going upstairs one tremendously hot afternoon, the daughter was driving away the flies, which were very troublesome, and was saying, "Thae flies will eat up a' that remains o' my puir mither." The old lady opened her eyes, and the last words she spoke were, "What's left o' me's guid eneuch for them."

The spirit of caution and wariness by which the Scottish character is supposed to be distinguished has given rise to many of these national anecdotes.

Certainly this cautious spirit thus pervaded the opinions of the Scottish architect who was called upon to erect a building in England upon the long-lease system, so common with Anglican proprietors, but quite new to our Scottish friend. When he found the proposal was to build upon the tenure of 999 years, he quietly suggested, " Culd ye no mak it a *thousand?* 999 years'll be slippin' awa'."

But of all the cautious and careful answers we ever heard of was one given by a carpenter to an old lady in Glasgow, for whom he was working, and the anecdote is well authenticated. She had offered him a dram, and asked him whether he would have it then or wait till his work was done : " Indeed, mem," he said, " there's been sic a power o' sudden deaths lately that I'll just tak' it now." He would guard against contingency and secure his dram.

The following is a good specimen of the same humour :—A minister had been preaching against covetousness and the love of money, and had frequently repeated how " love of money was the root of all evil." Two old bodies walking home from church—one said, " An' wasna the minister strang upo' the money ? " " Nae doubt," said the other, rather hesitatingly ; and added, " ay, but it's grand to hae the wee bit siller in your haund when ye gang an errand."

I have still another specimen of this national, cool, and deliberative view of a question, which seems characteristic of the temperament of our good countrymen. Some time back, when it was not uncommon for challenges to be given and accepted for insults, or

supposed insults, an English gentleman was entertaining a party at Inverness with an account of the
wonders he had seen and the deeds he had performed
in India, from whence he had lately arrived. He enlarged particularly upon the size of the tigers he had
met with at different times in his travels, and by way
of corroborating his statements, assured the company
that he had shot one himself considerably above forty
feet long. A Scottish gentleman present, who thought
that these narratives rather exceeded a traveller's
allowed privileges, coolly said that no doubt those
were very remarkable tigers; but that he could assure
the gentleman there were in that northern part of the
country some wonderful animals, and, as an example,
he cited the existence of a skate-fish captured off
Thurso, which exceeded half-an-acre in extent. The
Englishman saw this was intended as a sarcasm against
his own story, so he left the room in indignation,
and sent his friend, according to the old plan, to de-
mand satisfaction or an apology from the gentleman,
who had, he thought, insulted him. The narrator of
the skate story coolly replied, " Weel, sir, gin yer
freend will tak' a few feet aff the length o' his tiger,
we'll see what can be dune about the breadth o' the
skate." He was too cautious to commit himself to a
rash or decided course of conduct. When the tiger
was shortened, he would take into consideration a
reduction of superficial area in his skate.

A kind correspondent has sent me about as good a
specimen of dry Scottish quiet humour as I know.
A certain Aberdeenshire laird, who kept a very good
poultry-yard, could not command a fresh egg for his
breakfast, and felt much aggrieved by the want. One
day, however, he met his grieve's wife with a nice
basket, and very suspiciously going towards the

market; on passing and speaking a word, he was enabled to discover that her basket was full of beautiful white eggs. Next time he talked with his grieve, he said to him, " James, I like you very well, and I think you serve me faithfully, but I cannot say I admire your wife." To which the cool reply was, " Oh, 'deed, sir, I'm no' surprised at that, for I dinna muckle admire her mysel'."

An answer very much resembling this, and as much to the point, was that of a gudewife on Deeside, whose daughter had just been married and had left her for her new home. A lady asked the mother very kindly about her daughter, and said she hoped she liked her new home and new relations. " Ou, my lady, she likes the parish weel eneuch, but she doesna think muckle o' her *man*! "

The natives of Aberdeenshire are distinguished for the two qualities of being very acute in their remarks and very peculiar in their language. Any one may still gain a thorough knowledge of Aberdeen dialect and see capital examples of Aberdeen humour. I have been supplied with a remarkable example of this combination of Aberdeen shrewdness with Aberdeen dialect. In the course of the week after the Sunday on which several elders of an Aberdeen parish had been set apart for parochial offices, a knot of the parishioners had assembled at what was in all parishes a great place of resort for idle gossiping—the smiddy or blacksmith's workshop. The qualifications of the new elders were severely criticised. One of the speakers emphatically laid down that the minister should not have been satisfied, and had in fact made a most unfortunate choice. He was thus answered by another parish oracle—perhaps the schoolmaster, perhaps a weaver: " Fat better culd the man dee nir he's dune?

He bud tae big's dyke wi' the feal at fit o't." He meant there was no choice of material—he could only take what offered.

By the kindness of Dr Begg, I have a most amusing anecdote to illustrate how deeply long-tried associations were mixed up with the habits of life in the older generation. A junior minister having to assist at a church in a remote part of Aberdeenshire, the parochial minister (one of the old school) promised his young friend a good glass of whisky-toddy after all was over, adding slily and very significantly, " and gude *smuggled* whusky." His Southron guest thought it incumbent to say, " Ah, minister, that's wrong, is it not? You know it is contrary to Act of Parliament." The old Aberdonian could not so easily give up his fine whisky to what he considered an unjust interference; so he quietly said, " Oh, Acts o' Parliament lose their breath before they get to Aberdeenshire."

There is something very amusing in the idea of what may be called the " fitness of things," in regard to snuff-taking, which occurred to an honest Highlander, a genuine lover of sneeshin. At the door of the Blair-Athole Hotel he observed standing a magnificent man in full tartans, and noticed with much admiration the wide dimensions of his nostrils in a fine upturned nose. He accosted him, and, as his most complimentary act, offered him his mull for a pinch. The stranger drew up, and rather haughtily said : " I never take snuff." " Oh," said the other, " that's a peety, for there's grand *accommodation* ! " [1]

I don't know a better example of the sly sarcasm than the following answer of a Scottish servant to the

[1] This anecdote has been illustrated, as taken from these pages, by a very clever sketch of the Highlander and his admirer, in a curious publication at Liverpool called *The Tobacco Plant*, and devoted to the interests of smoking and snuffing.

violent command of his enraged master. A well-known coarse and abusive Scottish law functionary, when driving out of his grounds, was shaken by his carriage coming in contact with a large stone at the gate. He was very angry, and ordered the gatekeeper to have it removed before his return. On driving home, however, he encountered another severe shock by the wheels coming in contact with the very same stone, which remained in the very same place. Still more irritated than before, in his usual coarse language he called the gatekeeper, and roared out: "You rascal, if you don't send that beastly stone to h—, I'll break your head." "Well," said the man quietly, and as if he had received an order which he had to execute, and without meaning anything irreverent, "aiblins gin it were sent to heevan *it wad be mair out o' your Lordship's way.*"

I think about as cool a Scottish "aside" as I know, was that of the old dealer who, when exhorting his son to practise honesty in his dealings, on the ground of its being the "best policy," quietly added, "*I hae tried baith.*"

In this work frequent mention is made of a class of old *ladies*, generally residing in small towns, who retained till within the memory of many now living the special characteristics I have referred to. Owing to local connection, I have brought forward those chiefly who lived in Montrose and the neighbourhood. But the race is extinct; you might as well look for hoops and farthingales in society as for such characters now. You can scarcely imagine an old lady, however quaint, now making use of some of the expressions recorded in the text, or saying, for the purpose of breaking up a party of which she was tired, from holding bad cards, "We'll stop now, bairns; I'm no enter-

teened;" or urging more haste in going to church
on the plea, "Come awa, or I'll be ower late for the
'wicked man'"—her mode of expressing the commencement of the service.

Nothing could better illustrate the quiet pawky
style for which our countrymen have been distinguished, than the old story of the piper and the wolves.
A Scottish piper was passing through a deep forest.
In the evening he sat down to take his supper. He had
hardly begun, when a number of hungry wolves,
prowling about for food, collected round him. In
self-defence, the poor man began to throw pieces of
his victuals to them, which they greedily devoured.
When he had disposed of all, in a fit of despair he took
his pipes and began to play. The unusual sound
terrified the wolves, which, one and all, took to their
heels and scampered off in every direction: on observing which, Sandy quietly remarked, "Od, an I'd
kenned ye liket the pipes sae weel, I'd a gien ye a
spring *afore* supper."

This imperturbable mode of looking at the events
of life is illustrated by perhaps the *most* cautious answer
on record, of the Scotsman who, being asked if he
could play the fiddle, warily answered, "He couldna
say, for he had never tried." But take other cases.
For example: One tremendously hot day, during the
old stage-coach system, I was going down to Portobello, when the coachman drew up to take in a gentleman who had hailed him on the road. He was
evidently an Englishman—a fat man, and in a perfect
state of "thaw and dissolution" from the heat and
dust. He wiped himself, and exclaimed, as a remark
addressed to the company generally, "D—d hot it is."
No one said anything for a time, till a man in the
corner slily remarked, "I dinna doubt, sir, but it

may." The cautiousness against committing himself unreservedly to any proposition, however plausible, was quite delicious.

A more determined objection to giving a categorical answer occurred, as I have been assured, in regard to a more profound question. A party travelling on a railway got into deep discussion on theological questions. Like Milton's spirits in Pandemonium, they had

> " Reason'd high
> Of providence, fore-knowledge, will, and fate—
> Fix'd fate, free-will, fore-knowledge absolute ;
> And found no end, in wand'ring mazes lost."

A plain Scotsman present seemed much interested in these matters, and having expressed himself as not satisfied with the explanations which had been elicited in the course of discussion on a particular point regarding predestination, one of the party said to him that he had observed a minister, whom they all knew, in the adjoining compartment, and that when the train stopped at the next station a few minutes, he could go and ask *his* opinion. The good man accordingly availed himself of the opportunity to get hold of the minister, and lay their difficulty before him. He returned in time to resume his own place, and when they had started again, the gentleman who had advised him, finding him not much disposed to voluntary communication, asked if he had seen the minister. " O ay," he said, " he had seen him." " And did you propose the question to him ? " " O ay." " And what did he say ? " " Oh, he just said he didna ken ; and what was mair he didna *care* ! "

I have received the four following admirable anecdotes, illustrative of dry Scottish pawky humour, from an esteemed minister of the Scottish Church, the Rev.

W. Mearns of Kinneff. I now record them nearly in the same words as his own kind communication. The anecdotes are as follows :—An aged minister of the old school, Mr Patrick Stewart, one Sunday took to the pulpit a sermon without observing that the first leaf or two were so worn and eaten away that he couldn't decipher or announce the text. He was not a man, however, to be embarrassed or taken aback by a matter of this sort, but at once intimated the state of matters to the congregation : "My brethren, I canna tell ye the text, for the mice hae eaten it; but we'll just begin whaur the mice left aff, and when I come to it I'll let you ken."

In the year 1843, shortly after the Disruption, a parish minister had left the manse and removed to about a mile's distance. His pony got loose one day, and galloped down the road in the direction of the old glebe. The minister's man in charge ran after the pony in a great fuss, and when passing a large farm-steading on the way, cried out to the farmer, who was sauntering about, but did not know what had taken place : "Oh, sir, did *ye* see the minister's shault ? " "No, no," was the answer, " but what's happened ? " "Ou, sir, fat do ye think ? the minister's shault's *got lowse* frae his tether, an' I'm frichtened he's ta'en the road doun to the auld glebe." " Weel-a-wicht ! " was the shrewd clever rejoinder of the farmer, who was a keen supporter of the old parish church, "I wad *na* wonder *at that*. An' I'se warrant, gin the minister was gettin' *lowse* frae *his* tether, he wad just tak' the same road."

An old clerical friend upon Speyside, a confirmed bachelor, on going up to the pulpit one Sunday to preach, found, after giving out the psalm, that he had forgotten his sermon. I do not know what his objections were to his leaving the pulpit, and going to the manse for his sermon, but he preferred sending his old confidential housekeeper for it. He accordingly stood up in the pulpit, stopped the singing which had commenced, and thus accosted his faithful domestic: "Annie; I say, Annie, *we've* committed a mistak' the day. Ye maun just gang your waa's hame, and ye'll get my sermon oot o' my breek-pouch, an' we'll sing to the praise o' the Lord till ye come back again." Annie, of course, at once executed her important mission, and brought the sermon out of "the breek-pouch," and the service, so far as we heard, was completed without further interruption.

My dear friend, the late Rev. Dr John Hunter, told me an anecdote very characteristic of the unimaginative matter-of-fact Scottish view of matters. One of the ministers of Edinburgh, a man of dry humour, had a daughter who had for some time passed the period of youth and of beauty. She had become an Episcopalian, an event which the Doctor accepted with much good-nature, and he was asking her one day if she did not intend to be confirmed. "Well," she said, "I don't know. I understand Mr Craig always kisses the candidates whom he prepares, and I could not stand that." "Indeed, Jeanie," said the Doctor slily, "gin Edward Craig *were* to gie ye a kiss, I dinna think ye would be muckle the waur."

Many anecdotes characteristic of the Scottish peasant often turn upon words and ideas connected with Holy Scripture. This is not to be considered as in any sense profane or irreverent; but it arises from the Bible being to the peasantry of an older generation their library—their only book. We have constant indications of this almost exclusive familiarity with Scripture ideas. At the late ceremonial in the north, when the Archbishop of Canterbury laid the foundation of a Bishop's Church at Inverness, a number of persons, amid the general interest and kindly feeling displayed by the inhabitants, were viewing the procession from a hill as it passed along. When the clergy, to the number of sixty, came on, an old woman, who was watching the whole scene with some jealousy, exclaimed, at sight of the surplices, " There they go, the *whited* sepulchres ! " I received another anecdote illustrative of the same remark from an esteemed minister of the Free Church : I mean of the hold which Scripture expressions have upon the minds of our Scottish peasantry. One of his flock was a sick nervous woman, who hardly ever left the house. But one fine afternoon, when she was left alone, she fancied she would like to get a little air in the field adjoining the house. Accordingly she put on a bonnet and wrapped herself in a huge red shawl. Creeping along the dyke-side, some cattle were attracted towards her, and first one and then another gathered round, and she took shelter in the ditch till she was relieved by some one coming up to her rescue. She afterwards described her feelings to her minister in strong language, adding, " And eh, sir ! when I lay by the dyke, and the beasts round a' glowerin' at me, I thocht what Dauvid maun hae felt when he said—' Many bulls have compassed me ; strong bulls of Bashan have beset me round.' "

With the plainness and pungency of the old-fashioned Scottish language there was sometimes a coarseness of expression, which, although commonly repeated in the Scottish drawing-room of last century, could not now be tolerated. An example of a very plain and downright address of a laird has been recorded in the annals of " Forfarshire Lairdship." He had married one of the Misses Guthrie, who had a strong feeling towards the Presbyterian faith in which she had been brought up, although her husband was one of the zealous old school of Episcopalians. The young wife had invited her old friend, the parish minister, to tea, and had given him a splendid "*four hours.*" Ere the table was cleared the laird came in unexpectedly, and thus expressed his indignation, not very delicately, at what he considered an unwarrantable exercise of hospitality at his cost: "Helen Guthrie, ye'll no think to save yer ain saul at the expense of my meal-girnel!"

The answer of an old woman under examination by the minister to the question from the Shorter Catechism—"What are the *decrees* of God?" could not have been surpassed by the General Assembly of the Kirk, or even the Synod of Dort—"Indeed, sir, He kens that best Himsell." We have an answer analagous to that, though not so pungent, in a catechumen of the late Dr Johnston of Leith. She answered his own question, patting him on the shoulder: "'Deed, just tell it yersell, *bonny* doctor (he was a very handsome man); naebody can tell it better."

To pass from the answers of "persons come to years of discretion"—I have elsewhere given examples of peculiar traits of character set forth in the answers of mere *children,* and no doubt a most amusing collection might be made of very juvenile "Scottish Reminiscences." One of these is now a very old story, and has long been current amongst us:—A little boy who attended a day-school in the neighbourhood, when he came home in the evening was always asked how he stood in his own class. The invariable answer made was, "I'm second dux," which means in Scottish academical language second from the top of the class. As his habits of application at home did not quite

bear out the claim to so distinguished a position at school, one of the family ventured to ask what was the number in the class to which he was attached. After some hesitation he was obliged to admit : " Ou, there's jist me and *anither* lass." It was a very *practical* answer of the little girl, when asked the meaning of " darkness," as it occurred in Scripture reading : " Ou, just steek your een." On the question, What was the " pestilence that walketh in darkness " ? being put to a class, a little boy answered, after consideration : " Ou, it's just *bugs*." I did not anticipate when in a former edition I introduced this answer, which I received from my nephew, Sir Alexander Ramsay, that it would call forth a comment so interesting as one which I have received from Dr Barber of Ulverston. He sends me an extract from Matthew's *Translation of the Bible*, which he received from Rev. L. R. Ayre, who possesses a copy of date 1553, from which it appears that Psalm xci. 5 was thus translated by Matthew, who adopted his translation from Coverdale and Tyndale :—
" So that thou shalt not need to be afrayed for any bugge by nyght, nor for the arrow that flyeth by day." [1]
Dr Barber ingeniously remarks : " Is it possible the little boy's mother had one of these old Bibles, or is it merely a coincidence ? "

The innocent and unsophisticated answers of children on serious subjects are often very amusing. Many examples are recorded, and one I have received seems much to the point, and derives a good deal of its point from the Scottish turn of the expressions. An elder of the kirk having found a little boy and his sister playing marbles on Sunday, put his reproof in

---

[1] The truth is, in old English usage " bug " signifies a spectre or anything that is frightful. Thus in Henry VI., 3rd Part, Act v., Sc. ii.—" For Warwick was a *bug* that feared us all."

this form, not a judicious one for a child: " Boy, do ye know where children go to who play marbles on Sabbath-day ? " " Ay," said the boy, " they gang doun to the field by the water below the brig." " No," roared out the elder, " they go to hell, and are burned." The little fellow, really shocked, called to his sister, " Come awa', Jeanie, here's a man swearing awfully."

A Scotch story like that of the little boy, of which the humour consisted in the dry application of the terms in a sense different from what was intended by the speaker, was sent to me, but has got spoilt by passing through the press. It must be Scotch, or at least, is composed of Scottish materials—The Shorter Catechism and the bagpipes. A piper was plying his trade in the streets, and a strict elder of the kirk, desirous to remind him that it was a somewhat idle and profitless occupation, went up to him and proposed solemnly the first question of the Shorter Catechism, " What is the chief end of man ? " The good piper, thinking only of his own business, and supposing that the question had reference to some pipe melody, innocently answered, " Na, I dinna ken the tune, but if ye'll whistle it I'll try and play it for ye."

I have said before, and I would repeat the remark again and again, that the object of this work is *not* to string together mere funny stories, or to collect amusing anecdotes. We have seen such collections, in which many of the anecdotes are mere Joe Millers translated into Scotch. The purport of these pages has been throughout to illustrate Scottish life and character, by bringing forward those modes and forms of expression by which alone our national peculiarities can be familiarly illustrated and explained. Besides Scottish replies and expressions which are most characteristic—and in fact unique for dry humour, for quaint and exquisite wit—I have often referred to a consideration of dialect and proverbs. There can be no doubt there is a force and beauty in our Scottish *phraseology*, as well as a quaint humour, considered merely *as* phraseology, peculiar to itself. I have spoken of the phrase " Auld langsyne," and of other words, which may be compared in their Anglican and Scottish form. Take the familiar term common to many singing birds. The English word linnet does not, to my mind, convey so much of simple beauty and of pastoral ideas as belong to our Scottish word LINTIE.

I recollect hearing the Rev. Dr Norman Macleod give a most interesting account of his visit to Canada. In the course of his eloquent narrative he mentioned a conversation he had with a Scottish emigrant, who in general terms spoke favourably and gratefully of his position in his adopted country. But he could not help making this exception when he thought of the " banks and braes o' bonny Doon "—" But oh, sir," he said, " there are nae *linties* i' the wuds." How touching the words in his own dialect! The North American woods, although full of birds of beautiful plumage, it is well known have no singing-birds.

A worthy Scottish Episcopal minister one day met a townsman, a breeder and dealer in singing-birds. The man told him he had just had a child born in his family, and asked him if he would baptize it. He thought the minister could not resist the offer of a bird. " Eh, Maister Shaw," he said, " if ye'll jist do it, I hae a fine lintie the noo, and if ye'll do it, I'll gie ye the lintie." He quite thought that this would settle the matter!

By these remarks I mean to express the feeling that the word *lintie* conveys to my mind more of tenderness and endearment towards the little songster than linnet. And this leads me to a remark (which I do not remember to have met with) that Scottish dialects are peculiarly rich in such terms of endearment, more so than the pure Anglican. Without at all pretending to exhaust the subject, I may cite the following as examples of the class of terms I speak of. Take the names for parents—" Daddie " and " Minnie "; names for children, " My wee bit lady " or " laddie," " My wee bit lamb "; of a general nature, " My ain kind dearie." " Dawtie," especially used to young people, described by Jamieson a darling or favourite, one who is *dawted, i.e.,* fondled or caressed. My " joe " expresses affection with familiarity, evidently derived from *joy,* an easy transition—as " My Joe, Janet "; " John Anderson, my joe, John." Of this character is Burns's address to a wife, " My winsome "—*i.e.,* charming, engaging—" wee thing "; also to a wife, " My winsome marrow "—the latter word signifying a dear companion, one of a pair closely allied to each other; also the address of Rob the Ranter to Maggie Lauder, " My bonnie bird." Now, we would remark, upon this abundant nomenclature of kindly expressions in the Scottish dialect, that it assumes an interesting position as taken in connection with the Scottish Life and *Character,* and as a set-off against a frequent short and *grumpy* manner. It indicates how often there must be a current of tenderness and affection in the Scottish heart, which is so frequently represented to be, like its climate, " stern and wild." There could not be such *terms* were the feelings they express unknown. I believe it often happens that in the Scottish character there is a vein of deep and kindly feeling lying hid under a short, and hard and somewhat stern manner. Hence has arisen the Scottish saying which is applicable to such cases—" His girn's waur than his bite ": his disposition is of a softer nature than his words and manner would often lead you to suppose.

There are two admirable articles in *Blackwood's Magazine*, in the numbers for November and December 1870, upon this subject. The writer abundantly vindicates the point and humour of the Scottish tongue. Who can resist, for example, the epithet applied by Meg Merrilies to an unsuccessful probationer for admission to the ministry :—" a sticket stibbler "? Take the sufficiency of Holy Scripture as a pledge for any one's salvation :—" There's eneuch between the brods o' the Testament to save the biggest sinner i' the warld." I heard an old Scottish Episcopalian thus pithily describe the hasty and irreverent manner of a young Englishman :—" He ribbled aff the prayers like a man at the heid o' a regiment." A large family of young children has been termed " a great sma' family." It was a delicious dry rejoinder to the question— " Are you Mr So-and-so ? " " It's a' that's o' me " (*i.e.*, to be had for him). I have heard an old Scottish gentleman direct his servant to mend the fire by saying, " I think, Dauvid, we wadna be the waur o' some coals."

There is a pure Scottish term, which I have always thought more expressive than any English word of ideas connected with manners in society—I mean the word to blether, or blethering, or blethers. Jamieson defines it to " talk nonsense." But it expresses far more—it expresses powerfully, to Scottish people, a person at once shallow, chattering, conceited, tiresome, voluble.

There is a delicious servantgirlism, often expressed in an answer given at the door to an inquirer : " Is your master at home, or mistress ? " as the case may be. The problem is to save the direct falsehood, and yet evade the visit; so the answer is : " Ay, he or she is at hame; but he's no *in*."

The transition from Scottish *expressions* to Scottish Poetry is easy and natural. In fact, the most interesting feature now belonging to Scottish life and social habits is, to a certain extent, becoming with many a matter of reminiscence of *Poetry in the Scottish dialect*, as being the most permanent and the most familiar feature of Scottish characteristics. It is becoming a matter of history, in so far as we find that it has for some time ceased to be cultivated with much ardour, or to attract much popularity. In fact, since the time of Burns, it has been losing its hold on the public mind. It is a remarkable fact that neither Scott nor Wilson, both admirers of Burns, both copious writers of poetry themselves, both also so distinguished as writers of Scottish prose, should have written any poetry strictly in the form of pure Scottish dialect. " Jock o' Hazeldean " I hardly admit to be an exception. It is not Scottish. If, indeed, Sir Walter wrote the scrap of the beautiful ballad in the " Antiquary "—

> " Now haud your tongue, baith wife and carle,
>   And listen, great and sma',
>   And I will sing of Glenallan's Earl,
>   That fought at the red Harlaw "—

one cannot but regret that he had not written more of the same. Campbell, a poet and a Scotsman, has not attempted it. In short, we do not find poetry in the Scottish dialect at all *kept up* in Scotland. It is every year becoming more a matter of research and reminiscence. Nothing new is added to the old stock, and indeed it is surprising to see the ignorance and want of interest displayed by many young persons in this department of literature. How few read the works of

Allan Ramsay, once so popular, and still so full of pastoral imagery! There are occasionally new editions of the *Gentle Shepherd*, but I suspect for a limited class of readers. I am assured the boys of the High School, Academy, etc., do not care even for Burns. As poetry in the Scottish dialect is thus slipping away from the public Scottish mind, I thought it very suitable to a work of this character to supply a list of modern *Scottish dialect writers*. This I am able to provide by the kindness of our distinguished antiquary, Mr David Laing—the fulness and correctness of whose acquirements are only equalled by his readiness and courtesy in communicating his information to others :—

Scottish Poets of the Last Century.

Allan Ramsay. B. 1686. D. 1757. His *Gentle Shepherd*, completed in 1725, and his *Collected Poems* in 1721-1728.

It cannot be said there was any want of successors, however obscure, following in the same track. Those chiefly deserving of notice were—

Alexander Ross of Lochlee. B. 1700. D. 1783. *The Fortunate Shepherdess*.

Robert Fergusson. B. 1750. D. 1774. *Leith Races, Caller Oysters*, etc.

Rev. John Skinner. B. 1721. D. 1807. *Tullochgorum*.

Robert Burns. B. 1759. D. 1796.

Alexander, Fourth Duke of Gordon. B. 1743. D. 1827. *Cauld Kail in Aberdeen*.

Alexander Wilson of Paisley, who latterly distinguished himself as an American ornithologist. B. 1766. D. 1813. *Watty and Meg*.

Hector Macneill. B. 1746. D. 1818. *Will and Jean*.

Robert Tannahill. B. 1774. D. 1810. *Songs*.

James Hogg. B. 1772. D. 1835.
Allan Cunningham. B. 1784. D. 1842.

To this list we must add the names of Lady Nairne and Lady Anne Lindsay. To the former we are indebted for " The Land o' the Leal," " The Laird o' Cockpen," and " The Auld Hoose " ; to the latter for " Auld Robin Gray " : and our wonder is, how those who could write so charmingly should have written so little.

I have no intention of discussing the general question of Scottish poetry—of defending or eulogising, or of apologising for anything belonging to it. There are songs in broad Scottish dialect of which the beauty and the power will never be lost. Words of Burns, Allan Ramsay, and Lady Nairne, must ever speak to hearts that are true to nature. I am desirous of bringing before my readers at this time the name of a Scottish poet, which, though in Mr Lang's list, I fear is become rather a reminiscence. It is fifty years since his poetical pieces were published in a collected form. I am desirous of giving a special notice of a true-hearted Scotsman, and a genuine Scottish poet, under both characters. I look with a tender regard to the memory of the Rev. John Skinner of Langside. He has written little in quantity, but it is all charming. He was a good Christian minister. He was a man of learning—a man of liberal and generous feeling. In addition to all this, he has upon me the claim of having been a Scottish Episcopalian divine, and I am always rejoiced to see among learned men of our church sympathies with liberalism, besides what is patristic and theological. John Skinner's name and family are much mixed up with our church. " Tullochgorum " was father of Primus John Skinner, and grandfather of

35

Primus W. Skinner and of the Rev. John Skinner of
Forfar. The youngest brother of Tullochgorum was
James Skinner, W.S., who died at ninety-one, and
was grandfather of W. Skinner, W.S., Edinburgh.
The Rev. J. Skinner was born in Birse, a wild part of
Aberdeenshire, 1721. His father was parochial schoolmaster at Gight for nearly fifty years. He worked hard
under the care of his father, who was a good Latin
scholar. He gained a bursary at Aberdeen, where he
studied. When he left college he became schoolmaster
at Monymusk, where he wrote some pieces that
attracted attention, and Sir Archibald Grant took him
into the house, and allowed him the full use of a very
fine library. He made good use of this opportunity,
and indeed became a fair scholar and theologian.
Skinner had been brought up a Presbyterian, but at
Monymusk found reasons for changing his views. In
June 1740 he became tutor to the only son of Mrs
Sinclair in Shetland. Returning to Aberdeenshire in
1741, he completed his studies for the ministry, was
ordained by Bishop Dunbar, and in 1742 became pastor
of Langside. He worked for this little congregation
for nearly sixty-five years, and they were happy and
united under his pastoral charge. One very interesting
incident took place during his ministry, which bears
upon our general question of reminiscences and
changes. John Skinner was in his own person an example of that persecution for political opinion referred to in Professor Macgregor's account of the large
prayer-book in the library at Panmure. After the '45,
Episcopalians were treated with suspicion and severity.
The severe laws passed against Jacobites were put in
force, and poor Skinner fined.

However, better and more peaceful times came
round, and all that John Skinner had undergone did

not sour his temper or make him severe or misanthropical. As a pastor he seems to have had tact, as well as good temper, in the management of his flock, if we may judge from the following anecdote:—Talking with an obstinate self-confident farmer, when the conversation happened to turn on the subject of the motion of the earth, the farmer would not be convinced that the earth moved at all. "Hoot, minister," the man roared out, "d'ye see the earth never gaes oot o' the pairt, and it maun be that the sun gaes round: we a' ken he rises i' the east and sets i' the west." Then, as if to silence all argument, he added triumphantly, "As if the sun didna gae round the earth, when it is said in Scripture that the Lord commanded the sun to stand still!" Mr Skinner, finding it was no use to argue further, quietly answered, "Ay, it's verra true; the sun was commanded to stand still, and there he stands still, for Joshua never tauld him to tak' the road again." I have said John Skinner wrote little Scottish poetry, but what he wrote was rarely good. His prose works extended over three volumes when they were collected by his son, the Bishop of Aberdeen, but we have no concern with them. His poetical pieces, by which his name will never die in Scotland, are the "Reel of Tullochgorum" and the "Ewie with the Crooked Horn," charming Scottish songs—one the perfection of the lively, the other of the pathetic. It is quite enough to say of "Tullochgorum" (by which the old man is now always designated), what was said of it by Robert Burns, as "the first of songs," and as the best Scotch song Scotland ever saw.

I have brought in the following anecdote, exactly as it appeared in the *Scotsman* of October 4, 1859, because it introduces his name.

"The late Rev. John Skinner, author of 'Annals of Scottish Episcopacy,' was his grandson. He was first appointed to a charge in Montrose, from whence he was removed to Banff, and ultimately to Forfar. After he had left Montrose, it reached his ears that an ill-natured insinuation was circulating there that he had been induced to leave this town by the temptation of a better income and of fat pork, which, it would appear, was plentiful in the locality of his new incumbency. Indignant at such an aspersion, he wrote a letter, directed to his maligners, vindicating himself sharply from it, which he showed to his grandfather, John Skinner of Langside, for his approval. The old gentleman objected to it as too lengthy, and proposed the following pithy substitute :—

> "'Had Skinner been of carnal mind,
>   As strangely ye suppose,
> Or had he even been fond of swine,
>   He'd ne'er have left Montrose.'"

But there is an anecdote of John Skinner which should endear his memory to every generous and loving heart. On one occasion he was passing a small dissenting place of worship at the time when the congregation were engaged in singing : on passing the door—old-fashioned Scottish Episcopalian as he was—he reverently took off his hat. His companion said to him, "What! do you feel so much sympathy with this Anti-Burgher congregation?" "No," said Mr Skinner, "but I respect and love any of my fellow-Christians who are engaged in singing to the glory of the Lord Jesus Christ." Well done, old Tullochgorum! thy name shall be loved and honoured by every true liberal-minded Scotsman.

Yes! Mr Skinner's experience of the goodness of

God and of the power of grace, had led him to the conviction that the earnest song of praise, that comes from the heart of the sincere believer in Christ, can go up to Heaven from the humblest earthly house of prayer, and be received before the throne of grace as acceptably as the high and solemn service of the lofty cathedral,

"Where, from the long-drawn aisle and fretted vault,
The pealing anthem swells the note of praise."

We must firmly believe that, obsolete as the dialect of Scotland may become, and its words and expressions a matter of tradition and of reminiscence with many, still there are Scottish lines, and broad Scottish lines, which can never cease to hold their place in the affections and the admiration of innumerable hearts whom they have charmed. Can the choice and popular Scottish verses, endeared to us by so many kindly associations of the past, and by so many beauties and poetical graces of their own, ever lose their attractions for a Scottish heart? The charm of such strains can never die.

I think one subsidiary cause for permanency in the popularity still belonging to particular Scottish *songs* has proceeded from their association with Scottish *music*. The melodies of Scotland can never die. In the best of these compositions there is a pathos and a feeling which must preserve them, however simple in their construction, from being vulgar or commonplace. Mendelssohn did not disdain taking Scottish airs as themes for the exercise of his profound science and his exquisite taste. It must, I think, be admitted that singing of Scottish songs in the perfection of their style—at once pathetic, graceful, and characteristic— is not so often met with as to remove all apprehension

39

that ere long they may become matters only of reminiscence. Many accomplished musicians often neglect
entirely the cultivation of their native melodies, under
the idea of their being inconsistent with the elegance
and science of high-class music. They commit a
mistake. When judiciously and tastefully performed,
it is a charming style of music, and will always give
pleasure to the intelligent hearer. I have heard two
young friends, who have attained great skill in scien-
tific and elaborate compositions, execute the simple
song of " Low down in the Broom," with an effect I
shall not easily forget. Who that has heard the Countess of Essex, when Miss Stephens, sing " Auld Robin
Gray," can ever lose the impression of her heart-
touching notes? In the case of " Auld Robin Gray,"
the song composed by Lady Anne Lindsay, although
very beautiful in itself, has been, I think, a good deal
indebted to the air for its great and continued popularity. The history of that tender and appropriate
melody is somewhat curious, and not generally known.
The author was *not* a Scotsman. It was composed by
the Rev. Mr Leves, rector of Wrington in Somersetshire, either early in this century or just at the close of
the last. Mr Leves was fond of music, and composed
several songs, but none ever gained any notice except
his " Auld Robin Gray," the popularity of which has
been marvellous. I knew the family when I lived in
Somersetshire, and had met them in Bath. Mr Leves
composed the air for his daughter, Miss Bessy Leves,
who was a pretty girl and a pretty singer.

I cannot but deeply regret to think that I should
in these pages have any ground for classing Scottish
poetry and Scottish airs amongst " Reminiscences."
It is a department of literature where, of course, there
must be *selection*, but I am convinced it will repay a

careful cultivation. I would recommend, as a copious
and judicious selection of Scottish *tunes*, " The Scottish
Minstrel." by R. A. Smith (Purdie, Edinburgh).
There are the *words*, also, of a vast number of Scottish
songs, but the account of their *authorship* is very defective. Then, again, for the fine Scottish ballads of
an older period, we have two admirable collections—
one by Mr R. Chambers, and one by the late Professor
Aytoun. For Scottish dialect songs of the more
modern type, a copious collection will be found (exclusive of Burns and Allan Ramsay) in small volumes
published by David Robertson, Glasgow, at intervals
from 1832 to 1853, under the title of *Whistlebinkie*.

But there are more than lines of Scottish poetry
which may become matter of reminiscence, and more
than Scottish song melodies which may be forgotten.
There are strains of Scottish PSALMODY of which it
would be more sad to think that *they* possibly may
have lost their charm and their hold with Scottish
people. That such psalmody, of a peculiar Scottish
class and character, *has* existed, no one can doubt who
has knowledge or recollection of past days. In glens
and retired passes, where those who fled from persecution met together—on the moors and heaths, where
men suffering for their faith took refuge—in the humble
worship of the cottar's fireside—were airs of sacred
Scottish melody, which were well calculated to fan
the heavenward flame which was kindled in lays of
the " sweet Psalmist of Israel." These psalm-tunes
are in their way as peculiar as the song-tunes we have
referred to. Nothing can be more touching than the
description by Burns of the domestic psalmody of his
father's cottage. Mr R. Chambers, in his *Life of Burns*,
informs us that the poet, during his father's infirmity
and after his death, had himself sometimes conducted

family worship. Happy days, ere he had encountered the temptations of a world in which he had too often fallen before the solicitations of guilty passion! and then, beautifully does he describe the characteristic features of this portion of the cottar's worship. How solemnly he enumerates the psalm-tunes usually made use of on such occasions, and discriminates the character of each :—

> " They chant their artless notes in simple guise ;
>   They tune their hearts, by far the noblest aim :
> Perhaps DUNDEE's wild warbling measures rise
> Or plaintive MARTYRS, worthy of the name,
> Or noble ELGIN beets [1] the heavenward flame."

He was not, alas! always disposed in after life to reverence these sacred melodies as he had done in his youthful days. In his poem of " The Holy Fair," he less reverently adduces mention of these sacred airs :—

> " Now turn the Psalms o' David ower,
>   And lilt wi' holy clangour.
> O' double verse come gie us four,
>   An' skirl up the Bangor."

These tunes seem to have been strictly and exclusively national. In proof of such psalmody being quite national, I have been told that many of these tunes were composed by artisans, such as builders, joiners, blacksmiths, etc.

Several of the psalm-tunes more peculiar to Scotland are no doubt of an early date. In Ravenscroft's *Psalms*, published with the music in four parts in 1621, he gives the names of seven as purely Scottish—*King's Duke's, Abbey, Dunfermline, Dundee, Glasgow, Martyrs.* I was used to hear such psalmody in my early days in

[1] Adds fuel to fire.

42

the parish church of Fettercairn, where we always attended during summer. It had all the simple characteristics described by Burns, and there was a heartiness and energy too in the congregation when, as he expresses it, they used to " skirl up the Bangor," of which the effects still hang in my recollection. At that time there prevailed the curious custom, when some of the psalms were sung, of reading out a single line, and when that was sung another line was read, and so throughout.[1] Thus, on singing the 50th psalm, the first line sounded thus :—" *Our God shall come, and shall no more ;* " when that was sung, there came the next startling announcement—" *Be silent, but speak out.*" A rather unfortunate *juxtaposition* was suggested through this custom, which we are assured really happened in the church of Irvine. The precentor, after having given out the first line, and having observed some members of the family from the castle struggling to get through the crowd on a sacramental occasion, cried out, " Let the noble family of Eglinton pass," and then added the line which followed the one he had just given out rather mal-apropos—" *Nor stand in sinners' way.*" One peculiarity I remember, which was, closing the strain sometimes by an interval less than a semitone ; instead of the half-note preceding the close or key-note, they used to take the *quarter-*note, the effect of which had a peculiar gurgling sound, but I never heard it elsewhere. It may be said these Scottish tunes were unscientific, and their performance rude. It may be so, but the effect was striking, as I recall it through the vista of threescore years and ten. Great advances, no doubt, have been made in Scotland in congregational psalmody ; organs have in

---

[1] As far as I am aware the only place in which it is practised at present (July 1872), is in the Free Church, Brodick, Arran.

some instances been adopted; choirs have been organised with great effort by choirmasters of musical taste and skill. But I hope the spirit of PIETY, which in past times once accompanied the old Scottish psalm, whether sung in the church or at home, has not departed with the music. Its better emotions are not, I hope, to become a " Reminiscence."

There was no doubt sometimes a degree of noise in the psalmody more than was consistent with good taste, but this often proceeded from the earnestness of those who joined. I recollect at Banchory an honest fellow who sang so loud that he annoyed his fellow-worshippers, and the minister even rebuked him for " skirling " so loud. James was not quite patient under these hints, and declared to some of his friends that he was resolved to sing to the praise of God, as he said, " gin I should crack the waas o' the houss."

Going from sacred tunes to sacred words, a good many changes have taken place in the little history of our own psalmody and hymnology. When I first came to Edinburgh, for psalms we made use of the mild and vapid new version of Tate and Brady — for hymns, almost each congregation had its own selection —and there were hymn-books of Dundee, Perth, Glasgow, etc. The Established Church used the old rough psalter, with paraphrases by Logan, etc., and a few hymns added by authority of the General Assembly. There seems to be a pretty general tendency in the Episcopal Church to adopt at present the extensive collection called " Hymns Ancient and Modern," containing 386 pieces. Copies of the words alone are to be procured for one penny, and the whole, with tunes attached, to be procured for 1s. 6d. The Hymns Ancient and Modern are not set forth with any Ecclesiastical sanction. It is supposed, however, that there will be a Hymnal published by the Church of England on authority, and if so, our Church will be likely to adopt it. The Established Church Hymnal Committee have lately sanctioned a very interesting collection of 200 pieces. The compilation has been made with liberality of feeling as well as with good taste. There are several of Neale's translations from mediæval hymns, several from John Keble, and the whole concludes with the Te Deum taken literally from the Prayer-Book.

This mention of Scottish Psalmody and Scottish Hymnology, whether for private or for public worship, naturally brings us to a very important division of our subject; I mean the general question of reminiscences of Scottish religious feelings and observances; and first in regard to Scottish clergy.

My esteemed friend, Lord Neaves, who, it is well known, combines with his great legal knowledge and high literary acquirements a keen sense of the humorous, has sometimes pleasantly complained of my drawing so many of my specimens of Scottish humour from sayings and doings of Scottish ministers. They were a shrewd and observant race. They lived amongst their own people from year to year, and understood the Scottish type of character. Their retired habits and familiar intercourse with their parishioners gave rise to many quaint and racy communications. They were excellent men, well suited to their pastoral work, and did much good amongst their congregations; for it should be always remembered that a national church requires a sympathy and resemblance between the pastors and the flocks. Both will be found to change together. Nothing could be further from my mind in recording these stories, than the idea of casting ridicule upon such an order of men. My own feelings as a

Scotsman, with all their ancestral associations, lead me to cherish their memory with pride and deep interest. I may appeal also to the fact that many contributions to this volume are voluntary offerings from distinguished clergymen of the Church of Scotland, as well as of the Free Church and of other Presbyterian communities. Indeed, no persons enjoy these stories more than ministers themselves. I recollect many years ago travelling to Perth in the old stage-coach days, and enjoying the society of a Scottish clergyman, who was a most amusing companion, and full of stories, the quaint humour of which accorded with his own disposition. When we had come through Glen Farg, my companion pointed out that we were in the parish of Dron. With much humour he introduced an anecdote of a brother minister not of a brilliant order of mind, who had terminated in this place a course of appointments in the Church, the names of which, at least, were of an ominous character for a person of unimaginative temperament. The worthy man had been brought up at the school of *Dunse*; had been made assistant at *Dull*, a parish near Aberfeldy, in the Presbytery of Weem; and here had ended his days and his clerical career as minister of *Dron*.

There can be no doubt that the older school of national clergy supply many of our most amusing anecdotes; and our pages would suffer deplorably were all the anecdotes taken away which turn upon their peculiarities of dialect and demeanour. I think it will be found, however, that upon no class of society has there been a greater change during the last hundred years than on the Scottish clergy as a body. This, indeed, might, from many circumstances, have been expected. The improved facilities for locomotion have had effect upon the retirement and isolation of distant country parishes, the more liberal and extended course of study at Scottish colleges, the cheaper and wider diffusion of books on general literature, of magazines, newspapers, and reviews. Perhaps, too, we may add that candidates for the ministry now more generally originate from the higher educated classes of society. But honour to the memory of Scottish ministers of the days that are gone!

The Scottish clergy, from having mixed so little with life, were often, no doubt, men of simple habits and of very childlike notions. The opinions and feelings which they expressed were often of a cast, which amongst persons of more experience, would appear to be not always quite consistent with the clerical character. In them it arose from their having nothing *conventional* about them. Thus I have heard of an old bachelor clergyman whose landlady declared he used to express an opinion of his dinner by the grace which he made to follow. When he had had a good dinner which pleased him, and a good glass of beer with it, he poured forth the grace, " For the riches of Thy bounty and its blessings we offer our thanks." When he had had poor fare and poor beer, his grace was, " The least of these Thy mercies."

Many examples of the dry, quaint humour of the class occur in these pages, but there could not be a finer specimen than the instance recorded in the " Annals of the Parish " of the account given by the minister of his own ordination. The ministers were all assembled for the occasion; prayers had been offered, discourses delivered, and the time for the actual ordination had come. The form is for the candidate to kneel down and receive his sacred office by the imposition of hands, *i.e.*, the laying on of hands by the whole Presbytery. As the attendance of ministers

was large, a number of hands were stretched forth,
more than could quite conveniently come up to the
candidate. An old minister, of the quiet jocose turn
of mind we speak of, finding himself thus kept at a
little distance, stretched out his walking staff and put
it on the young man's head, with the quiet remark,
" That will do! Timmer to timmer "—timber to
timber.

Their style of preaching, too, was no doubt often
plain and homely. They had not the graces of elocu-
tion or elegance of diction. But many were faithful
in their office, and preached Christ as the poor man's
friend and the Saviour of the lowly and the suffering.
I have known Scottish ministers of the old school get
into a careless indifferent state of ministration; I have
also known the hoary head of many a Scottish minister
go down to the grave a crown of glory, in his day and
generation more honoured than many which had been
adorned by a mitre.

THE WEAVER

CHAPTER II

SCOTTISH RELIGIOUS FEELINGS AND OBSERVANCES

PASSING from these remarks on the Scottish Clergy of a past day, I would treat the more extensive subject of RELIGIOUS FEELINGS and RELIGIOUS OBSERVANCES generally with the caution and deference due to such a question, and I would distinctly premise that there is in my mind no intention of entering, in this volume, upon those great questions which are connected with certain church movements amongst us, or with national peculiarities of faith and discipline. It is impossible, however, to overlook entirely the fact of a gradual relaxation, which has gone on for some years, of the sterner features of the Calvinistic school of theology—at any rate, of keeping its theoretic peculiarities more in the background. What we have to notice in these pages are changes in the feelings with regard to religion and religious observances, which have appeared upon the *exterior* of society—the changes which belong to outward habits rather than to internal feelings. Of such changes many have taken place within my own experience. Scotland has ever borne the character of a moral and religious country; and the mass of the people are a more church-going race than the masses of English population. I am not at all prepared to say that in the middle and lower ranks of life our countrymen have undergone much change in regard to religious observances. But there can be no question that amongst the upper classes there are manifestations connected with religion now, which some years ago were not thought of. The attendance of *men* on public worship is of itself an example of the change we speak of. I am afraid that when Walter Scott described Monkbarns as being with difficulty " hounded out " to hear the sermons of good Mr Blattergowl, he wrote from a knowledge of the habits of church-going then generally prevalent among Scottish lairds. The late Bishop Sandford told me that when he first came to Edinburgh—I suppose fifty years ago—few gentlemen attended church—very few indeed were seen at the communion—so much so that it was a matter of conversation when a male communicant, not an aged man, was observed at the table for the first time. Sydney Smith, when preaching in Edinburgh some forty years ago, seeing how almost exclusively congregations were made up of ladies, took for his text the verse from the Psalms, " Oh that men would therefore praise the Lord ! " and with that touch of the facetious which marked everything he did, laid the emphasis on the word " men." Looking round the congregation and saying, " Oh that *men* would therefore praise the Lord ! " implying that he used the word, not to describe the human species generally, but the male individuals as distinguished from the female portion. In regard to attendance by young men, both at church and communion, a marked change has taken place in my own experience. In fact, there is an attention excited towards church subjects, which, thirty years ago, would have been hardly credited. Nor is it only in connection with churches and church services that these changes have been brought forth, but an interest has been raised on the subject from Bible societies, missionary associations at home and abroad, schools and reformatory institutions, most of which, as regard active operation, have grown up during fifty years.

Nor should I omit to mention, what I trust may be considered as a change belonging to religious feeling, viz., that conversation is now conducted without that accompaniment of those absurd and unmeaning oaths which were once considered an essential embellishment of polite discourse. I distinctly recollect an elderly gentleman, when describing the opinion of a refined and polished female upon a particular point, putting into her mouth an unmistakable round oath as the natural language in which people's sentiments and opinions would be ordinarily conveyed. This is a change wrought in men's feelings, which all must hail with great pleasure. Putting out of sight for a moment the sin of such a practice, and the bad influence it must have had upon all emotions of reverence for the name and attributes of the Divine Being, and the natural effect of profane swearing, to " harden a' within," we might marvel at the utter folly and incongruity of making swearing accompany every expression of anger or surprise, or of using oaths as mere expletives in common discourse. A quaint anecdote, descriptive of such senseless ebullition, I have from a friend who mentioned the names of parties concerned : A late Duke of Athole had invited a well-known character, a writer of Perth, to come up and meet him at Dunkeld for the transaction of some business. The Duke mentioned the day and hour when he should receive the man of law, who accordingly came punctually at the appointed time and place. But the Duke had forgotten the appointment, and gone to the hill, from which he could not return for some hours. A Highlander present described the Perth writer's indignation, and his mode of showing it by a most elaborate course of swearing. " But whom did he swear at ? " was the inquiry made of the narrator, who replied, "Oh, he didna sweer at ony thing particular, but juist stude in ta middle of ta road and swoor at lairge." I have from a friend also an anecdote which shows how entirely at one period the practice of swearing had become familiar even to female ears when mixed up with the intercourse of social life. A sister had been speaking of her brother as much addicted to this habit: "Oor John sweers awfu', and we try to correct him; but," she added in a candid and apologetic tone, "nae doubt it *is* a great set off to conversation." There was something of rather an *admiring* character in the description of an outbreak of swearing by a Deeside body. He had been before the meeting of Justices for some offence against the excise laws, and had been promised some assistance and countenance by my cousin, the laird of Finzean, who was unfortunately addicted to the practice in question. The poor fellow had not got off so well as he had expected, and on giving an account of what took place to a friend, he was asked, "But did not Finzean speak for you?" "Na," he replied, "he didna say muckle; but oh, he damned bonny!"

This is the place to notice a change which has taken place in regard to some questions of taste in the building and embellishing of Scottish places of worship. Some years back there was a great jealousy of ornament in connection with churches and church services, and, in fact, all such embellishments were considered as marks of a departure from the simplicity of old Scottish worship—they were distinctive of Episcopacy as opposed to the severer modes of Presbyterianism. The late Sir William Forbes used to give an account of a conversation, indicative of this feeling, which he had overheard between an Edinburgh inhabitant and his friend from the country.

They were passing St John's, which had just been finished, and the countryman asked, " Whatna kirk was that ? " " Oh," said the townsman, " that is an English chapel," meaning Episcopalian. " Ay," said his friend, " there'll be a walth o' *images* there." But, if unable to sympathise with architectural church ornament and embellishment, how much less could they sympathise with the performance of divine service, which included such musical accompaniments as intoning, chanting, and anthems ! On the first introduction of Tractarianism into Scotland, the full choir service had been established in an Episcopal church, where a noble family had adopted those views, and carried them out regardless of expense. The lady who had been instrumental in getting up these musical services was very anxious that a favourite female servant of the family—a Presbyterian of the old school —should have an opportunity of hearing them; accordingly, she very kindly took her down to church in the carriage, and on returning asked her what she thought of the music, etc. " Ou, it's verra bonny, verra bonny; but oh, my lady, it's an awfu' way of spending the Sabbath." The good woman could only look upon the whole thing as a musical performance. The organ was a great mark of distinction between Episcopalian and Presbyterian places of worship. I have heard of an old lady describing an Episcopalian clergyman, without any idea of disrespect, in these terms :—" Oh, he is a whistle-kirk minister." From an Australian correspondent I have an account of the difference between an Episcopal minister and a Presbyterian minister, as remarked by an old Scottish lady of his acquaintance. Being asked in what the difference was supposed to consist, after some consideration she replied, " Weel, ye see, the Presbyterian minister wears his sark under his coat, the Episcopal minister wears his sark aboon his coat." Of late years, however, a spirit of greater tolerance of such things has been growing up amongst us—a greater tolerance, I suspect, even of organs and liturgies. In fact, we may say a new era has begun in Scotland as to church architecture and church ornaments. The use of stained glass in churches—forming memorial windows for the departed,[1] a free use of crosses as architectural ornaments, and restoration of ancient edifices, indicate a revolution of feeling regarding this question. Beautiful and expensive churches are rising everywhere, in connection with various denominations. It is not long since the building or repairing a new church, or the repairing and adapting an old church, implied in Scotland simply a production of the greatest possible degree of ugliness and bad taste at the least possible expense, and certainly never included any notion of ornament in the details. Now, large sums are expended on places of worship, without reference to creed. First-rate architects are employed. Fine Gothic structures are produced. The rebuilding of the Greyfriars' Church, the restoration of South Leith Church and of Glasgow Cathedral, the very bold experiment of adopting a style little known amongst us, the pure Lombard, in a church for Dr W. L. Alexander, on George IV. Bridge, Edinburgh; the really splendid Free Churches, St Mary's, in Albany Street, and the Barclay Church, Bruntsfield, and many similar cases, mark the spirit of the times regarding the application of what is beautiful in art to the service of religion. One might hope that changes such as

[1] Distinguished examples of these are to be found in the Old Greyfriars' Church, Edinburgh, and in the Cathedral of Glasgow; to say nothing of the beautiful specimens in St John's Episcopal Church, Edinburgh.

these in the feelings, tastes, and associations, would have a beneficial effect in bringing the worshippers themselves into a more genial spirit of forbearance with each other. A friend of mine used to tell a story of an honest builder's views of church differences, which was very amusing, and quaintly professional. An English gentleman, who had arrived in a Scottish country town, was walking about to examine the various objects which presented themselves, and observed two rather handsome places of worship in course of erection nearly opposite to each other. He addressed a person, who happened to be the contractor for the chapels, and asked, "What was the difference between these two places of worship which were springing up so close to each other?"—meaning, of course, the difference of the theological tenets of the two congregations. The contractor, who thought only of architectural differences, innocently replied, "There may be a difference of sax feet in length, but there's no aboon a few inches in the breadth." Would that all our religious differences could be brought within so narrow a compass!

The variety of churches in a certain county of Scotland once called forth a sly remark upon our national tendencies to religious division and theological disputation. An English gentleman sitting on the box, and observing the great number of places of worship in the aforesaid borough, remarked to the coachman that there must be a great deal of religious feeling in a town which produced so many houses of God. "Na," said the man quietly, "it's no' religion, it's *curstness*," *i.e.*, crabbedness, insinuating that acerbity of temper, as well as zeal, was occasionally the cause of congregations being multiplied.

It might be a curious question to consider how far

motives founded on mere taste or sentiment may have operated in creating an interest towards religion, and in making it a more prominent and popular question than it was in the early portion of the present century. There are in this country two causes which have combined in producing these effects :—*First* : The great disruption which took place in the Church of Scotland no doubt called forth an attention to the subject which stirred up the public, and made religion at any rate a topic of deep interest for discussion and partisanship. Men's minds were not *allowed* to remain in the torpid condition of a past generation. *Second* : The æsthetic movement in religion, which some years since was made in England, has, of course, had its influence in Scotland; and many who showed little concern about religion, whilst it was merely a question of doctrines, of precepts, and of worship, threw themselves keenly into the contest when it became associated with ceremonial, and music, and high art. New ecclesiastical associations have been presented to Scottish tastes and feelings. With some minds, attachment to the church is attachment to her Gregorian tones, jewelled chalices, lighted candles, embroidered altar-cloths, silver crosses, processions, copes, albs, and chasubles. But, from whatever cause it proceeds, a great change has taken place in the general interest excited towards ecclesiastical questions. Religion now has numerous associations with the ordinary current of human life. In times past it was kept more as a thing apart. There was a false delicacy which made people shrink from encountering appellations that were usually bestowed upon those who made a more prominent religious profession than the world at large.

A great change has taken place in this respect with persons of *all* shades of religious opinions. With an increased attention to the *externals* of religion, we believe that in many points the heart has been more exercised also. Take, as an example, the practice of family prayer. Many excellent and pious households of the former generation would not venture upon the observance, I am afraid, because they were in dread of the sneer. There was a foolish application of the terms " Methodist," " saints," " over-righteous," where the practice was observed. It was to take up a rather decided position in the neighbourhood; and I can testify, that less than fifty years ago a family would have been marked and talked of for a usage of which now throughout the country the *exception* is rather the unusual circumstance. A little anecdote from recollections in my own family will furnish a good illustration of a state of feeling on this point now happily unknown. In a northern town of the east coast, where the earliest recollections of my life go back, there was usually a detachment of a regiment, who were kindly received and welcomed to the society, which in the winter months was very full and very gay. There was the usual measure of dining, dancing, supping, card-playing, and gossiping, which prevailed in country towns at the time. The officers were of course an object of much interest to the natives, and their habits were much discussed. A friend was staying in the family who partook a good deal of the Athenian temperament, viz., delight in hearing and telling some new thing. On one occasion she burst forth in great excitement with the intelligence that " Sir Nathaniel Duckinfield, the officer in command of the detachment, had family prayers *every* morning ! " A very near and dear relative of mine, knowing the tendency of the lady to gossip, pulled her up with the exclamation : " How can you repeat such things, Miss Ogilvy ?

Nothing in the world but the ill-natured stories of Montrose!" The remark was made quite innocently, and unconsciously of the bitter satire it conveyed upon the feeling of the place. The "ill-nature" of these stories was true enough, because ill-nature was the motive of those who raised them; not because it is an ill-natured thing of itself to say of a family that they have household worship, but the ill-nature consisted in their intending to throw out a sneer and a sarcasm upon a subject where all such reflections are unbecoming and indecorous. It is one of the best proofs of change of habits and associations on this matter, that the anecdote, exquisite as it is for our purpose, will hardly be understood by many of our young friends, or, at least, happily has lost much of its force and pungency.

These remarks apply perhaps more especially to the state of religious feeling amongst the upper classes of society. Though I am not aware of so much change in the religious habits of the Scottish peasantry, still the elders have yielded much from the sternness of David Deans; and upon the whole view of the question there have been many and great changes in the Scottish people during the last sixty years. It could hardly be otherwise, when we consider the increased facilities of communication between the two countries— a facility which extends to the introduction of English books upon religious subjects. The most popular and engaging works connected with the Church of England have now a free circulation in Scotland; and it is impossible that such productions as the "Christian Year," for example, and many others—whether for good or bad is not now the question—should not produce their effects upon minds trained in the strictest school of Calvinistic theology. I should be disposed to *extend* the boundaries of this division, and to include under "Religious Feelings and Religious Observances," many anecdotes which belong perhaps rather indirectly than directly to the subject. There is a very interesting reminiscence, and one of a sacred character also, which I think will come very suitably under this head. When I joined the Scottish Episcopal Church, nearly fifty years ago, it was quite customary for members of our communion to ask for the blessing of their Bishop, and to ask it especially on any remarkable event in their life, as marriage, loss of friends, leaving home, returning home, etc.; and it was the custom amongst the old Scottish Episcopalians to give the blessing in a peculiar form, which had become venerable from its traditionary application by our bishops. I have myself received it from my bishop, the late good Bishop Walker, and have heard him pronounce it on others. But whether the custom of asking the bishop's blessing be past or not, the form I speak of has become a reminiscence, and I feel assured is not known even by some of our own bishops. I shall give it to my readers as I received it from the family of the late Bishop Walker of Edinburgh :—

"God Almighty bless thee with his Holy Spirit;
Guard thee in thy going out and coming in;
Keep thee ever in His faith and fear;
Free from Sin, and safe from Danger."

I have been much pleased with a remark of my friend, the Rev. W. Gillespie of the U.P. Church, Edinburgh, upon this subject. He writes to me as follows :—"I read with particular interest the paragraph on the subject of the Bishop's Blessing, for certainly there seems to be in these days a general disbelief in the efficacy of blessings, and a neglect or disregard of the practice. If the spirit of God is in good men, as He certainly is, then who can doubt the value and the efficacy of the blessing which they bestow? I remember being blessed by a very venerable minister, John Dempster of Denny, while kneeling in his study, shortly before I left this country to go to China, and his prayer over me then was surely the effectual fervent prayer of a righteous man. Its effect upon me then and ever since will never be forgotten."

I quite agree with Mr Gillespie on the point, and think it not a good sign either of our religious belief or religious feeling that such blessings should become really a matter of reminiscence; for if we are taught to pray for one another, and if we are taught that the "prayer of the righteous availeth much," surely we ought to *bless* one another, and surely the blessing of those who are venerable in the church from their position, their age, and their piety, may be expected to avail as an aid and incentive to piety in those who in God's name are so blest. It has struck me that on a subject closely allied with religious feelings a great change has taken place in Scotland during a period of less than fifty years—I mean the attention paid to cemeteries as depositories of the mortal remains of those who have departed. In my early days I never recollect seeing any efforts made for the embellishment and adornment of our churchyards; if tolerably secured by fences, enough had been done. The English and Welsh practices of planting flowers, keeping the turf smooth and dressed over the graves of friends, were quite unknown. Indeed, I suspect such attention fifty years ago would have been thought by the sterner Presbyterians as somewhat savouring of superstition. The account given by Sir W. Scott, in "Guy Mannering," of an Edinburgh burial-place, was universally applicable to Scottish sepulchres.[1] A very different state of matters has grown up within the last few years. Cemeteries and churchyards are now as carefully ornamented in Scotland as in England. Shrubs, flowers, smooth turf, and neatly-kept gravel walks, are a pleasing accompaniment to head-stones, crosses, and varied forms of monumental memorials, in freestone, marble, and granite. Nay, more than these, not infrequently do we see an imitation of French sentiment, in wreaths of " everlasting " placed over graves as emblems of immortality ; and in more than one of our Edinburgh cemeteries I have seen these enclosed in glass cases to preserve them from the effects of wind and rain.

In consequence of neglect, the unprotected state of churchyards was evident from the number of stories in circulation connected with the circumstance of timid and excited passengers going amongst the tombs of the village. The following, amongst others, has been communicated. The *locale* of the story is unknown, but it is told of a weaver who, after enjoying his potations, pursued his way home through the churchyard, his vision and walking somewhat impaired. As he proceeded he diverged from the path, and unexpectedly stumbled into a partially made grave. Stunned for a while, he lay in wonder at his descent, and after some time he got out, but he had not proceeded much farther when a similar calamity befell him. At this second fall, he was heard, in a tone of wonder and surprise, to utter

---

[1] " This was a square enclosure in the Greyfriars' Churchyard, guarded on one side by a veteran angel without a nose, and having only one wing, who had the merit of having maintained his post for a century, while his comrade cherub, who had stood sentinel on the corresponding pedestal, lay a broken trunk, among the hemlock, burdock, and nettles, which grew in gigantic luxuriance around the walls of the mausoleum."

the following exclamation, referring to what he considered the untenanted graves : " Ay ! ir ye a' up an' awa' ? "

The kindly feelings and interest of the pastoral relation always formed a very pleasing intercourse between minister and people. I have received from an anonymous correspondent an anecdote illustrative of this happy connection, for which he vouches as authentic :—

John Brown, Burgher minister at Whitburn (son of the commentator, and father of the late Rev. Dr John Brown of Edinburgh, and grandfather of the present accomplished M.D. of the same name, author of " Rab and his Friends," etc.), in the early part of the century was travelling on a small sheltie[1] to attend the summer sacrament at Haddington. Between Musselburgh and Tranent he overtook one of his own people. " What are ye daein' here, Janet, and whaur ye gaun in this warm weather ? " " 'Deed, sir," quo' Janet, " I'm gaun to Haddington *for the occasion*,[2] an' expeck to hear ye preach this efternoon." " Very weel, Janet, but whaur ye gaun tae sleep ? " " I dinna ken, sir, but Providence is aye kind, an'll provide a bed." On Mr Brown jogged, but kindly thought of his humble follower ; accordingly, after service in the afternoon, before pronouncing the blessing, he said from the pulpit, " Whaur's the auld wifie that followed me frae Whitburn ? " " Here I'm, sir," uttered a shrill voice from a back seat. " Aweel," said Mr Brown, " I have fand ye a bed ; ye're to sleep wi' Johnnie Fife's lass."

There was at all times amongst the older Scottish peasantry a bold assertion of their religious opinions, and strong expression of their feelings. The spirit of

[1] A Shetland pony. [2] The Lord's Supper.

the Covenanters lingered amongst the aged people whom I remember, but which time has considerably softened down. We have some recent authentic instances of this readiness in Scotsmen to bear testimony to their principles :—

A friend has informed me that the late Lord Rutherfurd often told with much interest of a rebuke which he received from a shepherd, near Bonaly, amongst the Pentlands. He had entered into conversation with him, and was complaining bitterly of the weather, which prevented him enjoying his visit to the country, and said hastily and unguardedly, " What a d——d mist ! " and then expressed his wonder how or for what purpose there should have been such a thing created as east wind. The shepherd, a tall, grim figure, turned sharp round upon him. " What ails ye at the mist, sir ? It weets the sod, it slockens the yowes, and " —adding with much solemnity—" it's God's wull " ; and turned away with lofty indignation. Lord Rutherfurd used to repeat this with much candour as a fine specimen of a rebuke from a sincere and simple mind.

There was something very striking in the homely, quaint, and severe expressions on religious subjects which marked the old-fashioned piety of persons shadowed forth in Sir Walter Scott's Davie Deans. We may add to the rebuke of the shepherd of Bonaly of Lord Rutherfurd's remark about the east wind, his answer to Lord Cockburn, the proprietor of Bonaly. He was sitting on the hillside with the shepherd, and observing the sheep reposing in the coldest situation, he observed to him, " John, if I were a sheep, I would lie on the other side of the hill." The shepherd answered, " Ay, my lord, but if ye had been a sheep ye would hae had mair sense."

Of such men as this shepherd were formed the

elders—a class of men who were marked by strong features of character, and who, in former times, bore a distinguished part in all church matters.

The old Scottish elder was in fact quite as different a character from the modern elder, as the old Scottish minister was from the modern pastor. These good men were not disposed to hide their lights, and perhaps sometimes encroached a little upon the office of the minister. A clergyman had been remarking to one of his elders that he was unfortunately invited to two funerals on one day, and that they were fixed for the same hour. " Weel, sir," answered the elder, " if ye'll tak' the tane I'll tak' the tither."

Some of the elders were great humorists and originals in their way. An elder of the kirk at Muthill used to manifest his humour and originality by his mode of collecting the alms. As he went round with the ladle, he reminded such members of the congregation as seemed backward in their duty, by giving them a poke with the " brod," and making, in an audible whisper, such remarks as these—" Wife at the braid mailin, mind the puir " ; " Lass wi' the braw plaid, mind the puir," etc., a mode of collecting which marks rather a bygone state of things. But on no question was the old Scottish disciplinarian, whether elder or not, more sure to raise his testimony than on anything connected with a desecration of the Sabbath. In this spirit was the rebuke given to an eminent geologist, when visiting in the Highlands :—The professor was walking on the hills one Sunday morning, and partly from the effect of habit, and partly from not adverting to the very strict notions of Sabbath desecration entertained in Ross-shire, had his pocket hammer in hand, and was thoughtlessly breaking the specimens of minerals he picked up by the way. Under

THE SHEPHERD

these circumstances, he was met by an old man steadily pursuing his way to his church. For some time the patriarch observed the movements of the geologist, and at length, going up to him, quietly said, " Sir, ye're breaking something there forbye the stanes ! "

The same feeling, under a more fastidious form, was exhibited to a traveller by a Scottish peasant :— An English artist travelling professionally through Scotland, had occasion to remain over Sunday in a small town in the north. To while away the time, he walked out a short way in the environs, where the picturesque ruin of a castle met his eye. He asked a countryman who was passing to be so good as tell him the name of the castle. The reply was somewhat startling : " It's no' the day to be speerin' sic things ! "

A manifestation of even still greater strictness on the subject of Sabbath desecration, I have received from a relative of the family in which it occurred. About fifty years ago the Hon. Mrs Stewart lived in Heriot Row, who had a cook, Jeannie by name, a paragon of excellence. One Sunday morning when her daughter (afterwards Lady Elton) went into the kitchen, she was surprised to find a new jack (recently ordered, and which was constructed on the principle of going constantly without winding up) wholly paralysed and useless. Miss Stewart naturally inquired what accident had happened to the new jack, as it had stopped. The mystery was soon solved by Jeannie indignantly exclaiming that " she was nae gaeing to hae the fule thing clocking and rinning about in *her* kitchen a' the blessed Sabbath day."

There sometimes appears to have been in our countrymen an undue preponderance of zeal for Sabbath observance as compared with the importance attached to *other* religious duties, and especially as compared with the virtue of sobriety. The following dialogue between Mr Macnee of Glasgow, the celebrated artist, and an old Highland acquaintance whom he had met with unexpectedly, will illustrate the contrast between the severity of judgment passed upon treating the Sabbath with levity and the lighter censure attached to indulgence in whisky. Mr Macnee begins, " Donald, what brought you here ? " " Ou, weel, sir, it was a baad place yon ; they were baad folk—but they're a God-fearin' set o' folk here ! " " Well, Donald," said Mr M., " I'm glad to hear it." " Ou ay, sir, 'deed are they ; an' I'll gie ye an instance o't. Last Sabbath, just as the kirk was skailin', there was a drover chield frae Dumfries comin' along the road whustlin', an' lookin' *as happy* as if it was ta middle o' ta week ; weel, sir, oor laads is a God-fearin' set o' laads, an' they were just comin' oot o' the kirk—'od they yokit upon him, an' a'most killed him ! " Mr M., to whom their zeal seemed scarcely sufficiently well directed to merit his approbation, then asked Donald whether it had been drunkenness that induced the depravity of his former neighbours ? " Weel, weel, sir," said Donald, with some hesitation, " *may*-be ; I'll no' say but it micht." " Depend upon it," said Mr M., " it's a bad thing whisky." " Weel, weel, sir," replied Donald, " I'll no' say but it *may* " ; adding in a very decided tone—" speeciallie *baad* whusky ! "

I do not know any anecdote which illustrates in a more striking and natural manner the strong feeling which exists in the Scottish mind on this subject. At a certain time, the hares in the neighbourhood of a Scottish burgh had, from the inclemency of the season or from some other cause, become emboldened more than usual to approach the dwelling-places of men ;

so much so that on one Sunday morning a hare was seen skipping along the street as the people were going to church. An old man, spying puss in this unusual position, significantly remarked, " Ay, yon beast kens weel it is the Sabbath-day " ; taking it for granted that no one in the place would be found audacious enough to hurt the animal on a Sunday.

Lady Macneil supplies an excellent pendant to Miss Stewart's story about the jack going on the Sunday. Her henwife had got some Dorking fowls, and on Lady M. asking if they were laying many eggs, she replied with great earnestness, " Indeed my leddy, they lay every day, no' excepting the blessed Sabbath."

There were, however, old persons at that time who were not quite so orthodox on the point of Sabbath observance ; and of these a lady residing in Dumfries was known often to employ her wet Sundays in arranging her wardrobe. " Preserve us ! " she said on one occasion, " anither gude Sunday ! I dinna ken whan I'll get thae drawers redd up."

In connection with the awful subject of death and all its concomitants, it has been often remarked that the older generation of Scottish people used to view the circumstances belonging to the decease of their nearest and dearest friends with a coolness which does not at first sight seem consistent with their deep and sincere religious impressions. Amongst the peasantry this was sometimes manifested in an extraordinary and startling manner. I do not believe that those persons had less affection for their friends than a corresponding class in England, but they had less awe of the concomitants of death, and approached them with more familiarity. For example, I remember long ago at Fasque, my sister-in-law visiting a worthy and attached old couple, of whom the husband, Charles

Duncan, who had been gardener at Fasque for above thirty years, was evidently dying. He was sitting on a common deal chair, and on my sister proposing to send down for his use an old arm-chair which she recollected was laid up in a garret, his wife exclaimed against such a needless trouble: " Hout, my leddy, what would he be duin' wi' an arm-chair? He's just deein' fast awa'. " I have two anecdotes, illustrative of the same state of feeling, from a lady of ancient Scottish family accustomed to visit her poor dependants on the property, and to notice their ways. She was calling at a decent cottage, and found the occupant busy carefully ironing out some linens. The lady remarked, " Those are fine linens you have got there, Janet." " Troth, mem," was the reply, " they're just the gudeman's *deed* claes, and there are nane better i' the parish." On another occasion, when visiting an excellent woman, to condole with her on the death of her nephew, with whom she had lived, and whose loss must have been severely felt by her, she remarked, " What a nice white cap you have got, Margaret." " Indeed, mem, ay, sae it is; for ye see the gude lad's winding sheet was ower lang, and I cut aff as muckle as made twa bonny mutches " (caps).

There certainly was a quaint and familiar manner in which sacred and solemn subjects were referred to by the older Scottish race, who did not mean to be irreverent, but who no doubt appeared so to a more refined but not really a more religious generation.

It seems to me that this plainness of speech arose in part from the *sincerity* of their belief in all the circumstances of another condition of being. They spoke of things hereafter as positive certainties, and viewed things invisible through the same medium as they viewed things present. The following is illustrative of such a state of mind, and I am assured of its perfect authenticity and literal correctness :—" Joe M'Pherson and his wife lived in Inverness. They had two sons, who helped their father in his trade of a smith. They were industrious and careful, but not successful. The old man had bought a house, leaving a large part of the price unpaid. It was the ambition of his life to pay off that debt, but it was too much for him, and he died in the struggle. His sons kept on the business with the old industry, and with better fortune. At last their old mother fell sick, and told her sons she was dying, as in truth she was. The elder son said to her 'Mother, you'll soon be with my father; no doubt you'll have much to tell him; but dinna forget this mother, mind ye, tell him *the house is freed*. He'll be glad to hear that.' "

A similar feeling is manifest in the following conversation, which, I am assured, is authentic :—At Hawick the people used to wear wooden clogs, which make a *clanking* noise on the pavement. A dying old woman had some friends by her bed-side, who said to her, " Weel, Jenny, ye are gaun to heeven, an' gin you should see oor folk, you can tell them that we're a' weel." To which Jenny replied, " Weel, gin I should see them I'se tell them, but you manna expect that I am to gang clank clanking through heevan looking for your folk."

But of all stories of this class, I think the following deathbed conversation between a Scottish husband and wife is about the richest specimen of a dry Scottish matter-of-fact view of a very serious question :— An old shoemaker in Glasgow was sitting by the bed-side of his wife, who was dying. She took him by the hand. " Weel, John, we're gawin to part. I hae been a gude wife to you, John." " Oh, just middling, just middling, Jenny," said John, not disposed to commit himself. "John," says she, "ye maun promise to bury me in the auld kirk-yard at Stra'von, beside my mither. I couldna rest in peace among unco folk, in the dirt and smoke o' Glasgow." "Weel, weel, Jenny, my woman," said John soothingly, "we'll just pit you in the Gorbals *first*, and gin ye dinna lie quiet, we'll try you sine in Stra'von."

The same unimaginative and matter-of-fact view of things connected with the other world extended to a very youthful age, as in the case of a little boy who, when told of heaven, put the question, "An' will faather be there?" His instructress answered, "of course, she hoped he would be there"; to which he sturdily at once replied, "Then I'll no' gang."

We might apply these remarks in some measure to the Scottish pulpit ministrations of an older school, in which a minuteness of detail and a quaintness of expression were quite common, but which could not now be tolerated. I have two specimens of such antiquated language, supplied by correspondents, and I am assured they are both genuine.

The first is from a St Andrews professor, who is stated to be a great authority in such narratives.

In one of our northern counties, a rural district had its harvest operations affected by continuous rains. The crops being much laid, wind was desired in order to restore them to a condition fit for the sickle. A minister, in his Sabbath services, expressed their want in prayer as follows :—"O Lord, we pray Thee to send us wind; no' a rantin' tantin' tearin' wind, but a noohin' (noughin?) soughin' winnin' wind." More expressive words than these could not be found in any language.

The other story relates to a portion of the Presbyterian service on sacramental occasions, called "fencing the tables," *i.e.*, prohibiting the approach of those who were unworthy to receive.

This fencing of the tables was performed in the following effective manner by an old divine, whose flock transgressed the third commandment, not in a gross and loose manner, but in its minor details:—
"I debar all those who use such minced oaths as faith! troth! losh! gosh! and lovanendie!"

These men often showed a quiet vein of humour in their prayers, as in the case of the old minister of the Canongate, who always prayed, previous to the meeting of the General Assembly, that the Assembly might be so guided as "*no' to do ony harm.*"

A circumstance connected with Scottish church discipline has undergone a great change in my time— I mean the public censure from the pulpit, in the time of divine service, of offenders previously convicted before the minister and his kirk-session. This was performed by the guilty person standing up before the congregation on a raised platform, called the *cutty stool*, and receiving a rebuke. I never saw it done, but have heard in my part of the country of the discipline being enforced occasionally. Indeed, I recollect an instance where the rebuke was thus administered and received under circumstances of a touching character, and which made it partake of the moral sublime. The daughter of the minister had herself committed an offence against moral purity, such as usually called forth this church censure. The minister peremptorily refused to make her an exception to his ordinary practice. His child stood up in the congregation, and received, from her agonised father, a rebuke similar to that administered to other members of his congregation for a like offence. The spirit of the age became unfavourable in the practice. The rebuke on the cutty stool, like the penance in a white sheet in England, went out of use, and the circumstance is now a matter of " reminiscence." I have received some communications on the subject, which bear upon this point; and I subjoin the following remarks from a kind correspondent, a clergyman, to whom I am largely indebted, as indicating the great change which has taken place in this matter.

"Church discipline," he writes, " was much more vigorously enforced in olden time than it is now. A certain couple having been guilty of illicit intercourse, and also within the forbidden degrees of consanguinity, appeared before the Presbytery of Lanark, and made confession in sackcloth. They were ordered to return to their own session, and to stand at the kirkdoor, barefoot and barelegged, from the second bell to the last, and thereafter in the public place of repentance; and, at direction of the session, thereafter to go through the whole kirks of the presbytery, and to satisfy them in like manner. If such penance were now enforced for like offences, I believe the registration books of many parishes in Scotland would become more creditable in certain particulars than they unfortunately are at the present time."

But there was a less formidable ecclesiastical censure occasionally given by the minister from the pulpit against lesser misdemeanours, which took place under his own eye, such as levity of conduct or *sleeping* in church. A most amusing specimen of such censure was once inflicted by the minister upon his own wife for an offence not in our day visited with so heavy a penalty. The clergyman had observed one of his flock asleep during his sermon. He paused, and called him to order. " Jeems Robson, ye are sleepin';

72

I insist on your wauking when God's word is preached to ye." " Weel, sir, you may look at your ain seat, and ye'll see a sleeper forbye me," answered Jeems, pointing to the clergyman's lady in the minister's pew. " Then, Jeems," said the minister, " when ye see my wife asleep again, haud up your hand." By and by the arm was stretched out, and sure enough the fair lady was caught in the act. Her husband solemnly called upon her to stand up and receive the censure due to her offence. He thus addressed her : " Mrs B., a'body kens that when I got ye for my wife, I got nae beauty ; yer frien's ken that I got nae siller ; and if I dinna get God's grace, I shall hae a puir bargain indeed."

The quaint and original humour of the old Scottish minister came out occasionally in the more private services of his vocation as well as in church. As the whole service, whether for baptisms or marriages, is supplied by the clergyman officiating, there is more scope for scenes between the parties present than at similar ministrations by a prescribed form. Thus, a late minister of Caithness, when examining a member of his flock, who was a butcher, in reference to the baptism of his child, found him so deficient in what he considered the needful theological knowledge, that he said to him, " Ah, Sandy, I doubt ye're no' fit to haud up the bairn." Sandy, conceiving that reference was made not to spiritual but to physical incapacity, answered indignantly, " Hout, minister, I could haud him up an he were a twa-year-auld stirk." [1] A late humorous old minister, near Peebles, who had strong feelings on the subject of matrimonial happiness, thus prefaced the ceremony by an address to the parties who came to him :—" My friends, marriage is a bless-

[1] Bullock.

73

ing to a few, a curse to many, and a great uncertainty
to all. Do ye venture?" After a pause, he repeated
with great emphasis, " Do ye venture?" No objection
being made to the venture, he then said, " Let's
proceed."

The old Scottish hearers were very particular on the
subject of their minister's preaching old sermons;
and to repeat a discourse which they could recollect
was always made a subject of animadversion by those
who heard it. A beadle, who was a good deal of a wit
in his way, gave a sly hit in his pretended defence of
his minister on the question. As they were proceeding from church, the minister observed the beadle had
been laughing as if he had triumphed over some of
the parishioners with whom he had been in conversation. On asking the cause of this, he received for
answer, " Dod, sir, they were saying ye had preached
an auld sermon to-day, but I tackled them, for I tauld
them it was no' an auld sermon, for the minister had
preached it no' sax months syne."

I remember the minister of Banchory, Mr Gregory,
availed himself of the feelings of his people on this
subject for the purpose of accomplishing a particular
object. During the building of the new church the
service had to be performed in a schoolroom, which
did not nearly hold the congregation. The object was
to get part of the parish to attend in the morning, and
part in the afternoon. Mr Gregory prevented those
who had attended in the morning from returning in
the afternoon by just giving them, as he said, " cauld
kail het again."

It is somewhat remarkable, however, that notwithstanding this feeling in the matter of a repetition of
old sermons, there was amongst a large class of Scottish preachers of a former day such a sameness of

subject as really sometimes made it difficult to distinguish the discourse of one Sunday from amongst others. These were entirely doctrinal, and however they might commence, after the opening or introduction hearers were certain to find the preacher falling gradually into the old channel. The fall of man in Adam, his restoration in Christ, justification by faith, and the terms of the new covenant, formed the staple of each sermon, and without which it was not in fact reckoned complete as an orthodox exposition of Christian doctrine. Without omitting the essentials of Christian instruction, preachers now take a wider view of illustrating and explaining the gospel scheme of salvation and regeneration, without constant recurrence to the elemental and fundamental principles of the faith. From my friend, Dr Cook of Haddington, (who it is well known has a copious stock of old Scotch traditionary anecdotes), I have an admirable illustration of this state of things as regards pulpit instruction.

" Much of the preaching of the Scotch clergy," Dr Cook observes, " in the last century, was almost exclusively doctrinal—the fall : the nature, the extent, and the application of the remedy. In the hands of able men, no doubt, there might be much variety of exposition, but with weaker or indolent men preaching extempore, or without notes, it too often ended in a weekly repetition of what had been already said. An old elder of mine, whose recollection might reach back from sixty to seventy years, said to me one day, ' Now-a-days, people make a work if a minister preach the same sermon over again in the course of two or three years. When I was a boy, we would have wondered if old Mr W—— had preached anything else than what we heard the Sunday before.' My old friend used to tell of a clergyman who had held forth on the broken covenant till his people longed for a change. The elders waited on him to intimate their wish. They were examined on their knowledge of the subject, found deficient, rebuked, and dismissed, but after a little while they returned to the charge, and the minister gave in. Next Lord's Day he read a large portion of the history of Joseph and his brethren, as the subject of a lecture. He paraphrased it, greatly, no doubt, to the detriment of the original, but much to the satisfaction of his people, for it was something new. He finished the paraphrase, ' and now,' says he, ' my friends, we shall proceed to draw some lessons and inferences; and, *first*, you will observe that the sacks of Joseph's brethren were *ripit*, and in them was found the cup; so your sacks will be ripit at the day of judgment, and the first thing found in them will be the broken covenant '; and having gained this advantage, the sermon went off into the usual strain, and embodied the usual heads of elementary dogmatic theology."

In connection with this topic, I have a communication from a correspondent, who remarks :—The story about the minister and his favourite theme, " the broken covenant," reminds me of one respecting another minister whose staple topics of discourse were " Justification, Adoption, and Sanctification." Into every sermon he preached, he managed, by hook or by crook, to force these three heads, so that his general method of handling every text was not so much *expositio* as *impositio*. He was preaching on these words : " Is Ephraim my dear son? Is he a pleasant child? " and he soon brought the question into the usual formula by adding, Ephraim was a pleasant child— first, because he was a justified child; second, because he was an adopted child; and third, because he was a sanctified child.

It should be remembered, however, that the Scottish peasantry themselves—I mean those of the older school—delighted in expositions of *doctrinal* subjects, and in fact were extremely jealous of any minister who departed from their high standard of orthodox divinity, by selecting subjects which involved discussions of strictly moral or *practical* questions. It was condemned under the epithet of *legal* preaching; in other words, it was supposed to preach the law as independent of the gospel. A worthy old clergyman having, upon the occasion of a communion Monday, taken a text of such a character, was thus commented on by an ancient dame of the congregation, who was previously acquainted with his style of discourse: "If there's an ill text in a' the Bible, that creetur's aye sure to tak' it."

The great change—the great improvement, I would say—which has taken place during the last half-century in the feelings and practical relations of religion with social life is, that it has become more diffused through all ranks and all characters. Before that period many good sort of people were afraid of making their religious views very prominent, and were always separated from those who did. Persons who made a profession at all beyond the low standard generally adopted in society were marked out as objects of fear or of distrust. The anecdote on page 57 regarding the practice of family prayer fully proves this. Now, religious people and religion itself are not kept aloof from the ordinary current of men's thoughts and actions. There is no such marked line as used to be drawn round persons who make a decided profession of religion. Christian men and women have stepped over the line, and, without compromising their Christian principle, are not necessarily either morose, uncharitable, or exclusive. The effects of the old separation were injurious to men's minds. Religion was with many associated with puritanism, with cant, and unfitness for the world. The difference is marked also in the style of sermons prevalent at the two periods. There were sermons of two descriptions, viz., sermons by " *moderate* " clergy, of a purely moral or practical character; and sermons purely doctrinal, from those who were known as " evangelical " ministers. Hence arose an impression, and not unnaturally, on many minds, that an almost exclusive reference to doctrinal subjects, and a dread of upholding the law, and of enforcing its more minute details, were not favourable to the cause of moral rectitude and practical holiness of life. This was hinted in a sly way by a young member of the kirk to his father, a minister of the severe and high Calvinistic school. Old Dr Lockhart of Glasgow was lamenting one day, in the presence of his son John, the fate of a man who had been found guilty of immoral practices, and the more so that he was one of his own elders. " Well, father," remarked his son, " you see what you've driven him to." In our best Scottish preaching at the present day no such distinction is visible.

The same feeling came forth with much point and humour on an occasion referred to in Carlyle's Memoirs. In a company where John Home and David Hume were present, much wonder was expressed what *could* have induced a clerk belonging to Sir William Forbes' bank to abscond, and embezzle £900. " I know what it was," said Home to the historian; " for when he was taken there was found in his pocket a volume of your philosophical works and Boston's

78

' Fourfold State ' "—a hit, first, at the infidel, whose principles would have undermined Christianity; and second, a hit at the Church, which he was compelled to leave on account of his having written the tragedy of Douglas.

I can myself recollect an obsolete ecclesiastical custom, and which was always practised in the church of Fettercairn during my boyish days, viz., that of the minister bowing to the heritors in succession who occupied the front gallery seats; and I am assured that this bowing from the pulpit to the principal heritor or heritors after the blessing had been pronounced was very common in rural parishes till about forty years ago, and perhaps till a still later period. And when heritors chanced to be pretty equally matched, there was sometimes an unpleasant contest as to who was entitled to the precedence in having the *first* bow. A case of this kind once occurred in the parish of Lanark, which was carried so far as to be laid before the Presbytery; but they, not considering themselves " competent judges of the points of honour and precedency among gentlemen, and to prevent all inconveniency in these matters in the future, appointed the minister to forbear bowing to the lairds at all from the pulpit for the time to come "; and they also appointed four of their number " to wait upon the gentlemen, to deal with them, for bringing them to condescend to submit hereunto, for the success of the gospel and the peace of the parish."

In connection with this subject, we may mention a ready and complimentary reply once made by the late Reverend Dr Wightman of Kirkmahoe, on being rallied for his neglecting this usual act of courtesy one Sabbath in his own church. The heritor who was entitled to and always received this token of respect, was Mr Miller, proprietor of Dalswinton. One Sabbath the Dalswinton pew contained a bevy of ladies, but no gentleman, and the Doctor—perhaps because he was a bachelor and felt a delicacy in the circumstances—omitted the usual salaam in their direction. A few days after, meeting Miss Miller, who was widely famed for her beauty, and who afterwards became Countess of Mar, she rallied him, in presence of her companions, for not bowing to her from the pulpit on the previous Sunday, and requested an explanation; when the good Doctor immediately replied, " I beg your pardon, Miss Miller, but you surely know that angel-worship is not allowed in the Church of Scotland "; and lifting his hat, he made a low bow, and passed on.

Scottish congregations, in some parts of the country, contain an element in their composition quite unknown in English churches. In pastoral parts of the country, it was an established practice for each shepherd to bring his faithful *collie* dog—at least it was so some years ago. In a district of Sutherland, where the population is very scanty, the congregations are made up one-half of dogs, each human member having his canine companion. These dogs sit out the Gaelic services and sermon with commendable patience, till towards the end of the last psalm, when there is a universal stretching and yawning, and all are prepared to scamper out, barking in a most excited manner whenever the blessing is commenced. The congregation of one of these churches determined that the service should close in a more decorous manner, and steps were taken to attain this object. Accordingly, when a stranger clergyman was officiating, he found the people all sitting when he was about to pronounce the blessing. He hesitated, and paused, expecting them to rise, till an old shepherd, looking up to the pulpit, said, "Say awa', sir; we're a' sittin' to cheat the dowgs."

There must have been some curious specimens of Scottish humour brought out at the examinations or catechisings by ministers of the flock before the administrations of the communion. Thus, with reference to human nature before the fall, a man was asked, "What kind of man was Adam?" "Ou, just like ither fouk." The minister insisted on having a more special description of the first man, and pressed for more explanation. "Weel," said the catechumen, "he was just like Joe Simson the horse-couper." "How so?" asked the minister. "Weel, naebody got onything by him, and mony lost."

A lad had come for examination previous to his receiving his first communion. The pastor, knowing that his young friend was not very profound in his theology, and not wishing to discourage him, or keep him from the table unless compelled to do so, began by asking what he thought a safe question, and what would give him confidence. So he took the Old Testament, and asked him, in reference to the Mosaic law, how many commandments there were. After a little thought, he put his answer in the modest form of a supposition, and replied, cautiously, "Aiblins[1] a hunner." The clergyman was vexed, and told him such ignorance was intolerable, that he could not proceed in examination, and that the youth must wait and learn more; so he went away. On returning home he met a friend on his way to the manse, and on learning that he too was going to the minister for examination, shrewdly asked him, "Weel, what will ye say noo if the minister speers hoo mony commandments

[1] Perhaps.

F 81

there are?" "Say! why, I shall say ten to be sure."
To which the other rejoined, with great triumph,
"Ten! Try ye him wi' ten! I tried him wi' a hunner,
and he wasna satisfeed." Another answer from a little
girl was shrewd and reflective. The question was,
"Why did the Israelites make a golden calf?" "They
hadna as muckle siller as wad mak' a coo."

A kind correspondent has sent me, from personal
knowledge, an admirable pendant to stories of Scottish
child acuteness and shrewd observation. A young
lady friend of his, resident in a part of Ayrshire rather
remote from any very satisfactory administration of
the gospel, is in the habit of collecting the children of
the neighbourhood on Sundays at the " big hoose,"
for religious instruction. On one occasion the class
had repeated the paraphrase of the Lord's Prayer,
which contains these lines—

> " Give us this day our daily bread,
> And raiment *fit* provide."

There being no question as to what " daily bread "
was, the teacher proceeded to ask: " What do you
understand by ' raiment fit,' or as we might say, ' fit
raiment?'" For a short time the class remained puzzled
at the question; but at last one little girl sang out
" stockings and shune." The child knew that " fit,"
was Scotch for feet, so her natural explanation of the
phrase was equivalent to " feet raiment," or " stockings
and shune," as she termed it.

On the point of changes in religious feelings there
comes within the scope of these Reminiscences a
character in Aberdeenshire, which has now gone out
—I mean the popular and universally well-received
Roman Catholic priest. Although we cannot say
that Scotland is a more PROTESTANT nation than it

was in past days, still religious differences, and strong prejudices, seem at the present time to draw a more decided line of separation between the priest and his Protestant countryman. As examples of what is past, I would refer to the case of a genial Romish bishop in Ross-shire. It is well known that private stills were prevalent in the Highlands fifty or sixty years ago, and no one thought there was any harm in them. This good bishop, whose name I forget, was (as I heard the late W. Mackenzie of Muirton assure a party at Dunrobin Castle) several years previously a famous hand at brewing a good glass of whisky, and that he distributed his mountain-dew with a liberal and impartial hand alike to Catholic and to Protestant friends. Of this class, I recollect, certainly forty-five years ago, Priest Gordon, a genuine Aberdonian, and a man beloved by all, rich and poor. He was a sort of chaplain to Menzies of Pitfodels, and visited in all the country families round Aberdeen. I remember once his being at Banchory Lodge, and thus apologising to my aunt for going out of the room :—" I beg your pardon, Mrs Forbes, for leaving you, but I maun just gae doun to the garden and say my bit wordies "—these " bit wordies " being in fact the portion of the Breviary which he was bound to recite. So easily and pleasantly were those matters then referred to.

The following, however, is a still richer illustration, and I am assured it is genuine :—" Towards the end of the last century, a worthy Roman Catholic clergyman, well known as ' Priest Matheson,' and universally respected in the district, had charge of a mission in Aberdeenshire, and for a long time made his journeys on a piebald pony, the priest and his ' pyet shelty ' sharing an affectionate recognition wherever they came. On one occasion, however, he made his appearance on a steed of a different description, and passing near a Seceding meeting-house, he forgathered with the minister, who, after the usual kindly greetings, missing the familiar pony, said, ' Ou, Priest! fat's come o' the auld Pyet?' 'He's deid, minister.' 'Weel, he was an auld faithfu' servant, and ye wad nae doot gie him the offices o' the Church?' 'Na, minister,' said his friend, not quite liking this allusion to his priestly offices, ' I didna dee that, for ye see he *turned Seceder afore he dee'd, an' I buried him like a beast.*' He then rode quietly away. This worthy man, however, could, when occasion required, rebuke with seriousness as well as point. Always a welcome guest at the houses of both clergy and gentry, he is said on one occasion to have met with a laird whose hospitality he had thought it proper to decline, and on being asked the reason for the interruption of his visits, answered, ' Ye ken, an' I ken; but, laird, God kens!'"

One question connected with religious feeling, and the manifestation of religious feeling, has become a more settled point amongst us, since fifty years have expired. I mean the question of attendance by clergymen on theatrical representations. Dr Carlyle had been prosecuted before the General Assembly in 1757 for being present at the performance of the tragedy of Douglas, written by his friend John Home. He was acquitted, however, and writes thus on the subject in his Memoirs :—

"Although the clergy in Edinburgh and its neighbourhood had abstained from the theatre because it gave offence, yet the more remote clergymen, when occasionally in town, had almost universally attended the play-house. It is remarkable that in the year 1784, when the great actress Mrs Siddons first appeared in Edinburgh, during the sitting of the General Assembly, that court was obliged to fix all its important business for the alternate days when she did not act, as all the younger members, clergy as well as laity, took their stations in the theatre on those days by three in the afternoon."

Drs Robertson and Blair, although they cultivated the acquaintance of Mrs Siddons in private, were amongst those clergymen, referred to by Dr Carlyle, who abstained from attendance in the theatre; but Dr Carlyle states that they regretted not taking the opportunity of witnessing a display of her talent, and of giving their sanction to the theatre as a place of recreation. Dr Carlyle evidently considered it a narrow-minded intolerance and bigoted fanaticism that clergymen should be excluded from that amusement. At a period far later than 1784, the same opinion prevailed in some quarters. I recollect when such indulgence on the part of clergymen was treated with much leniency, especially for Episcopalian clergy. I do not mean to say that there was anything like a general feeling in favour of clerical theatrical attendance; but there can be no question of a feeling far less strict than what exists in our own time. As I have said, thirty-six years ago some clergymen went to the theatre; and a few years before that, when my brothers and I were passing through Edinburgh, in going backwards and forwards to school, at Durham, with our tutor, a licentiate of the Established Church of Scotland, and who afterwards attained considerable eminence in the Free Church, we certainly went with him to the theatre there, and at Durham very frequently. I feel quite assured, however, that no clergyman could expect to retain the respect of his people or of the public, to whom it was known that he frequently or habitually attended theatrical representations. It is so

understood. I had opportunities of conversing with
the late Mr Murray of the Theatre Royal, Edinburgh,
and with Mr Charles Kean, on the subject. Both
admitted the fact, and certainly if any men of the profession *could* have removed the feeling from the public
mind, these were the men to have done it.

There is a phase of religious observances which has
undergone a great change amongst us within fifty
years—I mean the services and circumstances connected with the administration of the Holy Communion. When these occurred in a parish they were
called " occasions," and the great interest excited by
these sacramental solemnities may be gathered from
" Peter's Letters," " The Annals of the Parish," and
Burns' " Holy Fair." Such ceremonials are now conducted, I believe, just as the ordinary church services.
Some years back they were considered a sort of preaching matches. Ministers vied with each other in order
to bear away the bell in popularity, and hearers em-
braced the opportunity of exhibiting to one another
their powers of criticism on what they heard and saw.
In the parish of Urr in Galloway, on one sacramental
occasion, some of the assistants invited were eminent
ministers in Edinburgh; Dr Scot of St Michael's,
Dumfries, was the only local one who was asked, and
he was, in his own sphere, very popular as a preacher.
A brother clergyman, complimenting him upon the
honour of being so invited, the old bald-headed divine
modestly replied, " Gude bless you, man, what can I
do? They are a' han' wailed [1] this time; I need never
show face among them." " Ye're quite mista'en,"
was the soothing encouragement; " tak' your *Resurrection* (a well-known sermon used for such occasions
by him), an I'll lay my lug ye'll beat every clute o'

[1] Carefully selected.

them." The Doctor did as suggested, and exerted himself to the utmost, and it appears he did not exert himself in vain. A batch of old women, on their way home after the conclusion of the services, were overheard discussing the merits of the several preachers who had that day addressed them from the tent. "Leeze me abune them a'," said one of the company, who had waxed warm in the discussion, "for yon auld clear-headed (bald) man, that said, 'Raphael sings an' Gabriel strikes his goolden harp, an' a' the angels clap their wings wi' joy.' O but it was gran', it just put me in min' o' our geese at Dunjarg when they turn their nebs to the south an' clap their wings when they see the rain's comin' after lang drooth."

There is a subject closely allied with the religious feelings of a people, and that is the subject of their *superstitions*. To enter upon that question, in a general view, especially in reference to the Highlands, would not be consistent with our present purpose, but I am induced to mention the existence of a singular superstition regarding swine which existed some years ago among the lower orders of the east coast of Fife. I can observe, in my own experience, a great change to have taken place amongst Scotch people generally on this subject. The old aversion to the "unclean animal" still lingers in the Highlands, but seems in the Lowland districts to have yielded to a sense of its thrift and usefulness.[1] The account given by my correspondent of the Fife swinophobia is as follows :—

Among the many superstitious notions and customs prevalent among the lower orders of the fishing towns on the east coast of Fife, till very recently, that class

---

[1] I recollect an old Scottish gentleman, who shared this horror, asking very gravely, "Were not swine forbidden under the law and cursed under the gospel?"

entertained a great horror of swine, and even at the very mention of the word. If that animal crossed their path when about to set out on a sea voyage, they considered it so unlucky an omen that they would not venture off. A clergyman of one of these fishing villages having mentioned the superstition to a clerical friend, and finding that he was rather incredulous on the subject, in order to convince him told him he would allow him an opportunity of testing the truth of it by allowing him to preach for him the following day. It was arranged that his friend was to read the chapter relating to the herd of swine into which the evil spirits were cast. Accordingly, when the first verse was read, in which the unclean beast was mentioned, a slight commotion was observable among the audience, each one of them putting his or her hand on any near piece of iron—a nail on the seat or bookboard, or to the nails on their shoes. At the repetition of the word again and again, more commotion was visible, and the words " cauld airn " (cold iron), the antidote to this baneful spell, were heard issuing from various corners of the church. And finally, on his coming over the hated word again, when the whole herd ran violently down the bank into the sea, the alarmed parishioners, irritated beyond bounds, rose and all left the church in a body.

It is some time now, however, since the Highlanders have begun to appreciate the thrift and comfort of swine-keeping and swine-killing. A Scottish minister had been persuaded by the laird to keep a pig, and the gudewife had been duly instructed in the mysteries of black puddings, pork chops, and pig's head. " Oh ! " said the minister, " nae doubt there's a hantle o' miscellawneous eating aboot a pig."

Amongst a people so deeply impressed with the

great truths of religion, and so earnest in their religious profession, any persons whose principles were
known to be of an *infidel* character would naturally be
looked on with abhorrence and suspicion. There is
a story traditionary in Edinburgh regarding David
Hume, which illustrates this feeling in a very amusing
manner, and which, I have heard it said, Hume himself often narrated. The philosopher had fallen from
the path into the swamp at the back of the Castle,
the existence of which I recollect hearing of from old
persons forty years ago. He fairly stuck fast, and
called to a woman who was passing, and begged her
assistance. She passed on apparently without attending to the request; at his earnest entreaty, however,
she came where he was, and asked him, " Are na ye
Hume the Atheist ? " " Well, well, no matter," said
Hume; " Christian charity commands you to do good
to every one." " Christian charity here, or Christian
charity there," replied the woman, " I'll do naething
for you till ye turn a Christian yoursel'—ye maun
repeat the Lord's Prayer and the Creed, or faith I'll
let ye grafel [1] there as I fand ye." The historian, really
afraid for his life, rehearsed the required formulas.

Notwithstanding the high character borne for so
many years by our countrymen as a people, and as
specially attentive to all religious observances, still
there can be no doubt that there has sprung up amongst
the inhabitants of our crowded cities, wynds, and
closes, a class of persons quite unknown in the old
Scottish times. It is a great difficulty to get them to
attend divine worship at all, and their circumstances
combine to break off all associations with public
services. Their going to church becomes a matter of
persuasion and of missionary labour.

[1] Lie in a grovelling attitude. *See* Jamieson.

A lady, who is most active in visiting the houses of these outcasts from the means of grace, gives me an amusing instance of self-complacency arising from performance of the duty. She was visiting in the West Port, not far from the church established by my illustrious friend the late Dr Chalmers. Having asked a poor woman if she ever attended there for divine service—" Ou ay," she replied; " there's a man ca'd Chalmers preaches there, and I whiles gang in and hear him, just to encourage him, puir body!"

From the religious opinions of a people, the transition is natural to their political partialities. One great political change has passed over Scotland, which none now living can be said to have actually *witnessed*; but they remember those who were contemporaries of the anxious scenes of '45, and many of us have known determined and thorough Jacobites. The poetry of that political period still remains, but we hear only as pleasant songs those words and melodies which stirred the hearts and excited the deep enthusiasm of a past generation. Jacobite anecdotes also are fading from our knowledge. To many young persons they are unknown. Of those stories illustrative of Jacobite feelings and enthusiasm, many are of a character not fit for me to record. The good old ladies who were violent partisans of the Stuarts had little hesitation in referring without reserve to the future and eternal destiny of William of Orange. One anecdote which I had from a near relative of the family may be adduced in illustration of the powerful hold which the cause had upon the views and consciences of Jacobites.

A former Mr Stirling of Keir had favoured the Stuart cause, and had, in fact attended a muster of forces at the Brig of Turk previous to the '15. This symptom of a rising against the Government occasioned some uneasiness, and the authorities were very active in their endeavours to discover who were the leaders of the movement. Keir was suspected. The miller of Keir was brought forward as a witness, and swore positively that the laird was *not* present. Now, as it was well known that he was there, and that the miller knew it, a neighbour asked him privately, when he came out of the witness-box, how he could on oath assert such a falsehood. The miller replied, quite undaunted, and with a feeling of confidence in the righteousness of his cause approaching the sublime: " I would rather trust my soul in God's mercy than Keir's head into their hands."

A correspondent has sent me an account of a curious ebullition of Jacobite feeling and enthusiasm, now I suppose quite extinct. My correspondent received it himself from Alexander, fourth Duke of Gordon, and he had entered it in a commonplace book when he heard it, in 1826.

" David Tulloch, tenant in Drumbenan, under the second and third Dukes of Gordon, had been ' *out* ' in the '45—or the *fufteen, or both*—and was a great favourite of his respective landlords. One day, having attended the young Lady Susan Gordon (afterwards Duchess of Manchester) to the ' Chapel ' at Huntly, David, perceiving that her ladyship had neither hassock nor carpet to protect her garments from the earthen floor, respectfully spread his plaid for the young lady to kneel upon, and the service proceeded; but when the prayer for the King and Royal Family was commenced, David, *sans cérémonie*, drew, or rather ' twitched,' the plaid from under the knees of the astonished young lady, exclaiming, *not sotto voce*, ' The deil a ane shall pray for *them* on *my* plaid! ' "

91

I have a still more pungent demonstration against praying for the king, which a friend in Aberdeen assures me he received from the son of the gentleman who *heard* the protest. In the Episcopal Chapel in Aberdeen, of which Primus *John* Skinner was incumbent, they commenced praying in the service for George III. immediately on the death of Prince Charles Edward. On the first Sunday of the prayer being used, this gentleman's father, walking home with a friend whom he knew to be an old and determined Jacobite, said to him, " What do you think of that, Mr ——? " The reply was, " Indeed, the less we say aboot that prayer the better." But he was pushed for " further answer as to his own views and his own ideas on the matter," so he came out with the declaration, " Weel, then, I say this—they may pray the kenees [1] aff their breeks afore I join in that prayer."

[1] So pronounced in Aberdeen.

The following is a characteristic Jacobite story. It must have happened shortly after 1745, when all manner of devices were fallen upon to display Jacobitism, without committing the safety of the Jacobite, such as having white knots on gowns; drinking, " The king, ye ken wha I mean " ; uttering the toast " The king," with much apparent loyalty, and passing the glass over the water-jug, indicating the esoteric meaning of majesty *beyond* the sea, etc., etc.; and various toasts, which were most important matters in those times, and were often given as tests of loyalty, or the reverse, according to the company in which they were given. Miss Carnegy of Craigo, well-known and still remembered amongst the old Montrose ladies as an uncompromising Jacobite, had been vowing that she would drink King James and his son in a company of staunch Brunswickers, and being strongly dissuaded from any such foolish and dangerous attempt by some of her friends present, she answered them with a text of Scripture, " The tongue no man can tame—James *Third* and *Aucht*," and drank off her glass ! [1]

[1] Implying that there was a James Third of England, Eighth of Scotland.

CHAPTER III

ON OLD SCOTTISH CONVIVIALITY

THE next change in manners which has been effected, in the memory of many now living, regards the habits of conviviality, or, to speak more plainly, regards the banishment of *drunkenness* from polite society. It is indeed a most important and blessed change. But it is a change the full extent of which many persons now alive can hardly estimate. Indeed, it is scarcely possible to realise the scenes which took place seventy or eighty years back, or even less. In many houses, when a party dined, the ladies going away was the signal for the commencement of a system of compulsory conviviality. No one was allowed to shirk—no daylight, no heeltaps— was the wretched jargon in which were expressed the propriety and the duty of seeing that the glass, when filled, must be emptied and drained. We have heard of glasses having the bottoms knocked off, so that no shuffling tricks might be played with them, and that they could only be put down—empty.

One cannot help looking back with amazement at the infatuation which could for a moment tolerate such a sore evil. To a man of sober inclinations it must have been an intolerable nuisance to join a dinner-party at many houses, where he knew he should have to witness the most disgusting excesses in others, and to fight hard to preserve himself from a compliance with the example of those around him.

The scenes of excess which occurred in the houses where deep drinking was practised must have been most revolting to sober persons who were unac-

94

customed to such conviviality; as in the case of a drinking Angus laird, entertaining as his guest a London merchant of formal manners and temperate habits. The poor man was driven from the table when the drinking set in hard, and stole away to take refuge in his bedroom. The company, however, were determined not to let the worthy citizen off so easily, but proceeded in a body, with the laird at their head, and invaded his privacy by exhibiting bottles and glasses at his bedside. Losing all patience, the wretched victim gasped out his indignation: " Sir, your hospitality borders upon brutality." It must have had a fatal influence also on many persons to whom drinking was most injurious, and who were yet not strongminded enough to resist the temptations to excess. Poor James Boswell, who certainly required no *extraordinary* urging to take a glass too much, is found in his letters, which have recently come to light, laying the blame of his excesses to " falling into a habit which still prevails in Scotland "; and then he remarks, with censorious emphasis, on the " drunken manners of his countrymen." This was about 1770.

A friend of mine, however, lately departed—Mr Boswell of Balmuto—showed more spirit than the Londoner, when he found himself in a similar situation. Challenged by the host to drink, urged and almost forced to swallow a quantity of wine against his own inclination, he proposed a counter-challenge in the way of eating, and made the following ludicrous and original proposal to the company—that two or three legs of mutton should be prepared, and he would then contest the point of who could devour most meat; and certainly it seems as reasonable to compel people to *eat*, as to compel them to drink, beyond the natural cravings of nature.

The situation of ladies, too, must frequently have been very disagreeable when, for instance, gentlemen came upstairs in a condition most unfit for female society. Indeed they were often compelled to fly from scenes which were most unfitting for them to witness. They were expected to get out of the way at the proper time, or when a hint was given them to do so. At Glasgow sixty years ago, when the time had come for the *bowl* to be introduced, some jovial and thirsty members of the company proposed as a toast, "The trade of Glasgow and *the outward bound*!" The hint was taken, and silks and satins moved off to the drawing-room.

In my part of the country the traditionary stories of drinking prowess are quite marvellous. On Deeside there flourished a certain Saunders Paul (whom I remember an old man), an innkeeper at Banchory. He was said to have drunk whisky, glass for glass, to the claret of Mr Maule and the Laird of Skene for a whole evening; and in those days there was a traditional story of his despatching, at one sitting, in company with a character celebrated for conviviality—one of the men employed to float rafts of timber down the Dee—three dozen of porter. Of this Mr Paul it was recorded, that on being asked if he considered porter as a wholesome beverage, he replied, "Oh yes, if you don't take above a dozen." Saunders Paul was, as I have said, the innkeeper at Banchory; his friend and *porter* companion was drowned in the Dee, and when told that the body had been found down the stream below Crathes, he coolly remarked, "I am surprised at that, for I never kenn'd him pass the inn before without comin' in for a glass."

Some relatives of mine travelling in the Highlands were amused by observing in a small road-side public-house a party drinking, whose apparatus for conviviality called forth the dry quaint humour which is so thoroughly Scottish. Three drovers had met together, and were celebrating their meeting by a liberal consumption of whisky; the inn could only furnish one glass without a bottom, and this the party passed on from one to another. A queer-looking pawky chield, whenever the glass came to his turn, remarked most gravely, "I think we wadna be the waur o' some water," taking care, however, never to add any of the simple element, but quietly drank off his glass.

There was a sort of infatuation in the supposed dignity and manliness attached to powers of deep potation, and the fatal effects of drinking were spoken of in a manner both reckless and unfeeling. Thus, I have been assured that a well-known old laird of the old school expressed himself with great indignation at the charge brought against hard drinking that it had actually *killed* people. " Na, na, I never knew onybody killed wi' drinking, but I hae kenn'd some that dee'd in the training." A positive *éclat* was attached to the accomplished and well-trained consumer of claret or of whisky toddy, which gave an importance and even merit to the practice of drinking, and which had a most injurious effect. I am afraid some of the Pleydells of the old school would have looked with the most ineffable contempt on the degeneracy of the present generation in this respect, and that the temperance movement would be little short of insanity in their eyes; and this leads me to a remark. In considering this portion of the subject, we should bear in mind a distinction. The change we now speak of involves more than a mere change of a custom or practice in social life. It is a change in men's sentiments and feelings on a certain great question of morals. Except we enter into this distinction we cannot appreciate the extent of the change which has really taken place in regard to intemperate habits.

I have an anecdote from a descendant of Principal Robertson, of an address made to him, which showed the real importance attached to all that concerned the system of drinking in his time. The Principal had been invited to spend some days in a country-house, and the minister of the parish (a jovial character) had been asked to meet him. Before dinner he went up to Dr Robertson and addressed him confidentially: "Doctor, I understand ye are a brother of my gude freend Peter Robertson of Edinburgh, therefore I'll gie you a piece of advice—Bend [1] weel to the Madeira at dinner, for here ye'll get little o't after." I have known persons who held that a man who could not drink must have a degree of feebleness and imbecility of character. But as this is an important point, I will adduce the higher authority of Lord Cockburn, and quote from him two examples, very different certainly in their nature, but both bearing upon the question. I refer to what he says of Lord Hermand:—" With Hermand drinking was a virtue; he had a sincere respect for drinking, indeed a high moral approbation, and a serious compassion for the poor wretches who *could* not indulge in it, and with due contempt of those who could but did not "; and, secondly, I refer to Lord Cockburn's pages for an anecdote which illustrates the perverted feeling I refer to, now happily no longer existing. It relates the opinion expressed by an old drunken writer of Selkirk (whose name is not mentioned) regarding his anticipation of professional success for Mr Cranstoun, afterwards Lord Corehouse. Sir Walter Scott, William Erskine, and Crans-

[1] Old Scotch for "drink hard."

toun, had dined with this Selkirk writer, and Scott—of hardy, strong, and healthy frame—had matched the writer himself in the matter of whisky punch. Poor Cranstoun, of refined and delicate mental and bodily temperament, was a bad hand at such work, and was soon off the field. On the party breaking up, the Selkirk writer expressed his admiration of Scott, assuring him that *he* would rise high in the profession, and adding : " I'll tell ye what, Maister Walter, that lad Cranstoun may get to the tap o' the Bar, if he can ; but tak' my word for't, it's no' be by drinking."

There was a sort of dogged tone of apology for excess in drinking, which marked the hold which the practice had gained on ordinary minds. Of this we have a remarkable example in the unwilling testimony of a witness who was examined as to the fact of drunkenness being charged against a minister. The person examined was beadle, or one of the church officials. He was asked, " Did you ever see the minister the worse of drink ? " " I canna say I've seen him the waur o' drink, but nae doubt I've seen him the *better* o't," was the evasive answer. The question, however, was pushed further ; and when he was urged to say if this state of being " the better for drink " ever extended to a condition of absolute helpless intoxication, the reply was : " Indeed, afore that cam', I was blind fou mysel', and I could see naething."

A legal friend has told me of a celebrated circuit where Lord Hermand was judge, and Clephane depute-advocate. The party got drunk at Ayr, and so continued (although quite able for their work) till the business was concluded at Jedburgh. Some years after, my informant heard that this circuit had, at Jedburgh, acquired the permanent name of the " *daft* circuit."

Lord Cockburn was fond of describing a circuit scene at Stirling, in his early days at the Bar, under the presidency of his friend and connection Lord Hermand. After the circuit dinner, and when drinking had gone on for some time, young Cockburn observed places becoming vacant in the social circle, but no one going out at the door. He found that the individuals had dropped down under the table. He took the hint, and by this ruse retired from the scene. He lay quiet till the beams of the morning sun penetrated the apartment. The judge and some of his staunch friends coolly walked upstairs, washed their hands and faces, came down to breakfast, and went into court quite fresh and fit for work.

The feeling of importance frequently attached to powers of drinking was formally attested by a well-known western baronet of convivial habits and convivial memory. He was desirous of bearing testimony to the probity, honour, and other high moral qualities of a friend whom he wished to commend. Having fully stated these claims to consideration and respect, he deemed it proper to notice also his *convivial* attainments. He added accordingly, with cautious approval on so important a point : " And he is a fair drinker." [1]

The following anecdote is an amusing example of Scottish servant humour and acuteness in measuring the extent of consumption by a convivial party in Forfarshire. The party had met at a farmer's house not far from Arbroath, to celebrate the reconciliation of two neighbouring farmers who had long been at

---

[1] A friend learned in Scottish history suggests an ingenious remark, that this might mean more than a mere *full drinker*. To drink " fair," used to imply that the person drank in the same proportion as the company ; to drink more would be unmannerly ; to drink less might imply some unfair motive. Either interpretation shows the importance attached to drinking and all that concerned it.

enmity. The host was pressing and hospitable; the party sat late, and consumed a vast amount of whisky toddy. The wife was penurious, and grudged the outlay. When at last, at a morning hour, the party dispersed, the lady, who had not slept in her anxiety, looked over the stairs and eagerly asked the servant girl, " How many bottles of whisky have they used, Betty ? " The lass, who had not to pay for the whisky, but had been obliged to go to the well to fetch the water for the toddy, coolly answered, " I dinna ken, mem, but they've drucken sax gang o' water."

We cannot imagine a better illustration of the general habits that prevailed in Scottish society in regard to drinking about the time we speak of than one which occurs in the recently published " Memoirs of a Banking House," that of the late Sir William Forbes, Bart., of Pitsligo. The book comprises much that is interesting to the family, and to Scotchmen. It contains a pregnant hint as to the manners of polite society and business habits in those days. Of John Coutts, one of four brothers connected with the house, Sir William records how he was " more correct in his conduct than the others; so much so, that Sir William *never but once* saw him in the counting-house disguised with liquor, and incapable of transacting business."

In the Highlands this sort of feeling extended to an almost incredible extent, even so much as to obscure the moral and religious sentiments. Of this a striking proof was afforded in a circumstance which took place in my own church soon after I came into it. One of our Gaelic clergy had so far forgotten himself as to appear in the church somewhat the worse of liquor. This having happened so often as to come to the ears of the bishop, he suspended him from the performance of divine service. Against this decision the people were a little disposed to rebel, because, according to their Highland notions, " a gentleman was no' the waur for being able to tak' a gude glass o' whisky." These were the notions of a people in whose eyes the power of swallowing whisky conferred distinction, and with whom inability to take the fitting quantity was a mark of a mean and futile character. Sad to tell, the funeral rites of Highland chieftains were not supposed to have been duly celebrated except there was an immoderate and often fatal consumption of whisky. It has been related that at the last funeral in the Highlands, conducted according to the traditions of the olden times, several of the guests fell victims to the usage, and actually died of the excesses.

This phase of old and happily almost obsolete Scottish intemperance at funeral solemnities must have been peculiarly revolting. Instances of this horrid practice being carried to a great extent are traditionary in every part of the country. I am assured of the truth of the following anecdote by a son of the gentleman who acted as chief mourner on the occasion :—About seventy years ago an old maiden lady died in Strathspey. Just previous to her death she sent for her grandnephew, and said to him, " Willy, I'm deein', and as ye'll hae the charge o' a' I have, mind now that as much whisky is to be used at my funeral as there was at my baptism." Willy neglected to ask the old lady what the quantity of whisky used at the baptism was, but when the day of the funeral arrived believed her orders would be best fulfilled by allowing each guest to drink as much as he pleased. The churchyard where the body was to be deposited was about ten miles distant from where the death occurred. It was a short day in November, and when the funeral party came to the churchyard the shades of night had considerably closed in. The grave-digger, whose patience had been exhausted in waiting, was not in the least willing to accept of Captain G——'s (the chief mourner) apology for delay. After looking about him he put the anxious question, " But, Captain, whaur's Miss Ketty ? " The reply was, " In her coffin, to be sure, and get it into the earth as fast as you can." There, however, was no coffin ; the procession had sojourned at a country inn by the way, had rested the body on a dyke, started without it, and had to postpone the interment until next day. My correspondent very justly adds the remark, " What would be thought of indulgence in drinking habits now that could lead to such a result ? "

Many scenes of a similar incongruous character are still traditionally connected with such occasions. Within the last thirty years, a laird of Dundonald, a small estate in Ross-shire, died at Inverness. There was open house for some days, and great eating and drinking. Here the corpse commenced its progress toward its appointed home on the coast, and people followed in multitudes to give it a partial convoy, all of whom had to be entertained. It took altogether a fortnight to bury poor Dundonald, and great expense must have been incurred. This, however, is looked back to at Inverness as the last of the real grand old Highland funerals. Such notions of what is due to the memory of the departed have now become un-usual if not obsolete. I myself witnessed the first decided change in this matter. I officiated at the funeral of the late Duke of Sutherland. The procession was a mile long. Refreshments were provided for 7000 persons—beef, bread, and beer—but not one glass of whisky was allowed on the property that day !

It may, perhaps, be said that the change we speak

of is not peculiar to Scotland; that in England the same change has been apparent; and that drunkenness has passed away in the higher circles, as a matter of course, as refinement and taste made an advancement in society. This is true. But there were some features of the question which were peculiar to Scotland, and which at one time rendered it less probable that intemperance would give way in the north. It seemed in some quarters to have taken deeper root amongst us. The system of pressing, or of *compelling*, guests to drink seemed more inveterate. Nothing can more powerfully illustrate the deep-rooted character of intemperate habits in families than an anecdote which was related to me, as coming from the late Mr Mackenzie, author of the *Man of Feeling*. He had been involved in a regular drinking party. He was keeping as free from the usual excesses as he was able, and as he marked companions around him falling victims to the power of drink, he himself dropped off under the table among the slain, as a measure of precaution; and lying there, his attention was called to a small pair of hands working at his throat; on asking what it was, a voice replied, " Sir, I'm the lad that's to lowse the neckcloths." Here, then was a family, where, on drinking occasions, it was the appointed duty of one of the household to attend, and, when the guests were becoming helpless, to untie their cravats in fear of apoplexy or suffocation.[1] We ought certainly to be grateful for the change which has taken place from such a system; for this change has made a great revolution in Scottish social life. The charm

---

[1] In Burt's *Letters from the North of Scotland*, written about 1730, similar scenes are related as occurring in Culloden House: as the company were disabled by drink, two servants in waiting took up the invalids with short poles in their chairs as they sat (if not fallen down), and carried them off to their beds.

and the romance long attached in the minds of some of our countrymen to the whole system and concerns of hard drinking was indeed most lamentable and absurd. At tavern suppers, where, nine times out of ten, it was the express *object* of those who went to get drunk, such stuff as "regal purple stream," "rosy wine," "quaffing the goblet," "bright sparkling nectar," "chasing the rosy hours," and so on, tended to keep up the delusion, and make it a monstrous fine thing for men to sit up drinking half the night, to have frightful headaches all next day, to make maudlin idiots of themselves as they were going home, and to become brutes amongst their family when they arrived. And here I may introduce the mention of a practice connected with the convivial habits of which we have been speaking, but which has for some time passed away, at least from private tables—I mean the absurd system of calling for toasts and sentiments each time the glasses were filled. During dinner not a drop could be touched, except in conjunction with others, and with each drinking to the health of each. But toasts came *after* dinner. I can just remember the practice in partial operation ; and my astonishment as a mere boy, when accidentally dining at table and hearing my mother called upon to "give the company a gentle-man," is one of my earliest reminiscences. Lord Cock-burn must have remembered them well, and I will quote his most amusing account of the effects :—
" After dinner, and before the ladies retired, there generally began what was called ' Rounds ' of toasts, when each gentleman named an absent lady, and each lady an absent gentleman, separately ; or one person was required to give an absent lady, and another per-son was required to match a gentleman with that lady, and the persons named were toasted, generally, with

allusions and jokes about the fitness of the union. And, worst of all, there were ' Sentiments.' These were short epigrammatic sentences, expressive of moral feelings and virtues, and were thought refined and elegant productions. A faint conception of their nauseousness may be formed from the following examples, every one of which I have heard given a thousand times, and which indeed I only recollect from their being favourites. The glasses being filled, a person was asked for his or for her sentiment, when this, or something similar, was committed : ' May the pleasures of the evening bear the reflections of the morning '; or, ' may the friends of our youth be the companions of our old age '; or, ' delicate pleasures to susceptible minds '; ' may the honest heart never feel distress '; ' may the hand of charity wipe the tear from the eye of sorrow.' The conceited, the ready, or the reckless, hackneyed in the art, had a knack of making new sentiments applicable to the passing incidents with great ease. But it was a dreadful oppression on the timid or the awkward. They used to shudder, ladies particularly; for nobody was spared when their turn in the *round* approached. Many a struggle and blush did it cost; but this seemed only to excite the tyranny of the masters of the craft; and compliance could never be avoided, except by more torture than yielding. . . . It is difficult for those who have been under a more natural system to comprehend how a sensible man, a respectable matron, a worthy old maid, and especially a girl, could be expected to go into company easily, on such conditions." [1]

This accompaniment of domestic drinking by a toast or sentiment—the practice of which is now con-

[1] Lord Cockburn's *Memorials of his Time*, p. 37, *et seq.*

fined to public entertainments—was then invariable in private parties, and was supposed to enliven and promote the good fellowship of the social circle. Thus Fergusson, in one of his poems, in describing a dinner, says—

> " The grace is said ; it's nae ower lang,
> The claret reams in bells.
> Quo' Deacon, ' Let the toast round gang ;
> Come, here's our noble sel's
> Weel met the day.' "

There was a great variety of these toasts, some of them exclusively Scottish. A correspondent has favoured me with a few reminiscences of such incentives to inebriety.

The ordinary form of drinking a health was in the address, " Here's t' ye."

Then such as the following were named by successive members of the company at the call of the host :—

The land o' cakes (Scotland).
Mair freens and less need o' them.
Thumping luck and fat weans.
When we're gaun up the hill o' fortune may we ne'er meet a freen' coming down.
May ne'er waur be amang us.
May the hinges o' freendship never rust, or the wings o' luve lose a feather.
Here's to them that lo'es us or lenns us a lift.
Here's health to the sick, stilts to the lame ; claise to the back, and brose to the wame.
Here's health, wealth, wit, and meal.
The deil rock them in a creel that does na' wish us a' weel.
Horny hands and weather-beaten haffets (cheeks).
The rending o' rocks and the pu'in' doun o' auld houses.

The last two belong to the mason craft; the first implies a wish for plenty of work, and health to do it; the second, to erect new buildings and clear away old ones.

May the winds o' adversity ne'er blaw open our door.

May poortith ne'er throw us in the dirt or gowd into the high saddle.[1]

May the mouse ne'er leave our meal-pock wi' the tear in its e'e.

Blythe may we a' be.

Ill may we never see.

Breeks and brochan (brose).

May we ne'er want a freend or a drappie to gie him.

Gude e'en to you a', an' tak' your nappy.

A willy-waught's a gude night cappy.[2]

May we a' be canty an' cosy.

An' ilk hae a wife in his bosy.

A cosy but, and a canty ben.

To couthie[3] *women and trusty men.*

The ingle neuk wi' routh[4] *o' bannocks and bairns.*

Here's to him wha winna beguile ye.

Mair sense and mair siller.

Horn, corn, wool, an' yarn.[5]

Sometimes certain toasts were accompanied by *Highland* honours. This was a very exciting, and to a stranger a somewhat alarming, proceeding. I recollect my astonishment the first time I witnessed the cere-mony—the company, from sitting quietly drinking their wine, seemed to assume the attitude of harmless maniacs, allowed to amuse themselves. The moment

---

[1] May we never be cast down by adversity, or unduly elevated by prosperity.

[2] A toast at parting or breaking-up of the party.

[3] Loving. [4] Plenty. [5] Toast for agricultural dinners.

the toast was given, and proposed to be drunk with Highland honours, the gentlemen all rose, and with one foot on their chair and another on the *table*, they drank the toast with Gaelic shrieks, which were awful to hear, the cheering being under the direction of a toast-master appointed to direct the proceedings. I am indebted to the kindness of the Rev. Duncan Campbell, the esteemed minister of Moulin, for the form used on such occasions. Here it is in the Gaelic and the Saxon :—

Gaelic.	*Translation.*
So !	Prepare !
Nish ! Nish !	Now ! Now !
Sud ris ! Sud ris !	Yon again ! Yon again !
Nish ! Nish !	Now ! Now !
Thig ris ! Thig ris !	At it again ! At it again !
A on uair eile !	Another time, or one cheer more !

The reader is to imagine these words uttered with yells and vociferations, and accompanied with frantic gestures.

The system of giving toasts was so regularly established, that collections of them were published to add brilliancy to the festive board. By the kindness of the librarian, I have seen a little volume which is in the Signet Library of Edinburgh. It is entitled, " The Gentleman's New Bottle Companion," Edinburgh, printed in the year MDCCLXXVII. It contains various toasts and sentiments which the writer considered to be suitable to such occasions. Of the taste and decency of the companies where some of them could be made use of, the less said the better.

I have heard also of large traditionary collections of toasts and sentiments, belonging to old clubs and societies, extending back above a century, but I have not seen any of them, and I believe my readers will think they have had quite enough.

The favourable reaction which has taken place in regard to the whole system of intemperance may very fairly, in the first place, be referred to an improved *moral* feeling. But other causes have also assisted; and it is curious to observe how the different changes in the modes of society bear upon one another. The alteration in the convivial habits which we are noticing in our own country may be partly due to alteration of hours. The old plan of early dining favoured a system of suppers, and after supper was a great time for convivial songs and sentiments. This of course induced drinking to a late hour. Most drinking songs imply the night as the season of conviviality—thus in a popular madrigal :—

> " By the gaily circling glass
> We can tell how minutes pass ;
> By the hollow cask we're told
> How the waning *night* grows old."

And Burns thus marks the time :—

> " It is the moon, I ken her horn,
> That's blinkin' in the lift sae hie ;
> She shines sae bright, to wyle us hame,
> But by my sooth she'll wait a wee."

The young people of the present day have no idea of the state of matters in regard to the supper system when it was the normal condition of society. The late dining hours may make the social circle more formal, but they have been far less favourable to drinking propensities. After such dinners as ours are now, suppers are clearly out of the question. One is astonished to look back and recall the scenes to which were attached associations of hilarity, conviviality, and enjoyment. Drinking parties were protracted beyond the whole Sunday, having begun by a dinner on Saturday; imbecility and prostrate helplessness were a common result of these bright and jovial scenes; and by what perversion of language, or by what obliquity of sentiment, the notions of pleasure could be attached to scenes of such excess—to the nausea, the disgust of sated appetite, and the racking headache—it is not easy to explain. There were men of heads so hard, and of stomachs so insensible, that, like my friend Saunders Paul, they could stand anything in the way of drink. But to men in general, and to the more delicate constitutions, such a life must have been a cause of great misery. To a certain extent, and up to a certain point, wine may be a refreshment and a wholesome stimulant; nay, it is a medicine, and a valuable one, and as such, comes recommended on fitting occasions by the physician. *Beyond* this point, as sanctioned and approved by nature, the use of wine is only degradation. Well did the sacred writer call wine, when thus taken in excess, "a mocker." It makes all men equal, because it makes them all idiotic. It allures them into a vicious indulgence, and then mocks their folly, by depriving them of any sense they may ever have possessed.

It has, I fear, been injurious to the cause of temperance, that emotions of true friendship, and the outpouring of human affections, should so frequently be connected with the obligation that the parties should *get drunk together*. Drunkenness is thus made to hold too close an association in men's minds with some of the best and finest feelings of their nature.

"Friend of my soul, this goblet sip,"

III

is the constant acknowledged strain of poetical friendship: our own Robert Burns calls upon the dear companion of his early happy days, with whom he had "paidl't i' the burn, frae mornin' sun till dine," and between whom "braid seas had roar'd sin' auld lang syne," to commemorate their union of heart and spirit, and to welcome their meeting after years of separation, by each one joining his pint-stoup, and by each taking a mutual "richt guid willie-waught," in honour of the innocent and happy times of "auld lang syne." David marks his recognition of friendship by tokens of a different character: "We took sweet counsel together, and walked *in the house of God* as friends."—Ps. lv. 14.

Reference has already been made to Lord Hermand's opinion of drinking, and to the high estimation in which he held a staunch drinker, according to the testimony of Lord Cockburn. There is a remarkable corroboration of this opinion in a current anecdote which is traditionary regarding the same learned judge. A case of some great offence was tried before him, and the counsel pleaded extenuation for his client in that he was *drunk* when he committed the offence. "Drunk!" exclaimed Lord Hermand, in great indignation; "if he could do such a thing when he was drunk, what might he not have done when he was *sober*!" evidently implying that the normal condition of human nature, and its most hopeful one, was a condition of intoxication.

Of the prevalence of hard drinking in certain houses as a system, a remarkable proof is given on page 95. The following anecdote still further illustrates the subject, and corresponds exactly with the story of the "loosing the cravats," which was performed for guests in a state of helpless inebriety by one of the household. There had been a carousing party at Castle Grant, many years ago, and as the evening advanced towards morning two Highlanders were in attendance to carry the guests upstairs, it being understood that none could by any other means arrive at their sleeping apartments. One or two of the guests, however, whether from their abstinence or their superior strength of head, were walking upstairs, and declined the proffered assistance. The attendants were quite astonished, and indignantly exclaimed, " Agh, it's sare cheenged times at Castle Grant, when shentlemens can gang to bed on their ain feet."

There was a practice in many Scottish houses which favoured most injuriously the national tendency to spirit-drinking, and that was a foolish and inconsiderate custom of offering a glass on all occasions as a mark of kindness or hospitality. I mention the custom only for the purpose of offering a remonstrance. It should never be done. Even now, I am assured, small jobs (carpenters' or blacksmiths', or such like) are constantly remunerated in the West Highlands of Scotland—and doubtless in many other parts of the country—not by a pecuniary payment, but by a *dram* ; if the said dram be taken from a *speerit*-decanter out of the family press or cupboard, the compliment is esteemed the greater, and the offering doubly valued.

A very amusing dialogue between a landlord and his tenant on this question of the dram has been sent to me. John Colquhoun, an aged Dumbartonshire tenant, is asked by his laird on Lochlomond side, to stay a minute till he *tastes*. " Now, John," says the laird. " Only half a glass, Camstraddale," meekly pleads John. " Which half," rejoins the laird, " the upper or the lower ? " John grins, and turns off *both —the upper and lower* too.

The upper and lower portions of the glass furnish another drinking anecdote. A very greedy old lady employed another John Colquhoun to cut the grass upon the lawn, and enjoined him to cut it very close, adding, as a reason for the injunction, that one inch at the bottom was worth two at the top. Having finished his work much to her satisfaction, the old lady got out the whisky-bottle and a tapering wineglass, which she filled about half full; John suggested that it would be better to fill it up, slily adding, " Fill it up, mem, for it's no' like the gress; an inch at the tap's worth twa at the boddom."

But the most whimsical anecdote connected with the subject of drink, is one traditionary in the south of Scotland, regarding an old Gallovidian lady disclaiming more drink under the following circumstances :—The old generation of Galloway lairds were a primitive and hospitable race, but their conviviality sometimes led to awkward occurrences. In former days, when roads were bad and wheeled vehicles almost unknown, an old laird was returning from a supper party, with his lady mounted behind him on horseback. On crossing the River Urr, at a ford at a point where it joins the sea, the old lady dropped off, but was not missed till her husband reached his door, when, of course, there was an immediate search made. The party who were despatched in quest of her arrived just in time to find her remonstrating with the advancing tide, which trickled into her mouth, in these words, " No anither drap; neither het nor cauld."

A lady, on one occasion, offering a dram to a porter in a rather small glass, said, " Take it off; it will do you no harm," on which the man, looking at the diminutive glass, observed, " Harm! Na, gin it were poushon " (poison).

I would now introduce, as a perfect illustration of this portion of our subject, two descriptions of clergymen, well known men in their day, which are taken from Dr Carlyle's work, already referred to. Of Dr Alexander Webster, a clergyman, and one of his contemporaries, he writes thus :—" Webster, leader of the high-flying party, had justly obtained much respect amongst the clergy, and all ranks indeed, for having established the Widows' Fund. . . . His appearance of great strictness in religion, to which he was bred under his father, who was a very popular minister of the Tolbooth Church, not acting in restraint of his convivial humour, he was held to be excellent company even by those of dissolute manners ; while, being a five-bottle man, he could lay them all under the table. This had brought on him the nickname of Dr Bonum Magnum in the time of faction. But never being indecently the worse of liquor ; and a love of claret, to any degree, not being reckoned in those days a sin in Scotland, all his excesses were pardoned."

Dr Patrick Cumming, also a clergyman and a contemporary, he describes in the following terms :— "Dr Patrick Cumming was, at this time (1751), at the head of the moderate interest, and had his temper been equal to his talents, might have kept it long, for he had both learning and sagacity, and very agreeable conversation, *with a constitution able to bear the conviviality of the times.*"

Now, of all the anecdotes and facts which I have collected, or of all which I have ever heard to illustrate the state of Scottish society in the past times, as regards its habits of intemperance, this assuredly surpasses them all :—Of two well-known, distinguished, and leading clergymen in the middle of the eighteenth century, one who had " obtained much respect," and "had the appearance of great strictness in religion," is described as an enormous drinker of claret; the other, an able leader of a powerful section in the Church, is described as *owing* his influence to his power of meeting the conviviality of the times. Suppose for a moment a future biographer should write in this strain of eminent divines, and should apply to distinguished members of the Scottish Church in 1863 such description as the following: "Dr —— was a man who took a leading part in all church affairs at this time, and was much looked up to by the evangelical section of the General Assembly; he could always carry off without difficulty his five bottles of claret. Dr —— had great influence in society, and led the opposite party in the General Assembly, as he could take his place in all companies, and drink on fair terms at the most convivial tables!" Why, this seems to us so monstrous, that we can scarcely believe Dr Carlyle's account of matters in his day to be possible.

There is a story which illustrates, with terrible force, the power which drinking had obtained in Scottish social life. I have been deterred from bringing it forward, as too shocking for production. But as the story is pretty well known, and its truth vouched for on high authority, I venture to give it, as affording a proof that, in those days, no consideration, not even the most awful that affects human nature, could be made to outweigh the claims of a determined conviviality. It may, I think, be mentioned also, in the way of warning men generally against the hardening and demoralising effects of habitual drunkenness. The story is this :—At a prolonged drinking bout, one of the party remarked, " What gars the laird of Garskadden look sae gash ? " [1] " Ou," says his neighbour,

[1] Ghastly.

the laird of Kilmardinny, " deil meane him! Garskadden's been wi' his Maker these twa hours; I saw him step awa', but I didna like to disturb gude company!"[1]

Before closing this subject of excess in *drinking*, I may refer to another indulgence in which our countrymen are generally supposed to partake more largely than their neighbours:—I mean snuff-taking. The popular southern ideas of a Scotchman and his snuff-box are inseparable. Smoking does not appear to have been practised more in Scotland than in England, and if Scotchmen are sometimes intemperate in the use of snuff, it is certainly a more innocent excess than intemperance in whisky. I recollect, amongst the common people in the north, a mode of taking snuff which showed a determination to make the *most* of it, and which indicated somewhat of intemperance in the enjoyment; this was to receive it not through a pinch between the fingers, but through a quill or little bone ladle, which forced it up the nose. But, besides smoking and snuffing, I have a reminiscence of a *third* use of tobacco, which I apprehend is now quite obsolete. Some of my readers will be surprised when I name this forgotten luxury. It was called *plugging*, and consisted (*horresco referens*) in poking a piece of pig-tail tobacco right into the nostril. I remember this distinctly; and now, at a distance of more than sixty years, I recall my utter astonishment as a boy, at seeing my grand-uncle, with whom I lived in early days, put a thin piece of tobacco fairly up his nose. I suppose the plug acted as a continued stimulant on the olfactory nerve, and was, in short, like taking a perpetual pinch of snuff.

[1] The scene is described and place mentioned in Dr Strang's account of Glasgow Clubs, p. 104, 2nd Edition.

The inveterate snuff-taker, like the dram-drinker, felt severely the being deprived of his accustomed stimulant, as in the following instance:—A severe snow-storm in the Highlands, which lasted for several weeks, having stopped all communication betwixt neighbouring hamlets, the snuff-boxes were soon reduced to their last pinch. Borrowing and begging from all the neighbours within reach were first resorted to, but when these failed, all were alike reduced to the longing which unwilling-abstinent snuff-takers alone know. The minister of the parish was amongst the unhappy number; the craving was so intense that study was out of the question, and he became quite restless. As a last resort the beadle was despatched, through the snow, to a neighbouring glen, in the hope of getting a supply; but he came back as unsuccessful as he went. "What's to be dune, John?" was the minister's pathetic inquiry. John shook his head, as much as to say that he could not tell; but immediately thereafter started up, as if a new idea had occurred to him. He came back in a few minutes, crying, "Hae!" The minister, too eager to be scrutinising, took a long, deep pinch, and then said, "Whaur did you get it?" "I soupit[1] the poupit," was John's expressive reply. The minister's accumulated superfluous Sabbath snuff now came into good use.

It does not appear that at this time a similar excess in *eating* accompanied this prevalent tendency to excess in drinking. Scottish tables were at that period plain and abundant, but epicurism or gluttony do not seem to have been handmaids to drunkenness. A humorous anecdote, however, of a full-eating laird, may well accompany those which appertain to the *drinking* lairds:—A lady in the north having watched the pro-

[1] Swept.

ceedings of a guest, who ate long and largely, she ordered the servant to take away, as he had at last laid down his knife and fork. To her surprise, however, he resumed his work, and she apologised to him, saying, " I thought, Mr ——, you had done." " Oh, so I had, mem ; but I just fan' a doo in the *redd* o' my plate." He had discovered a pigeon lurking amongst the bones and refuse of his plate, and could not resist finishing it.

CHAPTER IV

ON THE OLD SCOTTISH
DOMESTIC SERVANT

I COME now to a subject on which a great change has taken place in this country during my own experience, viz., those peculiarities of intercourse which some years back marked the connection between masters and servants. In many Scottish houses a great familiarity prevailed between members of the family and the domestics. For this many reasons might have been assigned. Indeed, when we consider the simple modes of life, which discarded the ideas of ceremony or etiquette; the retired and uniform style of living, which afforded few opportunities for any change in the domestic arrangements; and when we add to these a free, unrestrained, informal, and natural style of intercommunion, which seems rather a national characteristic, we need not be surprised to find in quiet Scottish families a sort of intercourse with old domestics which can hardly be looked for at a time when habits are so changed, and where much of the quiet eccentricity belonging to us as a national characteristic is almost necessarily softened down or driven out. Many circumstances conspired to promote familiarity with old domestics, which are now entirely changed. We take the case of a domestic coming early into service, and passing year after year in the same family. The servant grows up into old age and confirmed habits when the laird is becoming a man, a husband, father of a family. The domestic cannot forget the days when his master was a child, riding on his back, applying to him for help in difficulties about his fishing, his rabbits, his pony, his going to school. All the family know how attached he is; nobody likes to speak harshly to him. He is a privileged man. The faithful old servant of thirty, forty, or fifty years, if with a tendency to be jealous, cross, and interfering, becomes a great trouble. Still the relative position was the result of good feelings. If the familiarity sometimes became a nuisance, it was a wholesome nuisance, and relic of a simpler time gone by. But the case of the old servant, whether agreeable or trouble-some, was often so fixed and established in the house-holds of past days, that there was scarce a possibility of getting away from it. The well-known story of the answer of one of these domestic tyrants to the irritated master, who was making an effort to free himself from the thraldom, shows the idea entertained, by *one* of the parties at least, of the permanency of the tenure. I am assured by a friend that the true edition of the story was this:—An old Mr Erskine of Dun had one of these retainers, under whose language and un-reasonable assumption he had long groaned. He had almost determined to bear it no longer, when, walk-ing out with his man, on crossing a field, the master exclaimed, " There's a hare." Andrew looked at the place, and coolly replied, " What a big lee, it's a cauff." The master, quite angry now, plainly told the old domestic that they *must* part. But the tried servant of forty years, not dreaming of the possibility of *his* dismissal, innocently asked, " Ay, sir; whare ye gaun? I'm sure ye're aye best at hame "; supposing that, if there were to be any disruption, it must be the master who would change the place. An example of a similar fixedness of tenure in an old servant was afforded in an anecdote related of an old coachman long in the service of a noble lady, and who gave all the trouble and annoyance which he conceived were the privileges of his position in the family. At last the lady fairly gave him notice to quit, and told him he must go. The only satisfaction she got was the quiet answer, " Na, na, my lady ; I druve ye to your marriage, and I shall stay to drive ye to your burial." Indeed, we have heard of a still stronger assertion of his official position by one who met an order to quit his master's service by the cool reply, " Na, na ; I'm no gangin'. If ye dinna ken whan ye've a gude servant ; I ken whan I've a gude place."

It is but fair, however, to give an anecdote in which the master and the servant's position was *reversed*, in regard to a wish for a change :—An old servant of a relation of my own with an ungovernable temper, became at last so weary of his master's irascibility, that he declared he must leave, and gave as his reason the fits of anger which came on, and produced such great annoyance that he could not stand it any longer. His master, unwilling to lose him, tried to coax him by reminding him that the anger was soon off. " Ay," replied the other very shrewdly, " but it's nae suner aff that it's on again." I remember well an old servant of the old school, who had been fifty years domestic-ated in a family. Indeed I well remember the celebra-tion of the half-century service completed. There were rich scenes with Sandy and his mistress. Let me recall you both to memory. Let me think of you, the kind, generous, warm-hearted mistress ; a gentle-woman by descent and by feeling ; a true friend, a sincere Christian. And let me think, too, of you, Sandy, an honest, faithful, and attached member of the family. For you were in that house rather as a humble friend than a servant. But out of this fifty years of attached service there sprang a sort of domestic relation and freedom of intercourse which would surprise people in these days. And yet Sandy knew his place. Like Corporal Trim, who, although so familiar and admitted to so much familiarity with my Uncle Toby, never failed in the respectful address—never forgot to say "your honour." At a dinner party Sandy was very active about changing his mistress's plate, and whipped it off when he saw that she had got a piece of rich pâté upon it. His mistress, not liking such rapid movements, and at the same time knowing that remonstrance was in vain, exclaimed, "Hout, Sandy, I'm no dune," and dabbed her fork into the "pattee" as it disappeared, to rescue a morsel. I remember her praise of English mutton was a great annoyance to the Scottish prejudices of Sandy. One day she was telling me of a triumph Sandy had upon that subject. The smell of the joint roasting had become very offensive through the house. The lady called out to Sandy to have the doors closed, and added, "That must be some horrid Scotch mutton you have got." To Sandy's delight, this was a leg of *English* mutton his mistress had expressly chosen; and, as she significantly told me, "Sandy never let that down upon me."

On Deeside there existed, in my recollection, besides the Saunders Paul I have alluded to, a number of extraordinary acute and humorous Scottish characters amongst the lower classes. The native gentry enjoyed their humour, and hence arose a familiarity of intercourse which called forth many amusing scenes and quaint rejoinders. A celebrated character of this description bore the soubriquet of "Boaty," of whom I have already spoken. He had acted as Charon of the Dee at Banchory, and passed the boat over the river before there was a bridge. Boaty had many curious sayings recorded of him. When speaking of the gentry around, he characterised them according to their occupations and activity of habits, thus:—" As to Mr Russell of Blackha', he just works himsell like a paid labourer; Mr Duncan's a' the day fish, fish; but Sir Robert's a perfect gentleman—he does naething, naething." Boaty was a first-rate salmon-fisher himself, and was much sought after by amateurs who came to Banchory for the sake of the sport afforded by the beautiful Dee. He was, perhaps, a little spoiled, and presumed upon the indulgence and familiarity shown to him in the way of his craft—as, for example, he was in attendance with his boat on a sportsman who was both skilful and successful, for he caught salmon after salmon. Between each fish catching he solaced himself with a good pull from a flask, which he returned to his pocket, however, without offering to let Boaty have any participation in the refreshment. Boaty, partly a little professionally jealous, perhaps, at the success, and partly indignant at receiving less than his usual attention on such occasions, and seeing no prospect of amendment, deliberately pulled the boat to shore, shouldered the oars, rods, landing-nets, and all the fishing apparatus which he had provided, and set off homewards. His companion, far from considering his day's work to be over, and keen for more sport, was amazed, and peremptorily ordered him to come back. But all the answer made by the offended Boaty was, "Na, na; them 'at drink by themsells may just fish by themsells."

The charge these old domestics used to take of the interests of the family, and the cool way in which they took upon them to protect those interests, sometimes led to very provoking, and sometimes to very

ludicrous, exhibitions of importance. A friend told
me of a dinner scene illustrative of this sort of interference which had happened at Airth in the last
generation. Mrs Murray, of Abercairney, had been
amongst the guests, and at dinner one of the family
noticed that she was looking for the proper spoon to
help herself with salt. The old servant, Thomas, was
appealed to, that the want might be supplied. He did
not notice the appeal. It was repeated in a more peremptory manner, " Thomas, Mrs Murray has not a
salt-spoon! " to which he replied most emphatically,
" Last time Mrs Murray dined here we *lost* a salt-
spoon." An old servant who took a similar charge of
everything that went on in the family, having observed that his master thought he had drunk wine
with every lady at table, but had overlooked one,
jogged his memory with the question, " What ails ye
at her wi' the green gown ? "

In my own family I know a case of a very long
service, and where, no doubt, there was much interest
and attachment ; but it was a case where the temper
had not softened under the influence of years, but
had rather assumed that form of disposition which we
denominate *crusty*. My grand-uncle, Sir A. Ramsay,
died in 1806, and left a domestic who had been in his
service since he was ten years of age ; and being at
the time of his master's death past fifty or well on to
sixty, he must have been more than forty years a
servant in the family. From the retired life my grand-
uncle had been leading, Jamie Layal had much of his
own way, and, like many a domestic so situated, he
did not like to be contradicted, and, in fact, could not
bear to be found fault with. My uncle, who had succeeded to a part of my grand-uncle's property, succeeded also to Jamie Layal, and, from respect to his

late master's memory and Jamie's own services, he took him into his house, intending him to act as house servant. However, this did not answer, and he was soon kept on, more with the form than the reality of any active duty, and took any light work that was going on about the house. In this capacity it was his daily task to feed a flock of turkeys which were growing up to maturity. On one occasion, my aunt having followed him in his work, and having observed such a waste of food that the ground was actually covered with grain which they could not eat, and which would soon be destroyed and lost, naturally remonstrated, and suggested a more reasonable and provident supply. But all the answer she got from the offended Jamie was a bitter rejoinder, " Weel, then, neist time they sall get *nane ava* ! " On another occasion a family from a distance had called whilst my uncle and aunt were out of the house. Jamie came into the parlour to deliver the cards, or to announce that they had called. My aunt, somewhat vexed at not having been in the way, inquired what message Mr and Mrs Innes had left, as she had expected one. " No ; no message." She returned to the charge, and asked again if they had not told him *anything* he was to repeat. Still, " No ; no message." " But did they say nothing ? Are you sure they did nothing ? " Jamie, sadly put out and offended at being thus interrogated, at last burst forth, " They neither said ba nor bum," and indignantly left the room, banging the door after him. A characteristic anecdote of one of these old domestics I have from a friend who was acquainted with the parties concerned. The old man was standing at the sideboard and attending to the demands of a pretty large dinner party ; the calls made for various wants from the company became so numerous and frequent that the attendant got quite bewildered, and lost his patience and temper; at length he gave vent to his indignation in a remonstrance addressed to the whole company, "Cry a' thegither, that's the way to be served."

I have two characteristic and dry Scottish answers, traditional in the Lothian family, supplied to me by the late excellent and highly-gifted Marquis. A Marquis of Lothian of a former generation observed in his walk two workmen very busy with a ladder to reach a bell, on which they next kept up a furious ringing. He asked what was the object of making such a din, to which the answer was, "Oh, juist, my lord to ca' the workmen together!" "Why, how many are there?" asked his lordship. "Ou, juist Sandy and me," was the quiet rejoinder. The same Lord Lothian, looking about the garden, directed his gardener's attention to a particular plum-tree, charging him to be careful of the produce of that tree, and send the *whole* of it in marked, as it was of a very particular kind. "Ou," said the gardener, "I'll dae that, my lord; there's juist twa o' them."

These dry answers of Newbattle servants remind us of a similar state of communication in a Yester domestic. Lord Tweeddale was very fond of dogs, and on leaving Yester for London he instructed his head keeper, a quaint bodie, to give him a periodical report of the kennel, and particulars of his favourite dogs. Among the latter was an *especial* one, of the true Skye breed, called "Pickle," from which soubriquet we may form a tolerable estimate of his qualities.

It happened one day, in or about the year 1827, that poor Pickle, during the absence of his master, was taken unwell; and the watchful guardian immediately warned the Marquis of the sad fact, and of the progress of the disease, which lasted three days—for which he sent the three following laconic despatches :—

Yester, May 1st, 18—.

MY LORD,

Pickle's no' weel.

Your Lordship's humble servant, etc.

Yester, May 2nd, 18—.

MY LORD,

Pickle will no' do.

I am your Lordship's, etc.

Yester, May 3rd., 18—.

MY LORD,

Pickle's dead.

I am your Lordship's, etc.

I have heard of an old Forfarshire lady who, knowing the habits of her old and spoilt servant, when she wished a note to be taken without loss of time, held it open and read it over to him, saying, " There, noo, Andrew, ye ken a' that's in't ; noo dinna stop to open it, but just send it aff." Of another servant, when sorely tried by an unaccustomed bustle and hurry, a very amusing anecdote has been recorded. His mistress, a woman of high rank, who had been living in much quiet and retirement for some time, was called upon to entertain a large party at dinner. She consulted with Nichol, her faithful servant, and all the arrangements were made for the great event. As the company were arriving, the lady saw Nichol running about in great agitation, and in his shirt sleeves. She remonstrated, and said that as the guests were coming in he must put on his coat. " Indeed, my lady," was his excited reply, " indeed, there's sae muckle rinnin' here and rinnin' there, that I'm just distrackit. I hae cuist'n my coat and waistcoat, and faith I dinna ken how lang I can thole [1] my breeks."

[1] Bear.

There is often a ready wit in this class of character, marked by their replies. I have the following communicated from an ear-witness:—" Weel, Peggy," said a man to an old family servant, " I wonder ye're aye single yet ! " " Me marry," said she, indignantly ; " I wouldna gie my single life for a' the double anes I ever saw ! "

An old woman was exhorting a servant once about her ways. " You serve the deevil," said she. " Me ! " said the girl ; " na, na, I dinna serve the deevil ; I serve ae single lady."

A baby was out with the nurse, who walked it up and down the garden. " Is't a laddie or a lassie ? " said the gardener. " A laddie," said the maid. " Weel," says he, " I'm glad o' that, for there's ower mony women in the world." " Hech, man," said Jess, " div ye no' ken there's aye maist sawn o' the best crap ? "

The answers of servants used curiously to illustrate habits and manners of the time—as the economical modes of her mistress's life were well touched by the lass who thus described her ways and domestic habits with her household : " She's vicious upo' the wark ; but eh, she's vary mysterious o' the victualling."

A country habit of making the gathering of the congregation in the churchyard previous to and after divine service an occasion for gossip and business, which I remember well, is thoroughly described in the following :—A lady, on hiring a servant girl in the country, told her, as a great indulgence, that she should have the liberty of attending the church every Sunday, but that she would be expected to return home always immediately on the conclusion of service. The lady, however, rather unexpectedly found a positive objection raised against this apparently reasonable arrangement. " Then I canna engage wi'

ye, mem; for 'deed I wadna gie the crack i' the kirkyard for a' the sermon."

There is another story which shows that a greater
importance might be attached to the crack i' the kirkyard than was done even by the servant lass mentioned
above. A rather rough subject, residing in Galloway,
used to attend church regularly, as it appeared, for
the *sake* of the crack; for on being taken to task for
his absenting himself, he remarked, " There's nae need
to gang to the kirk noo, for everybody gets a newspaper."

The changes that many of us have lived to witness
in this kind of intercourse between families and old
servants is a part of a still greater change—the change
in that modification of the feudal system, the attachment of clans. This, also, from transfers of property
and extinction of old families in the Highlands, as
well as from more general causes, is passing away;
and it includes also changes in the intercourse between
landed proprietors and cottagers, and abolition of
harvest-homes, and such meetings. People are now
more independent of each other, and service has
become a pecuniary and not a sentimental question.
The extreme contrast of that old-fashioned Scottish
intercourse of families with their servants and dependants, of which I have given some amusing examples,
is found in the modern manufactory system. There
the service is a mere question of personal interest.
One of our first practical engineers, and one of the
first engine-makers in England, stated that he employed and paid handsomely on an average 1200
workmen; but that they held so little feeling for him
as their master, that not above half-a-dozen of the
number would notice him when passing him, either
in the works or out of work hours. Contrast this

advanced state of dependants' indifference with the familiarity of domestic intercourse we have been describing !

It has been suggested by my esteemed friend, Dr W. Lindsay Alexander, that Scottish anecdotes deal too exclusively with the shrewd, quaint, and pawky *humour* of our countrymen, and have not sufficiently illustrated the deep pathos and strong loving-kindness of the " kindly Scot "—qualities which, however little appreciated across the Border, abound in Scottish poetry and Scottish life. For example, to take the case before us of these old retainers, although snappy and disagreeable to the last degree in their replies, and often most provoking in their ways, they were yet deeply and sincerely attached to the family where they had so long been domesticated ; and the servant who would reply to her mistress's order to mend the fire by the short answer, " The fire's weel eneuch," would at the same time evince much interest in all that might assist her in sustaining the credit of her domestic economy, as, for example, whispering in her ear at dinner, " Press the jeelies ; they winna keep " ; and had the hour of real trial and of difficulty come to the family, would have gone to the death for them, and shared their greatest privations. Dr Alexander gives a very interesting example of kindness and affectionate attachment in an old Scottish domestic of his own family, whose quaint and odd familiarity was charming. I give it in his own words :—" When I was a child there was an old servant at Pinkieburn, where my early days were spent, who had been all her life, I may say, in the house, for she came to it a child, and lived, without ever leaving it, till she died in it, seventy-five years of age. Her feeling to her old master, who was just two years younger than herself, was a curious compound of the deference of a servant and the familiarity and affection of a sister. She had known him as a boy, lad, man, and old man, and she seemed to have a sort of notion that without her he must be a very helpless being indeed. ' I aye keepit the hoose for him, whether he was hame or awa',' was a frequent utterance of hers; and she never seemed to think the intrusion even of his own nieces, who latterly lived with him, at all legitimate. When on her deathbed, he hobbled to her room with difficulty, having just got over a severe attack of gout, to bid her farewell. I chanced to be present, but was too young to remember what passed, except one thing, which probably was rather recalled to me afterwards than properly recollected by me. It was her last request. ' Laird,' said she (for so she always called him, though his lairdship was of the smallest), ' will ye tell them to bury me whaur I'll lie across at your feet?' I have always thought this characteristic of the old Scotch servant, and as such I send it to you."

And here I would introduce another story which struck me very forcibly as illustrating the union of the qualities referred to by Dr Alexander. In the following narrative, how deep and tender a feeling is expressed in a brief dry sentence! I give Mr Scott's language [1] :—" My brother and I were, during our High School vacation, some forty years ago, very much indebted to the kindness of a clever young carpenter employed in the machinery workshop of New Lanark Mills, near to which we were residing during our six weeks' holidays. It was he—Samuel Shaw, our dear companion—who first taught us to saw, and to plane, and to turn too; and who made us the bows and arrows in which we so much delighted. The vacation

[1] Rev. R. Scott of Cranwell.

over, and our hearts very sore, but bound to Samuel Shaw for ever, our mother sought to place some pecuniary recompense in his hand at parting, for all the great kindness he had shown her boys. Samuel looked in her face, and gently moving her hand aside, with an affectionate look cast upon us, who were by, exclaimed, in a tone which had sorrow in it, ' Noo, Mrs Scott, *ye hae spoilt a*'.' " After such an appeal, it may be supposed no recompense, in silver or in gold, remained with Samuel Shaw.

On the subject of the old Scottish domestic, I have to acknowledge a kind communication from Lord Kinloch, which I give in his Lordship's words:—" My father had been in the counting-house of the well-known David Dale, the founder of the Lanark Mills, and eminent for his benevolence. Mr Dale, who it would appear was a short, stout man, had a person in his employment named Matthew, who was permitted that familiarity with his master which was so characteristic of the former generation. One winter day Mr Dale came into the counting-house, and complained that he had fallen on the ice. Matthew, who saw that his master was not much hurt, grinned a sarcastic smile. ' I fell all my length,' said Mr Dale. ' Nae great length, sir,' said Matthew. ' Indeed, Matthew, ye need not laugh,' said Mr Dale; ' I have hurt the sma' o' my back.' ' I wunner whaur *that* is,' said Matthew." Indeed, specimens like Matthew, of serving-men of the former time, have latterly been fast going out, but I remember one or two such. A lady of my acquaintance had one named John in her house at Portobello. I remember how my modern ideas were offended by John's familiarity when waiting at table. " Some more wine, John," said his mistress. " There's some i' the bottle, mem," said John. A little after, "Mend the fire, John." "The fire's weel eneuch, mem," replied the impracticable John. Another "John" of my acquaintance was in the family of Mrs Campbell of Ardnave, mother of the Princess Polignac and the Hon. Mrs Archibald Macdonald. A young lady visiting in the family asked John at dinner for a potato. John made no response. The request was repeated; when John, putting his mouth to her ear, said, very audibly, "There's jist twa in the dish, and they maun be keepit for the strangers."

The following was sent me by a kind correspondent —a learned Professor in India—as a sample of *squabbling* between Scottish servants. A mistress observing something peculiar in her maid's manner, addressed her, "Dear me, Tibbie, what are you so snappish about, that you go knocking the things as you dust them?" "Ou, mem, it's Jock." "Well, what has Jock been doing?" "Ou (with an indescribable, but easily imaginable toss of the head), he was angry at me, an' misca'd me, an' I said I was juist as the Lord had made me, an' ——" "Well, Tibbie?" "An' he said the Lord could hae had little to dae when he made me." The idea of Tibbie being the work of an idle moment was one, the deliciousness of which was not likely to be relished by the lassie.

The following characteristic anecdote of a Highland servant I have received from the same correspondent. An English gentleman, travelling in the Highlands, was rather late of coming down to dinner. Donald was sent upstairs to intimate that all was ready. He speedily returned, nodding significantly, as much as to say that it was all right. "But, Donald," said the master, after some further trial of a hungry man's patience, "are ye sure ye made the gentleman understand?" "*Understand?*" retorted Donald (who had peeped into the room and found the guest engaged at his toilet), " I'se warrant ye he understands; he's *sharping* his teeth,"—not supposing the tooth-brush could be for any other use.

There have been some very amusing instances given of the matter-of-fact obedience paid to orders by Highland retainers when made to perform the ordinary duties of domestic servants; as when Mr Campbell, a Highland gentleman, visiting in a country house, and telling Donald to bring everything out of the bedroom, found all its movable articles—fender, fire-irons, etc.—piled up in the lobby; so literal was the poor man's sense of obedience to orders! And of this he gave a still more extraordinary proof during his sojourn in Edinburgh, by a very ludicrous exploit. When the family moved into a house there, Mrs Campbell gave him very particular instructions regarding visitors, explaining that they were to be shown into the drawing-room, and no doubt used the Scotticism, " *Carry* any ladies that call upstairs." On the arrival of the first visitors, Donald was eager to show his strict attention to the mistress's orders. Two ladies came together, and Donald, seizing one in his arms, said to the other, " Bide ye there till I come for ye," and, in spite of her struggles and remonstrances, ushered the terrified visitor into Mrs Campbell's presence in this unwonted fashion.

Another case of *literal* obedience to orders produced a somewhat startling form of message. A servant of an old maiden lady, a patient of Dr Poole, formerly of Edinburgh, was under orders to go to the doctor every morning to report the state of her health, how she had slept, etc., with strict injunctions *always* to add, " with her compliments." At length, one morning the girl brought this extraordinary message:

" Miss S——'s compliments, and she dee'd last night at aicht o'clock ! "

I recollect, in Montrose (that fruitful field for old Scottish stories !), a most naïve reply from an honest lass, servant to old Mrs *Captain* Fullerton. A party of gentlemen had dined with Mrs Fullerton, and they had a turkey for dinner. Mrs F. proposed that one of the legs should be *devilled*, and the gentlemen have it served up as a relish for their wine. Accordingly one of the company skilled in the mystery prepared it with pepper, cayenne, mustard, ketchup, etc. He gave it to Lizzy, and told her to take it down to the kitchen, supposing, as a matter of course, she would know that it was to be broiled, and brought back in due time. But in a little while, when it was rung for, Lizzy very innocently replied that she had eaten it up. As it was sent back to the kitchen, her only idea was that it must be for herself. But on surprise being expressed that she had eaten what was so highly peppered and seasoned, she very quaintly answered, " Ou, I liket it a' the better."

A well-known servant of the old school was John, the servant of Pitfour, Mr Ferguson, M.P., himself a most eccentric character, long father of the House of Commons, and a great friend of Pitt. John used to entertain the tenants, on Pitfour's brief visits to his estate, with numerous anecdotes of his master and Mr Pitt ; but he always prefaced them with something in the style of Cardinal Wolsey's *Ego et rex meus*, with " Me, and Pitt, and Pitfour," went somewhere, or performed some exploit. The famous Duchess of Gordon once wrote a note to John (the name of this eccentric valet), and said, " John, put Pitfour into the carriage on Tuesday, and bring him up to Gordon Castle to dinner." After sufficiently scratching his head, and considering what he should do, he showed the letter to Pitfour, who smiled, and said drily, " Well, John, I suppose we must go."

An old domestic of this class gave a capital reason to his *young* master for his being allowed to do as he liked :—" Ye needna find faut wi' me, Maister Jeems ; *I hae been langer aboot the place than yersel'*."

It may seem ungracious to close this chapter with a communication which appears to convey an unfavourable impression of an old servant. But the truth is, real and attached domestic service does not offer its pleasures and advantages without some alloy of annoyance, and yet how much the solid benefits prevail over any occasional drawbacks !

The late Rev. Mr Leslie of St Andrew-Lhanbryd, a parish in Morayshire, in describing an old servant who had been with him thirty years, said, " The first ten years she was an excellent servant ; the second ten she was a good mistress ; but the third ten she was a perfect tyrant."

CHAPTER V

SCOTTISH JUDGES

THERE is no class of men which stands out more prominent in the reminiscences of the last hundred years than that of our SCOTTISH JUDGES. They form, in many instances, a type or representative of the leading *peculiarities* of Scottish life and manners. They are mixed up with all our affairs, social and political. There are to be found in the annals of the Bench rich examples of pure Scottish humour, the strongest peculiarity of Scottish phraseology, acuteness of intellect, cutting wit, eccentricity of manners, and abundant powers of conviviality. Their successors no longer furnish the same anecdotes of oddity or of intemperance. The Courts of the Scottish Parliament House, without lacking the learning or the law of those who sat there sixty years ago, lack not the refinement and the dignity that have long distinguished the Courts of Westminster Hall.

Stories still exist, traditionary in society, amongst its older members, regarding Lords Gardenstone, Monboddo, Hermand, Newton, Polkemmet, Braxfield, etc. But many younger persons do not know them. It may be interesting to some of my readers to devote a few pages to the subject, and to offer some judicial gleanings.[1]

I have two anecdotes to show that, both in social and judicial life, a remarkable change must have taken

---

[1] I have derived some information from a curious book, " Kay's Portraits," 2 vols. The work is scarcely known in England, and is becoming rare in Scotland. " Nothing can be more valuable in the way of engraved portraits than these representations of the distinguished men who adorned Edinburgh in the latter part of the eighteenth century."—*Chambers*.

place amongst the " fifteen." I am assured that the following scene took place at the *table* of Lord Polkemmet, at a dinner-party in his house. When the covers were removed, the dinner was seen to consist of veal broth, a roast fillet of veal, veal cutlets, a florentine (an excellent old Scottish dish composed of veal), a calf's head, calf's foot jelly. The worthy judge could not help observing a surprise on the countenance of his guests, and perhaps a simper on some; so he broke out in explanation : " Ou ay, it's a cauf; when we kill a beast we just eat up ae side, and down the tither." The expressions he used to describe his own *judicial* preparations for the bench were very characteristic : " Ye see I first read a' the pleadings, and then, after lettin' them wamble in my wame wi' the toddy twa or three days, I gie my ain interlocutor." For a moment suppose such anecdotes to be told now of any of our high legal functionaries. Imagine the feelings of surprise that would be called forth were the present Justice-Clerk to adopt such imagery in describing the process of preparing *his* legal judgment on a difficult case in his court !

In regard to the wit of the Scottish *Bar*.—It is a subject which I do not pretend to illustrate. It would require a volume for itself. One anecdote, however, I cannot resist, and I record it as forming a striking example of the class of Scottish humour which, with our dialect, has lost its distinctive characteristics. John Clerk (afterwards a judge by the title of Lord Eldin) was arguing a Scottish appeal case before the House of Lords. His client claimed the use of a millstream by a prescriptive right. Mr Clerk spoke broad Scotch, and argued that " the *watter* had rin that way for forty years. Indeed naebody kenn'd how long, and why should his client now be deprived of the watter?" etc. The chancellor, much amused at the pronunciation of the Scottish advocate, in a rather bantering tone asked him, "Mr Clerk, do you spell water in Scotland with two t's?" Clerk, a little nettled at this hit at his national tongue, answered, "Na, my Lord, we dinna spell watter (making the word as short as he could) wi' twa t's, but we spell mainners (making the word as long as he could) wi' twa n's."

John Clerk's vernacular version of the motto of the Celtic Club is highly characteristic of his humour and his prejudice. He had a strong dislike to the whole Highland race, and the motto assumed by the modern Celts, "Olim marte, nunc arte," Clerk translated "Formerly robbers, now thieves." Quite equal to Swift's celebrated remark on William III.'s motto—*Recepit, non rapuit*—"that the receiver was as bad as the thief." Very dry and pithy too was Clerk's legal *opinion* given to a claimant of the Annandale peerage, who, when pressing the employment of some obvious forgeries, was warned that if he persevered, nae doot he might be a peer, but it would be a peer o' anither *tree*!

The clever author of "Peter's Letters" gives an elaborate description of Clerk's character whilst at the Bar, and speaks of him as "the plainest, the shrewdest, and the most sarcastic of men." Nor could he entirely repress these peculiarities when raised to the Bench under the title of Lord Eldin.

His defence of a young friend, who was an advocate, and had incurred the displeasure of the Judges, has often been repeated. Mr Clerk had been called upon to offer his apologies for disrespect, or implied disrespect, in his manner of addressing the Bench. The advocate had given great offence by expressing his " *astonishment* " at something which had emanated from their Lordships, implying by it his disapproval. He got Lord Eldin, who was connected with him, to make an apology for him. But Clerk could not resist his humorous vein by very equivocally adding, " My client has expressed his astonishment, my Lords, at what he had met with here; if my young friend had known this court as long as I have, he would have been *astonished at nothing*."

A kind Perthshire correspondent has sent me a characteristic anecdote, which has strong internal evidence of being genuine. When Clerk was raised to the Bench he presented his credentials to the Court, and, according to custom, was received by the presiding Judge—who, on this occasion, in a somewhat sarcastic tone, referred to the delay which had taken place in his reaching a position for which he had so long been qualified, and to which he must have long aspired. He hinted at the long absence of the Whig party from political power as the cause of this delay, which offended Clerk; and he paid it off by intimating in his pithy and bitter tone, which he could so well assume, that it was not of so much consequence— " Because," as he said, " ye see, my Lord, I was not juist sae sune *doited* as some o' your Lordships."

The following account of his conducting a case is also highly characteristic. Two individuals, the one a mason, the other a carpenter, both residenters in West Portsburgh, formed a co-partnery, and commenced building houses within the boundaries of the burgh corporation. One of the partners was a freeman, the other not. The corporation, considering its rights invaded by a non-freeman exercising privileges only accorded to one of their body, brought an action in the Court of Session against the interloper, and his partner as aiding and abetting. Mr John Clerk, then an advocate, was engaged for the defendants. How the cause was decided matters little. What was really curious in the affair was the naïvely droll manner in which the advocate for the defence opened his pleading before the Lord Ordinary. " My Lord," commenced John, in his purest Doric, at the same time pushing up his spectacles to his brow and hitching his gown over his shoulders, " I wad hae thought naething o't (the action), had hooses been a new invention, and my clients been caught ouvertly impingin' on the patent richts o' the inventors ! "

Of Lord Gardenstone (Francis Garden) I have many early *personal* reminiscences, as his property of Johnstone was in the Howe of the Mearns, not far from my early home. He was a man of energy, and promoted improvements in the county with skill and practical sagacity. His favourite scheme was to establish a flourishing town upon his property, and he spared no pains or expense in promoting the importance of his village of Laurencekirk. He built an excellent inn, to render it a stage for posting. He built and endowed an Episcopal chapel for the benefit of his English immigrants, in the vestry of which he placed a most respectable library ; and he encouraged manufacturers of all kinds to settle in the place. Amongst others, as we have seen, came the hatter who found only three hats in the kirk. His lordship was much taken up with his hotel or inn, and for which he provided a large volume for receiving the written contributions of travellers who frequented it. It was the landlady's business to present this volume to the guests, and ask them to write in it during the evenings whatever occurred to their memory or their imagination. In the mornings it was a favourite amusement of Lord Gardenstone to look it over. I recollect Sir Walter Scott being much taken with this contrivance, and his asking me about it at Abbotsford. His son said to him, " You should establish such a book, sir, at Melrose "; upon which Sir W. replied, " No, Walter; I should just have to see a great deal of abuse of myself." On his son deprecating such a result, and on his observing my surprised look, he answered, " Well, well, I should have to read a great deal of foolish praise, which is much the same thing." An amusing account is given of the cause of Lord Gardenstone withdrawing this volume from the hotel, and of his determination to submit it no more to the tender mercies of the passing traveller. As Professor Stuart of Aberdeen was passing an evening at the inn, the volume was handed to him, and he wrote in it the following lines, in the style of the prophecies of Thomas the Rhymer :—

> " Frae sma' beginnings Rome of auld
> Became a great imperial city ;
> 'Twas peopled first, as we are tauld,
> By bankrupts, vagabonds, banditti.
> Quoth Thamas, Then the day may come,
> When Laurencekirk shall equal Rome."

These lines so nettled Lord Gardenstone, that the volume disappeared, and was never seen afterwards in the inn of Laurencekirk. There is another lingering reminiscence which I retain connected with the inn at Laurencekirk. The landlord, Mr Cream, was a man well-known throughout all the country, and was distinguished, in his later years, as one of the few men who continued to wear a *pigtail*. On one occasion the late Lord Dunmore (grandfather or great-grandfather of the present peer), who also still wore his queue, halted for a night at Laurencekirk. On the host leaving the room, where he had come to take orders for supper, Lord Dunmore turned to his valet and said, " Johnstone, do I look as like a fool in my pig-tail as Billy Cream does ? " " Much about it, my lord," was the valet's imperturbable answer. " Then," said his lordship, " cut off mine to-morrow morning when I dress."

Lord Gardenstone seemed to have had two favourite tastes : he indulged in the love of pigs and the love of snuff. He took a young pig as a pet, and it became quite tame, and followed him about like a dog. At first the animal shared his bed, but when, growing up to advanced swinehood, it became unfit for such companionship, he had it to sleep in his room, in which he made a comfortable couch for it of his own clothes. His snuff he kept not in a box, but in a leathern waist-pocket made for the purpose. He took it in enormous quantities, and used to say that if he had a dozen noses he would feed them all. Lord Garden-stone died 1793.

Lord Monboddo (James Burnet, Esq., of Mon-boddo) is another of the well-known members of the Scottish Bench, who combined, with many eccentrici-ties of opinion and habits, great learning and a most amiable disposition. From his paternal property being in the county of Kincardine, and Lord M. being a visitor at my father's house, and indeed a relation or clansman, I have many early reminiscences of stories which I have heard of the learned judge. His specula-tions regarding the origin of the human race have, in times past, excited much interest and amusement. His theory was that man emerged from a wild and savage condition, much resembling that of apes ; that man had then a tail like other animals, but which by pro-gressive civilisation and the constant habit of *sitting*, had become obsolete. This theory produced many a joke from facetious and superficial people, who had never read any of the arguments of the able and elaborate work, by which the ingenious and learned author maintained his theory.[1] Lord Kames, a brother judge, had his joke on it. On some occasion of their meeting, Lord Monboddo was for giving Lord Kames the precedency. Lord K. declined, and drew back, saying, " By no means, my lord; you must walk first, that I may *see your tail*." I recollect Lord Monboddo's coming to dine at Fasque caused a great excitement of interest and curiosity. I was in the nursery, too young to take part in the investigations; but my elder brothers were on the alert to watch his arrival, and get a glimpse of his tail. Lord M. was really a learned man, read Greek and Latin authors—not as a mere exercise of classical scholarship—but because he identified himself with their philosophical opinions, and would have revived Greek customs and modes of life. He used to give suppers after the manner of the ancients, and used to astonish his guests by the ancient cookery of Spartan broth, and of *mulsum*. He was an enthusiastic Platonist. On a visit to Oxford, he was received with great respect by the scholars of the University, who were much interested in meeting with one who had studied Plato as a pupil and follower. In accordance with the old custom at learned universities, Lord Monboddo was determined to address the Oxonians in Latin, which he spoke with much readiness. But they could not stand the numerous slips in prosody. Lord Monboddo shocked the ears of the men of Eton and of Winchester by dreadful false quantities—verse-making being, in Scotland, then quite neglected, and a matter little thought of by the learned judge.

[1] Origin and Progress of Language.

Lord Monboddo was considered an able lawyer, and on many occasions exhibited a very clear and correct judicial discernment of intricate cases. It was one of his peculiarities that he never sat on the bench with his brother judges, but always at the clerk's table. Different reasons for this practice have been given, but the simple fact seems to have been, that he was deaf, and heard better at the lower seat. His mode of travelling was on horseback. He scorned carriages, on the ground of its being unmanly to " sit in a box drawn by brutes." When he went to London he rode the whole way. At the same period, Mr Barclay of Ury (father of the well-known Captain Barclay), when he represented Kincardineshire in Parliament, always *walked* to London. He was a very powerful man, and could walk fifty miles a day, his usual refreshment on the road being a bottle of port wine, poured into a bowl, and drunk off at a draught. I have heard that George III. was much interested at these performances, and said, " I ought to be proud of my Scottish subjects, when my judges *ride*, and my Members of Parliament *walk*, to the metropolis."

On one occasion of his being in London, Lord Monboddo attended a trial in the Court of King's Bench. A cry was heard that the roof of the court-room was giving way, upon which judges, lawyers, and people made a rush to get to the door. Lord Monboddo viewed the scene from his corner with much composure. Being deaf and short-sighted, he knew nothing of the cause of the tumult. The alarm proved a false one; and on being asked why he had not bestirred himself to escape like the rest, he coolly answered that he supposed it was an *annual ceremony*, with which, as an alien to the English laws, he had no concern, but which he considered it interesting to witness as a remnant of antiquity! Lord Monboddo died 1799.

Lord Rockville (the Hon. Alexander Gordon, third son of the Earl of Aberdeen) was a judge distinguished in his day by his ability and decorum. " He adorned the bench by the dignified manliness of his appearance, and polished urbanity of his manners." [1] Like most lawyers of his time, he took his glass freely, and a whimsical account which he gave, before he was advanced to the bench, of his having fallen upon his face, after making too free with the bottle, was commonly current at the time. Upon his appearing late at a convivial club with a most rueful expression of countenance, and on being asked what was the matter, he exclaimed with great solemnity, " Gentlemen, I have just met with the most extraordinary adventure that ever occurred to a human being. As I was walking along the Grassmarket, all of a sudden *the street rose up and struck me on the face.*" He had, however, a more serious *encounter* with the street after he was a judge. In 1792, his foot slipped as he was going to the Parliament House; he broke his leg, was taken home, fevered, and died.

Lord Braxfield (Robert M'Queen of Braxfield) was one of the judges of the old school, well known in his day, and might be said to possess all the qualities united, by which the class were remarkable. He spoke the broadest Scotch. He was a sound and laborious lawyer. He was fond of a glass of good claret, and had a great fund of good Scotch humour. He rose to the dignity of Justice-Clerk, and, in consequence, presided at many important political criminal trials about the year 1793-4, such as those of Muir, Palmer, Skirving, Margarot, Gerrold, etc. He conducted these trials with much ability and great firmness, occasion-

[1] Douglas' Peerage, vol. i., p. 22.

ally, no doubt, with more appearance of severity and personal prejudice than is usual with the judges who in later times are called on to preside on similar occasions. The disturbed temper of the times and the daring spirit of the political offenders seemed, he thought, to call for a bold and fearless front on the part of the judge, and Braxfield was the man to show it, both on the Bench and in common life. He met, however, sometimes with a spirit as bold as his own from the prisoners before him. When Skirving was on trial for sedition, he thought Braxfield was threatening him and by gesture endeavouring to intimidate him; accordingly, he boldly addressed the Bench:— "It is altogether unavailing for your Lordship to menace me, for I have long learnt not to fear the face of man." I have observed that he adhered to the *broadest* Scottish dialect. "Hae ye ony coonsel, man?" he said to Maurice Margarot (who, I believe, was an Englishman). "No," was the reply. "Div ye want to hae ony appinted?" "No," replied Margarot; "I only want an *interpreter* to make me understand what your Lordship says." A prisoner, accused of stealing some linen garments, was one day brought up for trial before the old judge, but was acquitted because the prosecutor had charged him with stealing shirts, whereas the articles stolen were found to be shifts—female apparel. Braxfield indignantly remarked that the Crown Counsel should have called them by the Scottish name of *sarks*, which applied to both sexes.

Braxfield had much humour, and enjoyed wit in others. He was immensely delighted at a reply by Dr M'Cubbin, the minister of Bothwell. Braxfield, when Justice-Clerk, was dining at Lord Douglas's, and observed there was only port upon the table. In his usual off-hand brusque manner, he demanded of

the noble host if " there was nae claret i' the castle."
" Yes," said Lord Douglas ; " but my butler tells me
it is not good." " Let's pree't," said Braxfield in his
favourite dialect. A bottle was produced, and declared by all present to be quite excellent. " Noo,
minister," said the old judge, addressing Dr M'Cubbin,
who was celebrated as a wit in his day, " as a *fama
clamosa* has gone forth against this wine, I propose
that you *absolve* it,"—playing upon the terms made
use of in the Scottish Church Courts. " Ay, my Lord,"
said the minister, " you are first-rate authority for a
case of civil or criminal law, but you do not quite
understand our Church Court practice. We never
absolve *till after three several appearances*." The wit and
the condition of absolution were alike relished by
the judge. Lord Braxfield closed a long and useful
life in 1799.

Of Lord Hermand we have already had occasion to
speak, as in fact his name has become in some manner
identified with that conviviality which marked almost
as a characteristic the Scottish Bench of his time. He
gained, however, great distinction as a judge, and was
a capital lawyer. When at the bar, Lords Newton and
Hermand were great friends, and many were the convivial meetings they enjoyed together. But Lord
Hermand outlived all his old last-century contemporaries, and formed with Lord Balgray what we may
consider the connecting links between the past and
the present race of Scottish lawyers.

Lord Kames was a keen agricultural experiment-
alist, and in his *Gentleman Farmer* anticipated many
modern improvements. He was, however, occasionally too sanguine. " John," said he one day to his old
overseer, " I think we'll see the day when a man may
carry out as much chemical manure in his waistcoat

pocket as will serve for a whole field." "Weel," rejoined the other, "I am of opinion that if your lordship were to carry out the dung in your waistcoat pocket, ye might bring hame the crap in your greatcoat pocket."

We could scarcely perhaps offer a more marked difference between habits *once* tolerated on the Bench and those which now distinguish the august seat of Senators of Justice, than by quoting, from *Kay's Portraits*, vol. ii., p. 278, a sally of a Lord of Session of those days, which he played off, when sitting as judge, upon a young friend whom he was determined to frighten. "A young counsel was addressing him on some not very important point that had arisen in the division of a common (or commonty, according to law phraseology), when, having made some bold averment, the judge exclaimed, ' That's a lee, Jemmie.' ' My lord ! ' ejaculated the amazed barrister. ' Ay, ay, Jemmie ; I see by your face ye're leein'.' ' Indeed, my lord, I am not.' ' Dinna tell me that ; it's no' in your memorial (brief)—awa' wi' you '; and, overcome with astonishment and vexation, the discomfited barrister left the Bar. The judge thereupon chuckled with infinite delight ; and beckoning to the clerk who attended on the occasion, he said, ' Are ye no' Rabbie H——'s man ? ' ' Yes, my lord.' ' Wasna Jemmie —— leein' ? ' ' Oh no, my lord.' ' Ye're quite sure ? ' ' Oh yes.' ' Then just write out what you want, and I'll sign it ; my faith, but I made Jemmie stare.' So the decision was dictated by the clerk, and duly signed by the judge, who left the bench highly diverted with the fright he had given his young friend." Such scenes enacted in court *now* would astonish the present generation, both of lawyers and of suitors.

We should not do justice to our Scottish Reminiscences of judges and lawyers, if we omitted the once celebrated Court of Session *jeu d'esprit* called the "Diamond Beetle Case." This burlesque report of a judgment was written by George Cranstoun, advocate, who afterwards sat in court as judge under the title of Lord Corehouse. Cranstoun was one of the ablest lawyers of his time; he was a prime scholar, and a man of most refined taste and clear intellect. This humorous and clever production was printed in a former edition of these Reminiscences, and in a very flattering notice of the book which appeared in the *North British Review*, the reviewer—himself, as is well known, a distinguished member of the Scottish Judicial Bench—remarks : "We are glad that the whole of the 'Diamond Beetle' by Cranstoun has been given; for nothing can be more graphic, spirited, and ludicrous, than the characteristic speeches of the learned judges who deliver their opinions in the case of defamation." As copies of this very clever and jocose production are not now easily obtained, and as some of my younger readers may not have seen it, I have reprinted it in this edition. Considered in the light of a memorial of the Bench, as it was known to a former generation, it is well worth preserving ; for, as the editor of *Kay's Portraits* well observes, although it is a caricature, it is entirely without rancour, or any feeling of a malevolent nature towards those whom the author represents as giving judgment in the "Diamond Beetle" case. And in no way could the involved phraseology of Lord Bannatyne, the predilection for Latin quotation of Lord Meadowbank, the brisk manner of Lord Hermand, the anti-Gallic feeling of Lord Craig, the broad dialect of Lords Polkemmet and Balmuto, and the hesitating manner of Lord Methven, be more admirably caricatured.

FULL COPY OF THE FINDING OF THE COURT IN THE
ONCE CELEBRATED "DIAMOND BEETLE CASE." [1]

*Speeches taken at advising the Action of Defamation and
Damages* ALEXANDER CUNNINGHAM, *Jeweller in
Edinburgh, against* JAMES RUSSELL, *Surgeon there.*

"THE LORD PRESIDENT (SIR ILAY CAMPBELL).—
Your Lordships have the petition of Alexander
Cunningham against Lord Bannatyne's interlocutor.
It is a case of defamation and damages for calling the
petitioner's *Diamond Beetle* an *Egyptian Louse.* You
have the Lord Ordinary's distinct interlocutor, on
pages 29 and 30 of this petition :—' Having considered
the Condescendence of the pursuer, Answers for the
defender,' and so on ; ' Finds, in respect that it is not
alleged that the diamonds on the back of the Diamond
Beetle are real diamonds, or anything but shining
spots, such as are found on other Diamond Beetles,
which likewise occur, though in a smaller number, on
a great number of other Beetles, somewhat different
from the Beetle libelled, and similar to which there
may be Beetles in Egypt, with shining spots on their
backs, which may be termed Lice there, and may be
different not only from the common Louse, but from
the Louse mentioned by Moses as one of the plagues
of Egypt, which is admitted to be a filthy troublesome
Louse, even worse than the said Louse, which is clearly
different from the Louse libelled. But that the other
Louse is the same with, or similar to, the said Beetle,
which is also the same with the other Beetle ; and
although different from the said Beetle libelled, yet,
as the said Beetle is similar to the other Beetle, and
the said Louse to the other Louse libelled ; and the

[1] The version I have given of this amusing burlesque was revised by the
late Mr Pagan, Cupar-Fife, and corrected from his own manuscript copy,
which he had procured from authentic sources about forty years ago.

other Louse to the other Beetle, which is the same with, or similar to, the Beetle which somewhat resembles the Beetle libelled; assoilzies the defender, and finds expenses due.'

" Say away, my Lords.

" LORD MEADOWBANK.—This is a very intricate and puzzling question, my Lord. I have formed no decided opinion; but at present I am rather inclined to think the interlocutor is right, though not upon the *ratio* assigned in it. It appears to me that there are two points for consideration. *First*, whether the words libelled amount to a *convicium* against the Beetle; and *Secondly*, admitting the *convicium*, whether the pursuer is entitled to found upon it in this action. Now, my Lords, if there be a *convicium* at all, it consists in the *comparatio* or comparison of the *Scarabœus* or Beetle with the Egyptian *Pediculus* or *Louse*. My first doubt regards this point, but it is not at all founded on what the defender alleges, that there is no such animal as an Egyptian *Pediculus* or *Louse in rerum natura ;* for though it does not *actually* exist, it may *possibly* exist (if not in *actio*, yet in *potentia*—if not in actuality, yet in potentiality or capacity); and whether its existence be in *esse vel posse*, is the same thing to this question, provided there be *termini habiles* for ascertaining what it would be if it did exist. But my doubt is here :—How am I to discover what are the *essentia* of any Louse, whether Egyptian or not ? It is very easy to describe its accidents as a naturalist would do—to say that it belongs to the tribe of *Aptera* (or, that is, a yellow, little, greedy, filthy, despicable reptile), but we do not learn from this what the *proprium* of the animal is in a logical sense, and still less what its *differentia* are. Now, without these it is impossible to judge whether there is a *convicium* or not ; for, in a case of this kind, which *sequitur naturam delicti*, we must take them *meliori sensu*, and presume the *comparatio* to be *in melioribus tantum*. And here I beg that parties, and the Bar in general—[interrupted by Lord Hermand: *Your Lordship should address yourself to the Chair*]—I say, I beg it may be understood that I do not rest my opinion on the ground that *veritas convicii excusant*. I am clear that although this Beetle actually were an Egyptian Louse, it would accord no relevant defence, provided the calling it so were a *convicium*; and there my doubt lies.

"With regard to the second point, I am satisfied that the *Scarabœus* or Beetle itself has no *persona standi in judicio;* and therefore the pursuer cannot insist in the name of the *Scarabœus*, or for his behoof. If the action lie at all, it must be at the instance of the pursuer himself, as the *verus dominus* of the *Scarabœus*, for being calumniated through the *convicium* directed primarily against the animal standing in that relation to him. Now, abstracting from the qualification of an actual *dominium*, which is not alleged, I have great doubts whether a mere *convicium* is necessarily transmitted from one object to another, through the relation of a *dominium* subsisting between them; and if not necessarily transmissible, we must see the principle of its actual transmission here; and that has not yet been pointed out.

"LORD HERMAND.—We heard a little ago, my Lord, that there is a difficulty in this case; but I have not been fortunate enough, for my part, to find out where the difficulty lies. Will any man presume to tell me that a Beetle is not a Beetle, and that a Louse is not a Louse? I never saw the petitioner's Beetle, and what's more I don't care whether I ever see it or not; but I suppose it's like other Beetles, and that's enough for me.

"But, my Lord, I know the other reptile well. I have seen them, I have felt them, my Lord, ever since I was a child in my mother's arms; and my mind tells me that nothing but the deepest and blackest malice rankling in the human breast could have suggested this comparison, or led any man to form a thought so injurious and insulting. But, my Lord, there's more here than all that—a great deal more. One could have thought the defender would have gratified his spite to the full by comparing the Beetle to a common Louse—an animal sufficiently vile and abominable for the purpose of defamation—[*Shut that door there*]—but he adds the epithet *Egyptian*, and I know well what he means by that epithet. He means, my Lord, a Louse that has been fattened on the head of a *Gipsy or Tinker*, undisturbed by the comb or nail, and unmolested in the enjoyment of its native filth. He means a Louse grown to its full size, ten times larger and ten times more abominable than those with which *your Lordships and I are familiar*. The petitioner asks redress for the injury so atrocious and so aggravated; and, as far as my voice goes, he shall not ask it in vain.

"LORD CRAIG.—I am of the opinion last delivered. It appears to me to be slanderous and calumnious to compare a Diamond Beetle to the filthy and mischievous animal libelled. By an Egyptian Louse I understand one which has been formed on the head of a native Egyptian—a race of men who, after degenerating for many centuries, have sunk at last into the abyss of depravity, in consequence of having been subjugated for a time by the French. I do not find that Turgot, or Condorcet, or the rest of the economists, ever reckoned the combing of the head a species of productive labour; and I conclude, therefore, that wherever French principles have been propagated,

Lice grow to an immoderate size, especially in a warm climate like that of Egypt. I shall only add, that we ought to be sensible of the blessings we enjoy under a free and happy Constitution, where Lice and men live under the restraint of equal laws the only equality that can exist in a well-regulated state.

"LORD POLKEMMET.—It should be observed, my Lord, that what is called a Beetle is a reptile very well known in this country. I have seen mony ane o' them in Drumshorlin Muir; it is a little black beastie, about the size of my thoom-nail. The country-folks ca' them Clocks; and I believe they ca' them also Maggy-wi'-the-mony-feet; but they are not the least like any Louse that ever I saw; so that, in my opinion, though the defender may have made a blunder through ignorance, in comparing them, there does not seem to have been any *animus injuriandi*; therefore I am for refusing the petition, my Lords.

"LORD BALMUTO.—'Am [1] for refusing the petition. There's more Lice than Beetles in Fife. They ca' them Clocks there. What they ca' a Beetle is a thing as lang as my arm; thick at one end and sma' at the other. I thought, when I read the petition, that the Beetle or Bittle had been the thing that the women have when they are washing towels or napery with—things for dadding them with; and I see the petitioner is a jeweller till his trade; and I thought he had ane o' thae Beetles, and set it all round with diamonds; and I thought it a foolish and extravagant idea; and I saw no resemblance it could have to a Louse. But I find I was mistaken, my Lord; and I find it only a Beetle-clock the petitioner has; but my opinion's the same as it was before. I say, my Lords, 'am for refusing the petition, I say——

[1] His Lordship usually pronounced *I am—Aum*.

156

"LORD WOODHOUSELEE.—There is a case abridged in the third volume of the *Dictionary of Decisions*, Chalmers *v.* Douglas, in which it was found that *veritas convicii excusat*, which may be rendered not literally, but in a free and spirited manner, according to the most approved principles of translation, 'the truth of calumny affords a relevant defence.' If, therefore, it be the law of Scotland (which I am clearly of opinion it is) that the truth of the calumny affords a relevant defence, and if it be likewise true that the Diamond Beetle is really an Egyptian Louse, I am inclined to conclude (though certainly the case is attended with difficulty) that the defender ought to be assoilzied. —*Refuse*.

"LORD JUSTICE-CLERK (RAE).—I am very well acquainted with the defender in this action, and have respect for him, and esteem him likewise. I know him to be a skilful and expert surgeon, and also a good man ; and I would do a great deal to serve him or to be of use to him, if I had it in my power to do so. But I think on this occasion he has spoken rashly, and I fear foolishly and improperly. I hope he had no bad intention—I am sure he had not. But the petitioner (for whom I have likewise a great respect, because I knew his father, who was a very respectable baker in Edinburgh, and supplied my family with bread, and very good bread it was, and for which his accounts were regularly discharged), it seems, has a Clock or a Beetle, I think it is called a Diamond Beetle, which he is very fond of, and has a fancy for, and the defender has compared it to a Louse, or a Bug, or a Flea, or a worse thing of that kind, with a view to render it despicable or ridiculous, and the petitioner so likewise, as the proprietor or owner thereof. It is said that this is a Louse *in fact*, and that the *veritas convicii excusat* ;

and mention is made of a decision in the case of Chalmers *v.* Douglas. I have always had a great veneration for the decisions of your Lordships; and I am sure will always continue to have while I sit here; but that case was determined by a very small majority, and I have heard your Lordships mention it on various occasions, and you have always desiderated the propriety of it, and I think have departed from it in some instances. I remember the circumstances of the case well:—Helen Chalmers lived in Musselburgh, and the defender, Mrs Douglas, lived in Fisherrow; and at that time there was much intercourse between the genteel inhabitants of Fisherrow, and Musselburgh, and Inveresk, and likewise Newbigging; and there were balls, or dances, or assemblies every fortnight, or oftener, and also sometimes I believe every week; and there were card-parties, assemblies once a fortnight, or oftener; and the young people danced there also, and others played at cards, and there were various refreshments, such as tea and coffee, and butter and bread, and I believe, but I am not sure, porter and negus, and likewise small beer. And it was at one of these assemblies that Mrs Douglas called Mrs Chalmers very improper names. And Mrs Chalmers brought an action of defamation before the Commissaries, and it came by advocation into this Court, and your Lordships allowed a proof of the *veritas convicii*, and it lasted a very long time, and in the end answered no good purpose even to the defender herself, while it did much hurt to the pursuer's character. I am therefore for REFUSING such a proof in this case, and I think the petitioner in this case and his Beetle have been slandered, and the petition ought to be seen.

"LORD METHVEN.—If I understand this—a—a—a —interlocutor, it is not said that the—a—a—a—a—

Egyptian Lice are Beetles, but that they may be, or—
a—a—a—a—resemble Beetles. I am therefore for
sending the process to the Ordinary to ascertain the
fact, as I think it depends upon that whether there be
—a—a—a—a—*convicium* or not. I think also the
petitioner should be ordained to—a—a—a—produce
his Beetle, and the defender an Egyptian Louse or
Pediculus, and if he has not one, that he should take a
diligence—a—a—a—against havers to recover Lice
of various kinds; and these may be remitted to Dr
Monro, or Mr Playfair, or to some other naturalist,
to report upon the subject.

"Agreed to."

This is clearly a Reminiscence of a bygone state of
matters in the Court of Session. I think every reader
in our day, of the once famous Beetle case, will come
to the conclusion that, making all due allowance for
the humorous embellishment of the description, and
even for some exaggeration of caricature, it describes
what was once a real state of matters, which, he will
be sure, is real no more. The day of Judges of the
Balmuto-Hermand-Polkemmet class has passed away,
and is become a Scottish *Reminiscence*. Having thus
brought before my readers some Reminiscences of
past times from the Courts of Justice, let me advert
to one which belongs to, or was supposed to belong
to, past days of our Scottish universities. It is now a
matter of tradition. But an idea prevailed, whether
correctly or incorrectly, some eighty or a hundred
years ago, that at northern colleges degrees were regularly sold, and those who could pay the price obtained
them, without reference to the merits or attainments
of those on whom they were conferred. We have
heard of divers jokes being passed on those who were
supposed to have received such academical honours,

as well as on those who had given them. It is said Dr
Samuel Johnson joined in this sarcastic humour. But
his prejudices both against Scotland and Scottish
Literature were well known. Colman, in his amusing
play of the "Heir at Law," makes his Dr Pangloss
ludicrously describe his receiving an LL.D. degree, on
the grounds of his own celebrity (as he had never seen
the college), and his paying the heads one pound
fifteen shillings and threepence three farthings as a
handsome compliment to them on receiving his
diploma. Colman certainly had studied at a northern
university. But he might have gone into the idea in
fun. However this may be, an anecdote is current in
the East of Scotland, which is illustrative of this real
or supposed state of matters, to which we may indeed
apply the Italian phrase that if "non vero" it is "ben
trovato." The story is this:—An East Lothian minister, accompanied by his man, who acted as betheral
of his parish, went over to a northern university to
purchase his degree, and on their return home he gave
strict charge to his man, that as now he was invested
with academical honour, he was to be sure to say, if
any one asked for the minister, "O yes, the Doctor is
at home, or the Doctor is in the study, or the Doctor
is out, as the case might be." The man at once ac-
quiesced in the propriety of this observance on account
of his master's newly acquired dignity. But he quietly
added, "Ay, ay, minister; an' if ony ane speirs for
me, the servants maun be sure to say, Oh, the Doctor's
in the stable, or the Doctor's in the kitchen, or the
Doctor's in the garden or the field." "What do you
mean, Dauvid?" exclaimed his astonished master;
"what can *you* have to do with Doctor?" "Weel,
ye see, sir," said David, looking very knowing, "when
ye got your degree, I thought that as I had saved a

A GUID GANGIN' PLEA

little money, I couldna lay it out better, as being betheral of the church, than tak' out a degree to mysell." The story bears upon the practice, whether a real or a supposed one; and we may fairly say that under such principals as Shairp, Tulloch, Campbell, Barclay, who now adorn the Scottish universities, we have a guarantee that such reports must continue to be Reminiscence and traditional only.

CHAPTER VI

ON HUMOUR PROCEEDING FROM
SCOTTISH EXPRESSIONS, INCLUDING
SCOTTISH PROVERBS

WE come next to Reminiscences which are chiefly connected with peculiarities of our Scottish LANGUAGE, whether contained in words or in expressions. I am quite aware that the difference between the anecdotes belonging to this division and to the last division termed "Wit and Humour" is very indistinct, and must, in fact, in many cases, be quite arbitrary. Much of what we enjoy most in Scottish stories is not on account of wit properly so called, in the speaker, but I should say rather from the odd and unexpected view which is taken of some matter, or from the quaint and original turn of the expression made use of, or from the simple and matter-of-fact reference made to circumstances which are unusual. I shall not, therefore, be careful to preserve any strict line of separation between this division and the next. Each is conversant with what is amusing and with what is Scotch. What we have now chiefly to illustrate by suitable anecdotes is peculiarities of Scottish language—its various humorous turns and odd expressions.

We have now to consider stories where words and expressions, which are peculiarly Scotch, impart the humour and the point. Sometimes they are altogether incapable of being rendered in other language. As, for example, a parishioner in an Ayrshire village, meeting his pastor, who had just returned after a considerable absence on account of ill-health, congratu-

162

lated him on his convalescence, and added, anticipatory of the pleasure he would have in hearing him again, " I'm unco yuckie to hear a blaud o' your gab." This is an untranslatable form of saying how glad he should be to hear his minister's voice again speaking to him the words of salvation and of peace from the pulpit.

The two following are good examples of that Scottish style of expression which has its own character. They are kindly sent by Sir Archibald Dunbar. The first illustrates Scottish acute discernment. A certain titled lady, well-known around her country town for her long-continued and extensive charities, which are not withheld from those who least deserve them, had a few years since, by the unexpected death of her brother and of his only son, become possessor of a fine estate. The news soon spread in the neighbourhood, and a group of old women were overheard in the streets of Elgin discussing the fact. One of them said, " Ay, she may prosper, for she has baith the prayers of the good and of the bad."

The second anecdote is a delightful illustration of Mrs Hamilton's *Cottagers of Glenburnie*, and of the old-fashioned Scottish pride in the *midden*. About twenty years ago, under the apprehension of cholera, committees of the most influential inhabitants of the county of Moray were formed to enforce a more complete cleansing of its towns and villages, and to induce the cottagers to remove their dunghills or dung-pits from too close a proximity to their doors or windows. One determined woman, on the outskirts of the town of Forres, no doubt with her future potato crop in view, met the M.P. who headed one of these committees, thus, " Noo, Major, ye may tak' our lives, but ye'll no' tak' our middens."

The truth is, many of the peculiarities which marked

163

Scottish society departed with the disuse of the Scottish dialect in the upper ranks. I recollect a familiar example of this, which I may well term a Reminiscence. At a party assembled in a county house, the Earl of Elgin (grandfather of the present Earl) came up to the tea-table, where Mrs Forbes of Medwyn, one of the finest examples of the past Scottish *lady*, was sitting, evidently much engaged with her occupation. " You are fond of your tea, Mrs Forbes ? " The reply was quite a characteristic one, and a pure reminiscence of such a place and such interlocutors : " 'Deed, my Lord, I wadna gie my tea for your yerldom."

My aunt, the late Lady Burnett of Leys, was one of the class of Scottish ladies I have referred to—thoroughly a good woman and a gentlewoman, but in dialect quite Scottish. For example, being shocked at the sharp Aberdonian pronunciation adopted by her children, instead of the broader Forfarshire model in which she had been brought up, she thus adverted to their manner of calling the *floor* of the room where they were playing : " What gars ye ca' it ' *fleer* ' ? Canna ye ca' it ' *flure* ' ? But I needna speak ; Sir Robert winna let me correc' your language."

In respect of language, no doubt, a very important change has taken place in Scotland during the last seventy years, and which, I believe, influences, in a greater degree than many persons would imagine, the turn of thought and general modes and aspects of society. In losing the old racy Scottish tongue, it seems as if much originality of *character* was lost. I suppose at one time the two countries of England and Scotland were considered as almost speaking different languages, and I suppose also, that from the period of the union of the crowns the language has been assimilating. We see the process of assimilation going on, and ere long amongst persons of education and birth very little difference will be perceptible. With regard to that class, a great change has taken place in my own time. I recollect old Scottish ladies and gentlemen who really *spoke Scotch*. It was not, mark me, speaking English with an accent. No; it was downright Scotch. Every tone and every syllable was Scotch. For example, I recollect old Miss Erskine of Dun, a fine specimen of a real lady, and daughter of an ancient Scottish house, so speaking. Many people now would not understand her. She was always *the lady*, notwithstanding her dialect, and to none could the epithet vulgar be less appropriately applied. I speak of more than forty years ago, and yet I recollect her accost to me as well as if it were yesterday: " I didna ken ye were i' the toun." Taking word and accents together, an address how totally unlike what we now meet with in society. Some of the old Scottish words which we can remember are charming; but how strange they would sound to the ears of the present generation! Fancy that in walking from church, and discussing the sermon, a lady of rank should now express her opinion of it by the description of its being, " but a hummelcorn discourse." Many living persons can remember Angus old ladies who would say to their nieces and daughters, " Whatna hummeldoddie o' a mutch hae ye gotten? " meaning a flat and low-crowned cap. In speaking of the dryness of the soil on a road in Lanarkshire, a farmer said, " It stoors in an oor." [1] How would this be as tersely translated into English? The late Duchess of Gordon sat at dinner

---

[1] Stoor is, Scotticé, dust in motion, and has no English synonym; oor is hour. Sir Walter Scott is said to have advised an artist, in painting a battle, not to deal with details, but to get up a good *stoor*; then put in an arm and a sword here and there, and leave all the rest to the imagination of the spectator.

165

next an English gentleman who was carving, and who made it a boast that he was thoroughly master of the Scottish language. Her Grace turned to him and said, " Rax me a spaul o' that bubbly jock." [1] The unfortunate man was completely *nonplussed*. A Scottish gentleman was entertaining at his house an English cousin who professed himself as rather knowing in the language of the north side of the Tweed. He asked him what he supposed to be the meaning of the expression, " ripin the ribs."[2] To which he readily answered, " Oh, it describes a very fat man." I profess myself an out-and-out Scotchman. I have strong national partialities—call them if you will national prejudices. I cherish a great love of old Scottish language. Some of our pure Scottish ballad poetry is unsurpassed in any language for grace and pathos. How expressive, how beautiful are its phrases! You can't translate them. Take an example of power in a Scottish expression, to describe with tenderness and feeling what is in human life. Take one of our most familiar phrases, as thus: We meet an old friend, we talk over bygone days, and remember many who were dear to us both, once bright, and young, and gay, of whom some remain, honoured, prosperous, and happy—of whom some are under a cloud of misfortune or disgrace—some are broken in health and spirit—some sunk into the grave; we recall old familiar places—old companions, pleasures, and pursuits; as Scotchmen our hearts are touched with these remembrances of

AULD LANG SYNE.

Match me the phrase in English. You can't translate it. The fitness and the beauty lie in the felicity of the

---

[1] Reach me a leg of that turkey.
[2] Clearing ashes out of the bars of the grate.

language. Like many happy expressions, it is not trans-
ferable into another tongue, just like the " simplex
munditiis " of Horace, which describes the natural
grace of female elegance, or the ἀνηξίθμον γελασμα of
Æschylus, which describes the bright sparkling of the
ocean in the sun.

I think the power of Scottish dialect was happily
exemplified by the late Dr Adam, rector of the High
School of Edinburgh, in his translation of the Horatian
expression " *desipere in loco*," which he turned by the
Scotch phrase " Weel-timed daffin' " ; a translation,
however, which no one but a Scotchman could appreciate. The following humorous Scotch translation of
an old Latin aphorism has been assigned to the late
Dr Hill of St Andrews : " *Qui bene cepit dimidium facti
fecit*," the witty Principal expressed in Scotch, " Weel
saipet (well soaped) is half shaven."

What mere *English* word could have expressed a
distinction so well in such a case as the following ?
I heard once a lady in Edinburgh objecting to a
preacher that she did not understand him. Another
lady, his great admirer, insinuated that probably he
was too " deep " for her to follow. But her ready
answer was, " Na, na, he's no' just deep, but he's
drumly." [1]

We have a testimony to the value of our Scottish
language from a late illustrious Chancellor of the
University of Edinburgh, the force and authority of
which no one will be disposed to question. Lord
Brougham, in speaking of improvements upon the
English language, makes these striking remarks :—

" The pure and classical language of Scotland must
on no account be regarded as a provincial dialect, any
more than French was so regarded in the reign of

[1] Mentally confused. Muddy when applied to water.

Henry V., or Italian in that of the first Napoleon, or Greek under the Roman Empire. Nor is it to be in any manner of way considered as a corruption of the Saxon; on the contrary, it contains much of the old and genuine Saxon, with an intermixture from the Northern nations, as Danes and Norse, and some, though a small portion from the Celtic. But in whatever way composed, or from whatever sources arising, it is a national language, used by the whole people in their early years, by many learned and gifted persons throughout life, and in which are written the laws of the Scotch, their judicial proceedings, their ancient history; above all, their poetry.

" There can be no doubt that the English language would greatly gain by being enriched with a number both of words and of phrases, or turns of expression, now peculiar to the Scotch. It was by such a process that the Greek became the first of tongues, as well written as spoken. . . .

" Would it not afford means of enriching and improving the English language, if full and accurate glossaries of improved Scotch words and phrases—those successfully used by the best writers, both in prose and verse—were given, with distinct explanation and reference to authorities? This has been done in France and other countries, where some dictionaries accompany the English, in some cases with Scotch synonyms, in others with varieties of expression."—*Installation Address*, p. 63.

The Scotch, as a people, from their more guarded and composed method of speaking, are not so liable to fall into that figure of speech for which our Irish neighbours are celebrated—usually called the Bull; some specimens, however, of that confusion of thought, very like a bull, have been recorded of Scottish interlocutors.

Of this the two following examples have been sent to me by a kind friend.

It is related of a Scottish judge (who has supplied several anecdotes of Scottish stories), that on going to consult a dentist, who, as is usual, placed him in the professional chair, and told his lordship that he must let him put his fingers into his mouth, he exclaimed, " Na! na! ye'll aiblins *bite me*."

A Scottish laird, singularly enough the grandson of the learned judge mentioned above, when going his round to canvass for the county, at the time when the electors were chiefly confined to resident proprietors, was asked at one house where he called if he would not take some refreshment, hesitated, and said, ." I doubt it's treating, and may be ca'd *bribery*."

But a still more amusing specimen of this figure of speech was supplied by an honest Highlander, in the days of sedan chairs. For the benefit of my young readers I may describe the sedan chair as a comfortable little carriage fixed to two poles, and carried by two men, one behind and one before. A dowager lady of quality had gone out to dinner in one of these " leathern conveniences." and whilst she herself enjoyed the hospitality of the mansion upstairs, her bearers were profusely entertained downstairs, and partook of the abundant refreshment offered to them. When my lady was to return, and had taken her place in the sedan, her bearers raised the chair, but she found no progress was made—she felt herself sway first to one side, then to the other, and soon came bump upon the ground, when Donald behind was heard shouting to Donald before (for the bearers of sedans were always Highlanders), " Let her down, Donald, man, *for she's drunk*."

I cannot help thinking that a change of national

language involves to some extent change of national character. Numerous examples of great power in Scottish Phraseology, to express the picturesque, the feeling, the wise, and the humorous, might be taken from the works of Robert Burns, Ferguson, or Allan Ramsay, and which lose their charms altogether when *unscottified*. The speaker certainly seems to take a strength and character from his words. We must now look for specimens of this racy and expressive tongue in the more retired parts of the country. It is no longer to be found in high places. It has disappeared from the social circles of our cities. I cannot, however, omit calling my reader's attention to a charming specimen of Scottish prose and of Scottish humour of our own day, contained in a little book, entitled *Mystifications*, by Clementina Stirling Graham. The scenes described in that volume are matters of pleasing remininiscence, and to some of us who still remain " will recall that blithe and winning face, sagacious and sincere, that kindly, cheery voice, that rich and quiet laugh, that mingled sense and sensibility, which met, and still to our happiness meet, in her who, with all her gifts, never gratified her consciousness of these powers so as to give pain to any human being." [1] These words, written more than ten years ago, might have been penned yesterday; and those who, like myself, have had the privilege of seeing the authoress presiding in her beautiful mansion of Duntrune, will not soon forget how happy, how gracious, and how young, old age may be.

> " No fears to beat away—no strife to heal;
> The past unsighed for, and the future sure."

In my early days the intercourse with the peasantry

---

[1] Preface to 4th Edition of *Mystifications*, by Dr John Brown.

of Forfarshire, Kincardineshire, and especially Deeside, was most amusing,—not that the things said were
so much out of the common, as that the language in
which they were conveyed was picturesque, and odd,
and taking. And certainly it does appear to me that
as the language grows more uniform and conventional,
less marked and peculiar in its dialect and expressions,
so does the character of those who speak it become so.
I have a rich sample of Mid-Lothian Scotch from a
young friend in the country, who describes the conversation of an old woman on the property as amusing
her by such specimens of genuine Scottish raciness
and humour. On one occasion, for instance, the young
lady had told her humble friend that she was going to
Ireland, and would have to undergo a sea voyage.
"Weel, noo, ye dinna mean that! Ance I thocht to
gang across to tither side o' the Queensferry wi' some
ither folks to a fair, ye ken; but just whene'er I pat
my fit in the boat, the boat gae wallop, and my heart
gae a loup, and I thocht I'd gang oot o' my judgment
athegither; so says I, Na, na, ye gang awa' by yoursells to tither side, and I'll bide here till sic times as ye
come awa' back." When we hear our Scottish language
at home, and spoken by our own countrymen, we are
not so much struck with any remarkable effects; but
it takes a far more impressive character when heard
amongst those who speak a different tongue, and when
encountered in other lands. I recollect hearing the late
Sir Robert Liston expressing this feeling in his own
case. When our ambassador at Constantinople, some
Scotchmen had been recommended to him for a purpose of private or of government business; and Sir
Robert was always ready to do a kind thing for a
countryman. He found them out in a barber's shop,
waiting for being shaved in turn. One came in rather

late, and seeing he had scarcely room at the end of the seat, addressed his countryman, "Neebour, wad ye sit a bit *wast*?" What strong associations must have been called up, by hearing in an eastern land such an expression in Scottish tones.

We may observe here, that marking the course any person is to take, or the direction in which any object is to be met with, by the points of the compass, was a prevailing practice amongst the older Scottish race. There could hardly be a more ludicrous application of the test, than was furnished by an honest Highlander in describing the direction which his medicine would *not* take. Jean Cumming of Altyre, who, in common with her three sisters, was a true *sœur de charité*, was one day taking her rounds as usual, visiting the poor sick, among whom there was a certain Donald MacQueen, who had been some time confined to his bed. Miss Cumming, after asking him how he felt, and finding that he was "no better," of course inquired if he had taken the medicine which she had sent him; "Troth no, me lady," he replied. "But why not, Donald?" she answered; "it was *very wrong*; how can you expect to get better if you do not help yourself with the remedies which heaven provides for you?" "*V*right or *V*rang," said Donald, "it wadna gang *wast* in spite o' me." In all the north country, it is always said, "I'm ganging east or west," etc., and it happened that Donald on his sick-bed was lying east and west, his feet pointing to the latter direction, hence his reply to indicate that he could not swallow the medicine!

We may fancy the amusement of the officers of a regiment in the West Indies, at the innocent remark of a young lad who had just joined from Scotland. On meeting at dinner, his salutation to his Colonel

was, " Anither het day, Cornal," as if " het days "
were in Barbadoes few and far between, as they were
in his dear old stormy, cloudy Scotland. Or take the
case of a Scottish saying, which indicated at once the
dialect and the economical habits of a hardy and
struggling race. A young Scotchman, who had been
some time in London, met his friend recently come up
from the north to pursue his fortune in the great
metropolis. On discussing matters connected with
their new life in London, the more experienced visitor
remarked upon the greater *expenses* there than in the
retired Scottish town which they had left. " Ay,"
said the other, sighing over the reflection, " when ye
get cheenge for a saxpence here, it's soon slippit awa'."
I recollect a story of my father's which illustrates the
force of dialect, although confined to the inflections of
a single monosyllable. On riding home one evening,
he passed a cottage or small farmhouse, where there
was a considerable assemblage of people, and an
evident incipient merry-making for some festive
occasion. On asking one of the lasses standing about,
what it was, she answered, " Ou, it's just a wedding
o' Jock Thamson and Janet Frazer." To the question,
" Is the bride rich? " there was a plain quiet " Na."
" Is she young? " a more emphatic and decided
" Naa! " but to the query, " Is she bonny? " a most
elaborate and prolonged shout of " Naaa! "

It has been said that the Scottish dialect is peculiarly powerful in its use of *vowels*, and the following
dialogue between a shopman and a customer has been
given as a specimen. The conversation relates to a
plaid hanging at the shop door.

Cus.   (inquiring the material), Oo ? (wool ?)
Shop.   Ay, oo (yes, of wool).
Cus.   A' oo ? (all wool ?)

Shop. Ay, a' oo (yes, all wool).
Cus. A' ae oo? (all same wool?)
Shop. Ay, a' ae oo (yes, all same wool).

An amusing anecdote of a pithy and jocular reply, comprised in one syllable, is recorded of an eccentric legal Scottish functionary of the last century. An advocate, of whose professional qualifications he had formed rather a low estimate, was complaining to him of being passed over in a recent appointment to the Bench, and expressed his sense of the injustice with which he had been treated. He was very indignant at his claims and merit being overlooked in their not choosing him for the new judge, adding with much acrimony, " And I can tell you they might have got a ' waur.' "[1] To which, as if merely coming over the complainant's language again, the answer was a grave " Whaur? "[2] The merit of the impertinence was, that it sounded as if it were merely a repetition of his friend's last words, waur and whaur. It was as if " *echo* answered whaur? " As I have said, the oddity and acuteness of the speaker arose from the manner of expression, not from the thing said. In fact, the same thing said in plain English would be mere commonplace. I recollect being much amused with a dialogue between a late excellent relative of mine and his man, the chief manager of a farm which he had just taken, and, I suspect in a good measure manager of the *farmer* as well. At any rate he committed to this acute overseer all the practical details; and on the present occasion had sent him to market to dispose of a cow and a pony, a simple enough transaction, and with a simple enough result. The cow was brought back, the pony was sold. But the man's description of it forms the point. " Well, John, have you sold the

[1] Worse. [2] Where.

cow ? " " Na, but I *grippit* a chiel for the powny ! "
" *Grippit* " was here most expressive. Indeed, this
word has a significance hardly expressed by any
English one, and used to be very prevalent to indicate
keen and forcible tenacity of possession; thus a
character noted for avarice or sharp looking to self-
interest was termed " grippy." In mechanical contrivances, anything taking a close adherence was called
having a gude *grip*. I recollect in boyish days, when on
Deeside taking wasp-nests, an old man looking on
was sharply stung by one, and his description was,
" Ane o' them's grippit me fine." The following had
an indescribable piquancy, which arose from the *Scotticism* of the terms and the manners. Many years ago,
when accompanying a shooting party on the Gram-
pians, not with a gun like the rest, but with a botanical
box for collecting specimens of mountain plants, the
party got very hot, and very tired, and very cross.
On the way home, whilst sitting down to rest, a
gamekeeper sort of attendant, and a character in his
way, said, " I wish I was in the dining-room of
Fasque." Our good cousin the Rev. Mr Wilson,
minister of Farnel, who liked well a quiet shot at the
grouse, rather testily replied, " Ye'd soon be *kickit* out
o' that " ; to which the other replied, not at all daunted,
" Weel, weel, then I wadna be far frae the kitchen."
A quaint and characteristic reply I recollect from an
other farmservant. My eldest brother had just been
constructing a piece of machinery which was driven
by a stream of water running through the home farm-
yard. There was a thrashing machine, a winnowing
machine, and circular saw for splitting trees into pal-
ing, and other contrivances of a like kind. Observing
an old man, who had long been about the place, looking very attentively at all that was going on, he said,

" Wonderful things people can do now, Robby ! "
" Ay," said Robby; " indeed, Sir Alexander, I'm
thinking gin Solomon were alive noo he'd be thocht
naething o' ! "

The two following derive their force entirely from
the Scottish turn of the expressions. Translated into
English, they would lose all point—at least, much of
the point which they now have :—

At the sale of an antiquarian gentleman's effects in
Roxburghshire, which Sir Walter Scott happened to
attend, there was one little article, a Roman *patina*,
which occasioned a good deal of competition, and was
eventually knocked down to the distinguished baronet
at a high price. Sir Walter was excessively amused
during the time of bidding to observe how much it
excited the astonishment of an old woman, who had
evidently come there to buy culinary utensils on a
more economical principle. " If the parritch-pan,"
she at last burst out—" If the parritch-pan gangs at
that, what will the kail-pat gang for ? "

An ancestor of Sir Walter Scott joined the Stuart
Prince in 1715, and, with his brother, was engaged in
that unfortunate adventure which ended in a skirmish
and captivity at Preston. It was the fashion of those
times for all persons of the rank of gentlemen to wear
scarlet waistcoats. A ball had struck one of the
brothers, and carried part of this dress into his body,
and in this condition he was taken prisoner with a
number of his companions, and stripped, as was too
often the practice in those remorseless wars. Thus
wounded, and nearly naked, having only a shirt on,
and an old sack about him, the ancestor of the great
poet was sitting, along with his brother and a hundred and fifty unfortunate gentlemen, in a granary at
Preston. The wounded man fell sick, as the story

THE BONNET LAIRD

goes, and vomited the scarlet cloth which the ball had passed into the wound. " O man, Wattie," cried his brother, " if you have a wardrobe in your wame, I wish you would vomit me a pair o' breeks." But, after all, it was amongst the old ladies that the great abundance of choice pungent Scottish expressions, such as you certainly do not meet with in these days, was to be sought. In their position of society, education either in England, or education conducted by English teachers, has so spread in Scottish families, and intercourse with the south has been so increased, that all these colloquial peculiarities are fast disappearing. Some of the ladies of this older school felt some indignation at the change which they lived to see was fast going on. One of them being asked if an individual whom she had lately seen was " Scotch," answered with some bitterness, " I canna say; ye a' speak sae *genteel* now that I dinna ken wha's Scotch." It was not uncommon to find, in young persons, examples, some years ago, of an attachment to the Scottish dialect, like that of the old lady. In the life of P. Tytler, lately published, there is an account of his first return to Scotland from a school in England. His family were delighted with his appearance, manners, and general improvement; but a sister did not share this pleasure unmixed, for being found in tears, and the remark being made, " Is he not charming?" her reply was, in great distress, " Oh yes, but he speaks English!"

The class of old Scottish ladies, marked by so many peculiarities, generally lived in provincial towns, and never dreamt of going from home. Many had never been in London, or had even crossed the Tweed. But as Lord Cockburn's experience goes back further than mine, and as he had special opportunities of being acquainted with their characteristic peculiarities I will quote his animated description on a page of his *Memorials*. " There was a singular race of old Scotch ladies. They were a delightful set—strong-headed, warm-hearted, and high-spirited—merry even in solitude; very resolute; indifferent about the modes and habits of the modern world, and adhering to their own ways, so as to stand out like primitive rocks above ordinary society. Their prominent qualities of sense, humour, affection, and spirit, were embodied in curious outsides, for they all dressed, and spoke, and did exactly as they chose. Their language, like their habits, entirely Scotch, but without any other vulgarity than what perfect naturalness is sometimes mistaken for." [1]

This is a masterly description of a race now all but passed away. I have known several of them in my early days; and amongst them we must look for the racy Scottish peculiarities of diction and of expression which, with them, are also nearly gone. Lord Cockburn has given some illustrations of these peculiarities; and I have heard others, expecially connected with Jacobite partialities, of which I say nothing, as they are in fact rather *strong* for such a work as this. One, however, I heard lately as coming from a Forfarshire old lady of this class, which bears upon the point of " resolute " determination referred to in the learned judge's description. She had been very positive in the disclaiming of some assertion which had been attributed to her, and on being asked if she had not written it, or something very like it, she replied, " Na, na; I never *write* onything of consequence—I may deny what I say, but I canna deny what I write."

Mrs Baird of Newbyth, the mother of our distinguished countryman the late General Sir David Baird,

---

[1] Lord Cockburn's *Memorials*, p. 48.

was always spoken of as a grand specimen of the class. When the news arrived from India of the gallant but unfortunate action of '84 against Hyder Ali, in which her son, then Captain Baird, was engaged, it was stated that he and other officers had been taken prisoners and chained together two and two. The friends were careful in breaking such sad intelligence to the mother of Captain Baird. When, however, she was made fully to understand the position of her son and his gallant companions, disdaining all weak and useless expressions of her own grief, and knowing well the restless and athletic habits of her son, all she said was, " Lord pity the chiel that's chained to our Davie ! "

It is only due to the memory of " our Davie," however, to add that the " chiel " to whom he was chained, had, in writing home to his friends, borne the highest testimony to the kindness and consideration of Captain Baird, which he exercised towards him in this uncomfortable alliance. General Baird was a first-rate officer, and a fine noble character. He left home for active service so soon (before he was fifteen) that his education had necessarily been very imperfect. This deficiency he had always himself through life deeply regretted. A military friend, and great admirer of Sir David, used jocularly to tell a story of him—that having finished the despatch which must carry home the news of his great action, the capture of Seringapatam, as he was preparing to sign it in great form, he deliberately took off his coat. " Why do you take off your coat ? " said his friend. To which the General quietly answered, " Oh, it's to turn the muckle D in Dauvid."

The ladies of this class had certainly no affectation in speaking of those who came under their displeasure, even when life and death were concerned. I had an anecdote illustrative of this characteristic in a well-known old lady of the last century, Miss Johnstone of Westerhall. She had been extremely indignant that, on the death of her brother, his widow had proposed to sell off the old furniture of Westerhall. She was attached to it from old associations, and considered the parting with it little short of sacrilege. The event was, however, arrested by death, or, as she describes the result, " The furniture was a' to be roupit, and we couldna persuade her. But before the sale cam' on, in God's gude providence she just clinkit aff hersell." Of this same Miss Johnstone another characteristic anecdote has been preserved in the family. She came into possession of Hawkhill, near Edinburgh, and died there. When dying, a tremendous storm of rain and thunder came on, so as to shake the house. In her own quaint eccentric spirit, and with no thought of profane or light allusions, she looked up, and, listening to the storm, quietly remarked, in reference to her departure, " Eh, sirs! what a nicht for me to be fleein' through the air! " Of fine acute sarcasm I recollect hearing an expression from a *modern* sample of the class, a charming character, but only to a certain degree answering to the description of the *older* generation. Conversation turning, and with just indignation, on the infidel remarks which have been heard from a certain individual, and on his irreverent treatment of Holy Scripture, all that this lady condescended to say of him was, " Gey impudent of him, I think."

A recorded reply of old Lady Perth to a French gentleman is quaint and characteristic. They had been discussing the respective merits of the cookery of each country. The Frenchman offended the old Scottish peeress by some disparaging remarks on Scottish dishes, and by highly preferring those of France. All she would answer was, " Weel, weel, some fowk like parritch and some like paddocks." [1]

Of this older race—the ladies who were aged, fifty years ago—no description could be given in bolder or stronger outline than that which I have quoted from Lord Cockburn. I would pretend to nothing more than giving a few further illustrative details from my own experience, which may assist the representation by adding some practical realities to the picture.

Several of them whom I knew in my early days certainly answered to many of the terms made use of by his lordship. Their language and expressions had a zest and peculiarity which are gone, and which would not, I fear, do for modern life and times.

I have spoken of Miss Erskine of Dun, which is near Montrose. She, however, resided in Edinburgh. But those I knew best had lived many years in the then retired society of a country town. Some were my own relations; and in boyish days (for they had not generally much patience with boys) were looked up to with considerable awe as very formidable personages. Their characters and modes of expression in many respects remarkably corresponded with Lord Cockburn's idea of the race. There was a dry Scottish humour which we fear their successors do not inherit. One of these Montrose ladies, Miss Nelly Fullerton, had many anecdotes told of her quaint ways and sayings. Walking in the street one day, slippery from frost, she fairly fell down. A young officer with much politeness came forward and picked her up, earnestly asking her at the same time, " I hope, ma'am, you are no worse ? " to which she very drily answered, looking at him very steadily, " 'Deed, sir, I'm just as little the better." A few days after, she met her military sup-

[1] Frogs.

porter in a shop. He was a fine tall youth, upwards of six feet high, and by way of making some grateful recognition for his late polite attention, she eyed him from head to foot, and as she was of the opinion of the old Scotch lady who declared she " aye liked bonny fowk," she viewed her young friend with much satisfaction, but which she only evinced by the quaint remark, " Od, ye're a lang lad ; God gie ye grace."

I had from a relative or intimate friend of two sisters of this school, well known about Glasgow, an odd account of what it seems, from their own statement, had passed between them at a country house, where they had attended a sale by auction. As the business of the day went on, a dozen of silver spoons had to be disposed of ; and before they were put up for competition, they were, according to the usual custom, handed round for inspection to the company. When returned into the hands of the auctioneer, he found only eleven. In great wrath, he ordered the door to be shut, that no one might escape, and insisted on every one present being searched to discover the delinquent. One of the sisters, in consternation, whispered to the other, " Esther, ye hae nae gotten the spune ? " to which she replied, " Na ; but I hae gotten Mrs Siddons in my pocket." She had been struck by a miniature of the great actress, and had quietly pocketed it. The cautious reply of the sister was, " Then just drop her, Esther." One of the sisterhood, a connection of my own, had much of this dry Scottish humour. She had a lodging in the house of a respectable grocer ; and on her niece most innocently asking, " if she was not very fond of her landlord," in reference to the excellence of her apartments and the attention he paid to her comfort, she demurred to the question on the score of its propriety, by replying,

" Fond of my landlord! that would be an *unaccountable* fondness."

An amusing account was given of an interview and conversation between this lady and the provost of Montrose. She had demurred at paying some municipal tax with which she had been charged, and the provost, anxious to prevent her getting into difficulty on the subject, kindly called to convince her of the fairness of the claim, and the necessity of paying it. In his explanation he referred back to his own bachelor days when a similar payment had been required from him. " I assure you, ma'am," he said, " when I was in your situation I was called upon in a similar way for this tax "; to which she replied, in quiet scorn, " In my situation! an' what were ye in my situation? —an auld maid leevin' in a flat wi' an ae lass." But the complaints of such imposts were urged in a very humorous manner by another Montrose old lady, Miss Helen Carnegy of Craigo; she hated paying taxes, and always pretended to misunderstand their nature. One day, receiving a notice of such payment signed by the provost (Thom), she broke out: " I dinna understand thae taxes; but I just think that when Mrs Thom wants a new gown, the provost sends me a tax paper!" The good lady's naïve rejection of the idea that she could be in any sense " fond of her landlord," already referred to, was somewhat in unison with a similar feeling recorded to have been expressed by the late Mr Wilson, the celebrated Scottish vocalist. He was taking lessons from the late Mr Finlay Dun, one of the most accomplished musicians of the day. Mr Dun had just returned from Italy, and, impressed with admiration of the deep pathos, sentiment, and passion of the Italian school of music, he regretted to find in his pupil so lovely a voice and so much talent losing much of its effect for want of feeling. Anxious, therefore, to throw into his friend's performance something of the Italian expression, he proposed to bring it out by this suggestion : " Now, Mr Wilson, just suppose that I am your lady love, and sing to me as you could imagine yourself doing were you desirous of impressing her with your earnestness and affection." Poor Mr Wilson hesitated, blushed, and, under doubt how far such a personification even in his case was allowable, at last remonstrated, " Ay, Mr Dun, ye forget I'm a married man ! "

A case has been reported of a country girl, however, who thought it possible there might be an excess in such scrupulous regard to appearances. On her marriage-day, the youth to whom she was about to be united said to her in a triumphant tone, " Weel, Jenny, haven't I been unco ceevil ? " alluding to the fact that during their whole courtship he had never even given her a kiss. Her quiet reply was, " Ou, ay, man ; *senselessly* ceevil."

One of these Montrose ladies and a sister lived together ; and in a very quiet way they were in the habit of giving little dinner-parties, to which occasionally they invited their gentlemen friends. However, gentlemen were not always to be had ; and on one occasion, when such a difficulty had occurred, they were talking over the matter with a friend. The one lady seemed to consider such an acquisition almost essential to the having a dinner at all. The other, who did not see the same necessity, quietly adding, " But, indeed, oor Jean thinks a man *perfect salvation.*"

Very much of the same class of remarks was the following sly observation of one of the sisterhood. At a well-known tea-table in a country town in Forfarshire, the events of the day, grave and gay, had been fully discussed by the assembled sisterhood. The occasion was improved by an elderly spinster, as follows :—" Weel, weel, sirs, these are solemn events —death and marriage—but ye ken they're what we must a' come till." " Eh, Miss Jeany ! ye have been lang spared," was the arch reply of a younger member.

There was occasionally a pawky semi-sarcastic humour in the replies of some of the ladies we speak of, that was quite irresistible, of which I have from a friend a good illustration in an anecdote well known at the time. A late well-known member of the Scottish Bar, when a youth, was somewhat of a dandy, and, I suppose, somewhat short and sharp in his temper. He was going to pay a visit in the country, and was making a great fuss about his preparing and putting up his habiliments. His old aunt was much annoyed at all this bustle, and stopped him by the somewhat contemptuous question, " Whar's this you're gaun, Robby, that ye mak sic a grand wark about yer claes ? " The young man lost temper, and pettishly replied : " I'm going to the devil." " 'Deed, Robby, then," was the quiet answer, " ye needna be sae nice, he'll juist tak' ye as ye are."

Ladies of this class had a quiet mode of expressing themselves on very serious subjects, which indicated their quaint power of description, rather than their want of feeling. Thus, of two sisters, when one had died, it was supposed that she had injured herself by an imprudent indulgence in strawberries and cream, of which she had partaken in the country. A friend was condoling with the surviving sister, and, expressing her sorrow, had added, " I had hoped your sister was to live many years." To which her relative replied : " Leeve ! hoo could she leeve ? she juist felled [1]

---

[1] Killed.

hersell at Craigo wi' straeberries and 'ream!" However, she spoke with the same degree of coolness of her own decease. For when her friend was comforting her in illness, by the hopes that she would, after winter, enjoy again some of their country spring butter, she exclaimed, without the slightest idea of being guilty of any irreverence, " Spring butter! by that time I shall be buttering in heaven." When really dying, and when friends were round her bed she overheard one of them saying to another, " Her face has lost its colour; it grows like a sheet of paper." The quaint spirit even then broke out in the remark, " Then I'm sure it maun be *broon* paper." A very strong-minded lady of the class, and, in Lord Cockburn's language, " indifferent about modes and habits," [1] had been asking from a lady the character of a cook she was about to hire. The lady naturally entered a little upon her moral qualifications, and described her as a very decent woman; the response to which was, " Oh, d——n her decency; can she make good collops?"—an answer which would somewhat surprise a lady of Moray Place now, if engaged in a similar discussion of a servant's merits.

The Rev. Dr Cook of Haddington supplies an excellent anecdote, of which the point is in the dry Scottish answer: An old lady of the Doctor's acquaintance, about seventy, sent for her medical attendant to consult him about a sore throat, which had troubled her for some days. Her medical man was ushered into her room, decked out with the now prevailing fashion, a mustache and flowing beard. The old lady, after exchanging the usual civilities, described her complaint to the worthy son of Æsculapius. " Well," says he, " do you know, Mrs Macfarlane, I

[1] Miss Jenny Methven.

used to be much affected with the very same kind of sore throat, but ever since I allowed my mustache and beard to grow, I have never been troubled with it." " Aweel, aweel," said the old lady drily, " that may be the case, but ye maun prescribe some other method for me to get quit o' the sair throat; for ye ken, doctor, I canna adopt *that* cure."

Then how quaint the answer of old Mrs Robison, widow of the eminent professor of natural philosophy, and who entertained an inveterate dislike to everything which she thought savoured of *cant*. She had invited a gentleman to dinner on a particular day, and he had accepted, with the reservation, " If I am spared." " Weel, weel," said Mrs Robison; " if ye're deed, I'll no' expect ye."

I had two grand-aunts living at Montrose at that time—two Miss Ramsays of Balmain. They were somewhat of the severe class—Nelly especially, who was an object rather of awe than of affection. She certainly had a very awful appearance to young apprehensions, from the strangeness of her headgear. Ladies of this class Lord Cockburn has spoken of as " having their peculiarities embodied in curious outsides, as they dressed, spoke, and did exactly as they chose." As a sample of such " curious outside and dress," my good aunt used to go about the house with an immense pillow strapped over her head—warm but formidable. These two maiden grand-aunts had invited their niece to pay them a visit—an aunt of mine, who had made what they considered a very imprudent marriage, and where considerable pecuniary privations were too likely to accompany the step she had taken. The poor niece had to bear many a taunt directed against her improvident union, as for example :— One day she had asked for a piece of tape for some

187

work she had in hand as a young wife expecting to become a mother. Miss Nelly said, with much point, " Ay, Kitty, ye shall get a bit knittin' (*i.e.*, a bit of tape). We hae a'thing ; we're no married." It was this lady who, by an inadvertent use of a term, showed what was passing in her mind in a way which must have been quite transparent to the bystanders. At a supper which she was giving, she was evidently much annoyed at the reckless and clumsy manner in which a gentleman was operating upon a ham which was at table, cutting out great lumps, and distributing them to the company. The lady said, in a very querulous tone, " Oh, Mr *Divot*, will you help Mrs So-and-So ? "— divot being a provincial term for a turf or sod cut out of the green, and the resemblance of it to the pieces carved out by the gentleman evidently having taken possession of her imagination. Mrs Helen Carnegy of Craigo, already mentioned, was a thorough specimen of this class. She lived in Montrose, and died in 1818, at the advanced age of ninety-one. She was a Jacobite, and very aristocratic in her feelings, but on social terms with many burghers of Montrose, or Munross as it was called. She preserved a very nice distinction of addresses, suited to the different individuals in the town, according as she placed them in the scale of her consideration. She liked a party at quadrille, and sent out her servant every morning to invite the ladies required to make up the game, and her directions were graduated thus :—" Nelly, ye'll gang to Lady Carnegy's and mak' my compliments, and ask the *honour* of her ladyship's company, and that of the Miss Carnegys, to tea this evening ; and if they canna come, ging to the Miss Mudies, and ask the *pleasure* of their company ; and if they canna come, ye may ging to Miss Hunter and ask the *favour* of her company ; and if she canna come, ging to Lucky Spark and *bid her come*."

A great confusion existed in the minds of some of those old-fashioned ladies on the subject of modern inventions and usages. A Montrose old lady protested against the use of steam-vessels, as counteracting the decrees of Providence in going against wind and tide, vehemently asserting, " I would hae naething to say to thae *im-pious* vessels." Another lady was equally discomposed by the introduction of gas, asking, with much earnestness, " What's to become o' the puir whales ? " deeming their interests materially affected by this superseding of their oil. A lady of this class, who had long lived in country retirement, coming up to Edinburgh, was, after an absence of many years, going along Princes Street about the time when the water-carts were introduced for preventing the dust, and seeing one of them passing, rushed from off the pavement to the driver, saying, " Man, ye're *skailin'* a' the water." Such being her ignorance of modern improvements.

There used to be a point and originality in expressions made use of in regard to common matters, unlike what one finds now ; for example : A country minister had been invited, with his wife, to dine and spend the night at the house of one of his lairds. Their host was very proud of one of the very large beds which had just come into fashion, and in the morning asked the lady how she had slept in it. " Oh, vary well, sir ; but, indeed, I thought I'd lost the minister, a'thegither."

Nothing, however, in my opinion, comes up to the originality and point of the Montrose old maiden lady's most " exquisite reason " for not subscribing to the proposed fund for organising a volunteer corps in that town. It was at the time of expected invasion at the beginning of the century, and some of the town magistrates called upon her and solicited her subscription to raise men for the service of the king—" Indeed," she answered right sturdily, " I'll dae nae sic thing; I ne'er could raise a man *for myself*, and I'm no' ga'in to raise men for King George."

Some curious stories are told of ladies of this class, as connected with the novelties and excitement of railway travelling. Missing their luggage, or finding that something has gone wrong about it, often causes very terrible distress, and might be amusing, were it not to the sufferer so severe a calamity. I was much entertained with the earnestness of this feeling, and the expression of it from an old Scotch lady whose box was not forthcoming at the station where she was to stop. When urged to be patient, her indignant exclamation was: " I can bear ony pairtings that may be ca'ed for in God's providence; but I *canna stan' pairtin' frae my claes*."

The following anecdote from the west exhibits a curious confusion of ideas arising from the old-fashioned prejudice against Frenchmen and their language, which existed in the last generation. During the long French war, two old ladies in Stranraer were going to the kirk; the one said to the other, " Was it no' a wonderfu' thing that the Breetish were aye victorious ower the French in battle?" " Not a bit," said the other old lady; " dinna ye ken the Breetish aye say their prayers before ga'in into battle?" The other replied, " But canna the French say their prayers as weel?" The reply was most characteristic, " Hoot! jabbering bodies, wha could *understan'* them?"

Some of these ladies, as belonging to the old county families, had very high notions of their own importance, and a great idea of their difference from the burgher families of the town. I am assured of the truth of the following naïve specimen of such family pride :—One of the olden maiden ladies of Montrose called one day on some ladies of one of the families in the neighbourhood, and on being questioned as to the news of the town, said, " News ! oh, Bailie ——'s eldest son is to be married." " And pray," was the reply, " and pray, Miss ——, an' fa' ever heard o' a merchant i' the toon o' Montrose *ha'in* an *eldest son* ? " The good lady thought that any privilege of primo-geniture belonged only to the family of *laird*.

It is a dangerous experiment to try passing off ungrounded claims upon characters of this description. Many a clever sarcastic reply is on record from Scottish ladies, directed against those who wished to impose upon them some false sentiment. I often think of the remark of the outspoken ancient lady, who, when told by her pastor, of whose disinterestedness in his charge she was not quite sure, that he "had a call from his Lord and Master to go," replied, " 'Deed, sir, the Lord might hae ca'ed and ca'ed to ye lang eneuch to Ouchtertoul (a very small stipend), and ye'd ne'er hae letten on that ye heard him."

At the beginning of this century, when the fear of invasion was rife, it was proposed to mount a small battery at the water-mouth by subscription, and Miss Carnegy was waited on by a deputation from the town-council. One of them having addressed her on the subject, she heard him with some impatience, and when he had finished, she said, " Are ye ane o' the toon-council ? " He replied, " I have that honour, ma'am." To which she rejoined, " Ye may hae that *profit*, but honour ye hae nane " ; and then to the point, she added, " But I've been tell't that ae day's wark o' twa or three men wad mount the cannon, and that it may be a' dune for twenty shillings; now there's twa punds to ye." The councillor pocketed the money and withdrew. On one occasion, as she sat in an easy-chair, having assumed the habits and privileges of age, Mr Mollison, the minister of the Established Kirk, called on her to solicit for some charity. She did not like being asked for money, and, from her Jacobite principles, she certainly did not respect the Presbyterian Kirk. When he came in she made an inclination of the head, and he said, "Don't get up, madam." She replied, "Get up! I wadna rise out o' my chair for King George himsell, let abee a whig minister."

This was plain speaking enough, but there is something quite inimitable in the matter-of-factness of the following story of an advertisement, which may tend to illustrate the Antiquary's remark to Mrs Macleuchar, anent the starting of a coach or fly to Queensferry. A carrier, who plied his trade between Aberdeen and a village considerably to the north of it, was asked by one of the villagers, " Fan are ye gaen to the toon ? " (Aberdeen). To which he replied, " I'll be in on Monanday, God willin' and weather permittin', an' on Tiseday, *fither or no'*.

It is a curious subject the various shades of Scottish dialect and Scottish expressions, commonly called Scotticisms. We mark in the course of fifty years how some disappear altogether; others become more and more rare, and of all of them we may say, I think, that the specimens of them are to be looked for every year more in the descending classes of society. What was common amongst peers, judges, lairds, advocates, and people of family and education, is now found in humbler ranks of life. There are few persons perhaps who have been born in Scotland, and who have lived long in Scotland, whom a nice southern ear might not detect as from the north. But far beyond such nicer shades of distinction, there are strong and character-istic marks of a Caledonian origin, with which some of us have had practical acquaintance. I possess two curious, and now, I believe, rather scarce, publications on the prevalent Scotticisms of our speaking and writing. One is entitled "Scotticisms designed to Correct Improprieties of Speech and Writing," by Dr Beattie of Aberdeen. The other is to the same purpose, and is entitled, "Observations on the Scottish Dialect," by the late Right Honourable Sir John Sinclair. Expressions which were common in their days, and used by persons of all ranks, are not known by the rising generation. Many amusing equivoques used to be current, arising from Scotch people in England applying terms and expressions in a manner rather surprising to southern ears. Thus, the story was told of a public character long associated with the affairs of Scotland, Henry Dundas (first Viscount Melville), applying to Mr Pitt for the loan of a horse " *the length* of Highgate "; a very common expression in Scotland, at that time, to signify the distance to which the ride was to extend. Mr Pitt good-humouredly wrote back to say that he was afraid he had not a horse in his possession *quite so long* as Mr Dundas had mentioned, but he had sent the longest he had. There is a well-known case of mystification, caused to English ears by the use of Scottish terms, which took place in the House of Peers during the examination of the Magis-trates of Edinburgh touching the particulars of the Porteous Mob in 1736. The Duke of Newcastle having asked the Provost with what kind of shot the town-guard commanded by Porteous had loaded their muskets, received the unexpected reply, " Ou, juist sic as ane shutes dukes and sic like fules wi'." The answer was considered as a contempt of the House of Lords, and the poor provost would have suffered from misconception of his patois, had not the Duke of Argyle (who must have been exceedingly amused) explained that the worthy magistrate's expression, when rendered into English, did not apply to Peers and Idiots but to *ducks* and *water-fowl*. The circumstance is referred to by Sir W. Scott in the notes to the *Heart of Mid-Lothian*. A similar equivoque upon the double meaning of "Deuk" in Scottish language supplied material for a poor woman's honest compliment to a benevolent Scottish nobleman. John, Duke of Roxburghe, was one day out riding, and at the gate of Floors he was accosted by an importunate old beggar woman. He gave her half-a-crown, which pleased her so much that she exclaimed, "Weel's me on your *guse* face, for Duke's ower little tae ca' ye."

A very curious list may be made of words used in Scotland in a sense which would be quite unintelligible to Southerns. Such applications are going out, but I remember them well amongst the old-fashioned people of Angus and the Mearns quite common in conversation. I subjoin some specimens :—

Bestial signifies amongst Scottish agriculturists cattle generally, the whole aggregate number of beasts on the farm. Again, a Scottish farmer, when he speaks of his " hogs " or of buying " hogs," has no reference to swine, but means young sheep, *i.e.*, sheep before they have lost their first fleece.

Discreet does not express the idea of a prudent or cautious person so much as of one who is not rude, but considerate of the opinions of others. Such application of the word is said to have been made by Dr Chalmers to the late Henry, Bishop of Exeter.

These two eminent individuals had met for the first time at the hospitable house of the late Mr Murray, the publisher. On the introduction taking place, the Bishop expressed himself so warmly as to the pleasure it gave him to meet so distinguished and excellent a man as Dr Chalmers, that the Doctor, somewhat surprised at such an unexpected ebullition from an English Church dignitary, could only reply, " Oh, I am sure your lordship is very ' discreet.' " [1]

Enterteening has in olden Scottish usage the sense not of amusing, but interesting. I remember an honest Dandie Dinmont on a visit to Bath. A lady, who had taken a kind charge of him, accompanied him to the theatre, and in the most thrilling scene of Kemble's acting, what is usually termed the dagger scene in " Macbeth," she turned to the farmer with a whisper, " Is not that fine ? " to which the confidential reply was, " Oh, mem, its verra *enterteening* ! " Enterteening expressing his idea of the effect produced.

Pig, in old-fashioned Scotch, was always used for a coarse earthenware jar or vessel. In the Life of the late Patrick Tytler, the amiable and gifted historian of Scotland, there occurs an amusing exemplification of the utter confusion of ideas caused by the use of Scottish phraseology. The family, when they went to London, had taken with them an old Scottish servant who had no notion of any terms beside her own. She came in one day greatly disturbed at the extremely backward state of knowledge of domestic affairs amongst the Londoners. She had been to so many shops and could not get " a great broon pig to haud the butter in."

From a relative of the family I have received an account of a still worse confusion of ideas, caused by

---

[1] " Civil," " obliging."—Jamieson.

the inquiry of a Mrs Chisholm of Chisholm, who died in London in 1825, at an advanced age. She had come from the country to be with her daughter, and was a genuine Scottish lady of the old school. She wished to purchase a tablecloth of a cheque pattern, like the squares of a chess or draught board. Now a draught-board used to be called (as I remember) by old Scotch people a " dam [1] brod." [2] Accordingly, Mrs Chisholm entered the shop of a linen-draper, and asked to be shown table-linen a *dam-brod pattern*. The shopman, although taken aback by a request, as he considered it, so strongly worded, by a respectable old lady, brought down what he assured her was the largest and widest made. No; that would not do. She repeated her wish for a dam-brod pattern, and left the shop surprised at the stupidity of the London shopman not having the pattern she asked for.

Silly has in genuine old Scottish use reference to weakness of body only, and not of mind. Before knowing the use of the word, I remember being much astonished at a farmer of the Mearns telling me of the strongest-minded man in the county that he was " uncommon silly," not insinuating any decline of mental vigour, but only meaning that his bodily strength was giving way.

Frail, in like manner, expresses infirmity of body, and implies no charge of any laxity in moral principle; yet I have seen English persons looking with considerable consternation when an old-fashioned Scottish lady, speaking of a young and graceful female, lamented her being so *frail*.

Fail is another instance of different use of words. In Scotland it used to be quite common to say of a person whose health and strength had declined, that

---

[1] *Dam*, the game of draughts.   [2] *Brod*, the board.

he had *failed*. To say this of a person connected with mercantile business has a very serious effect upon southern ears, as implying nothing short of bankruptcy and ruin. I recollect many years ago at Monmouth, my dear mother creating much consternation in the mind of the mayor, by saying of a worthy man, the principal banker in the town, whom they both concurred in praising, that she was " sorry to find he was *failing*."

Honest has in Scotch a peculiar application, irrespective of any integrity of moral character. It is a kindly mode of referring to an individual, as we would say to a stranger, " Honest man, would you tell me the way to —— ? " or as Lord Hermand, when about to sentence a woman for stealing, began remonstratively, " Honest woman, whatever garr'd ye steal your neighbour's tub ? "

Superstitious : A correspondent informs me that in some parts of Mid-Lothian the people constantly use the word " superstitious " for " bigoted " ; thus, speaking of a very keen Free Church person, they will say, " He is awfu' supperstitious."

Kail in England simply expresses cabbage, but in Scotland represents the chief meal of the day. Hence the old-fashioned easy way of asking a friend to dinner was to ask him if he would take his kail with the family. In the same usage of the word, the Scottish proverb expresses distress and trouble in a person's affairs, by saying that " he has got his kail through the reek." In like manner haddock, in Kincardineshire and Aberdeenshire, used to express the same idea, as the expression is, " Will ye tak' your haddock wi' us the day ? " that fish being so plentiful and so excellent that it was a standing dish. There is this difference, however, in the local usage, that to say in

Aberdeen, Will you take your haddock? implies an invitation to dinner; whilst in Montrose the same expression means an invitation to *supper*. Differences of pronunciation also caused great confusion and misunderstanding. Novels used to be pronounced no*vels*; envy, en*vy*; a cloak was a clock, to the surprise of an English lady, to whom the maid said, on her leaving the house, " Mem, winna ye tak' the *clock* wi' ye?"

The names of children's diseases were a remarkable item in the catalogue of Scottish words :—Thus, in 1775, Mrs Betty Muirhead kept a boarding-school for young ladies in the Trongate of Glasgow, near the Tron steeple. A girl on her arrival was asked whether she had had smallpox. " Yes, mem, I've had the sma'-pox, the nirls,[1] the blabs,[2] the scaw,[3] the kinkhost[4] and the fever, the branks[5] and the worm." [6]

There is indeed a case of Scottish pronunciation which adds to the force and copiousness of our language, by discriminating four words which, according to English speaking, are undistinguishable in mere pronunciation. The words are—wright (a carpenter), to write (with a pen), right (the reverse of wrong), rite (a ceremony). The four are, however, distinguished in old-fashioned Scotch pronunciation thus—1, He's a wiricht; 2, to wireete; 3, richt; 4, rite.

I can remember a peculiar Scottish phrase very commonly used, which now seems to have passed away. I mean the expression " to let on," indicating the notice or observation of something, or of some person. For example, " I saw Mr —— at the meeting, but I never let on that I knew he was present." A form of expression which has been a great favourite in Scotland in my recollection has much gone out of

---

[1] Measles. [2] Nettle-rash. [3] The itch.
[4] Whooping-cough. [5] Mumps. [6] Toothache.

practice—I mean the frequent use of diminutives, generally adopted either as terms of endearment or of contempt. Thus it was very common to speak of a person whom you meant rather to undervalue, as a *mannie*, a *boddie*, a *bit boddie*, or a *wee bit mannie*. The Bailie in Rob Roy, when he intended to represent his party as persons of no importance, used the expression, "We are bits o' Glasgow bodies."

An admirable Scotch expression I recollect from one of the Montrose ladies before referred to. Her niece was asking a great many questions on some point concerning which her aunt had been giving her information, and coming over and over the ground, demanding an explanation how this had happened, and why something else was so-and-so. The old lady lost her patience, and at last burst forth: "I winna be *back-speired* noo, Pally Fullerton." Back-speired! how much more pithy and expressive than cross-examined! "He's not a man to ride the water on," expresses your want of confidence and of trust in the character referred to. Another capital expression to mark that a person has stated a point rather under than over the truth, is, "The less I lee," as in Guy Mannering, where the precentor exclaims to Mrs MacCandlish, "Aweel, gudewife, then the less I lee." We have found it a very amusing task collecting together a number of these phrases, and forming them into a connected epistolary composition. We may imagine the sort of puzzle it would be to a young person of the present day—one of what we may call the new school. We will suppose an English young lady, or an English educated young lady, lately married, receiving such a letter as the following from the Scottish aunt of her husband. We may suppose it to be written by a very old lady, who, for the last fifty years has not moved from home, and has changed nothing of her early days. I can safely affirm that every word of it I have either seen written in a letter, or have heard in ordinary conversation :—

"*Montrose*, 1858.*

"MY DEAR NIECE—I am real glad to find my *nevy* has made so good a choice as to have secured you for his wife; and I am sure this step will add much to his comfort, and we *behove* to rejoice at it. He will now look forward to his evening at home, and you will be happy when you find you never *want* him. It will be a great pleasure when you hear him in the *trance*, and wipe his feet upon the *bass*. But Willy is not strong, and you must look well after him. I hope you do not let him *snuff* so much as he did. He had a sister, poor thing, who died early. She was remarkably clever, and well read, and most intelligent, but was always uncommonly *silly*.[1] In the autumn of '40 she had a *sair host*, and was aye *speaking through a cold*, and at dinner never did more than to *sup a few family broth*. I am afraid she did not *change her feet* when she came in from the wet one evening. I never *let on* that I observed anything to be wrong; but I remember asking her to come and *sit upon* the fire. But she went out, and did not *take* the door with her. She lingered till next spring, when she had a great *income*,[2] and her parents were then too poor to take her south, and she died. I hope you will like the lassie Eppie we have sent you. She is a *discreet* girl, and comes of a decent family. She has a sister *married upon* a Seceding minister at Kirkcaldy. But I hear he expects to be *transported* soon. She was brought up in one of the *hospitals* here. Her father had been a *souter* and a *pawky chiel* enough,

---

* The Scotticisms are printed in italics.
[1] Delicate in health.   [2] Ailment.

but was *doited* for many years, and her mother was *sair dottled*. We have been greatly interested in the hospital where Eppie was *educate*, and intended getting up a bazaar for it, and would have asked you to help us, as we were most anxious to raise some additional funds, when one of the Bailies died and left it *feuing-stances* to the amount of 5000 pounds, which was really a great *mortification*. I am not a good *hand of write*, and therefore shall stop. I am very tired, and have been *gantin'* [1] for this half-hour, and even in correspondence gantin' may be *smittin'*.[2] The *kitchen* [3] is just coming in, and I *feel* a *smell of tea*, so when I get my *four hours*, that will refresh me and set me up again.—I am, your affectionate aunt,   ISABEL DINGWALL."

This letter, then, we suppose written by a very old Forfarshire lady to her niece in England, and perhaps the young lady who received it might answer it in a style as strange to her aunt as her aunt's is to her, especially if she belonged to that lively class of our young female friends who indulge a little in phraseology which they have imbibed from their brothers, or male cousins, who have, perhaps for their amusement, encouraged them in its use. The answer, then, might be something like this; and without meaning to be severe or satirical upon our young lady friends, I may truly say that, though I never heard from one young lady *all* these fast terms, I have heard the most of them separately from many :—

" MY DEAR AUNTY—Many thanks for your kind letter and its enclosure. From my not knowing Scotch, I am not quite up to the mark, and some of the expressions I don't *twig* at all. Willie is absent for a few days, but when he returns home he will explain it; he is

---

[1] Yawning.   [2] Catching.   [3] Tea-urn.

quite *awake* on all such things. I am glad you are
pleased that Willie and I are now *spliced*. I am well
aware that you will hear me spoken of in some quarters
as a *fast* young lady. A man here had the impudence
to say that when he visited my husband's friends he
would tell them so. I quietly and civilly replied, " You
be blowed ! " So don't believe him. We get on
famously at present. Willie comes home from the
office every afternoon at five. We generally take a
walk before dinner, and read and work if we don't go
out ; and I assure you we are very *jolly*. We don't
know many people here yet. It is rather a *swell* neighbourhood ; and if we can't get in with the *nobs*, depend
upon it we will never take up with any society that is
decidedly *snobby*. I daresay the girl you are sending
will be very useful to us ; our present one is an awful
slow coach. In fact, the sending her to us was a regular
do. But we hope some day to sport *buttons*. My father
and mother paid us a visit last week. The *governor* is
well, and, notwithstanding years and infirmities, comes
out quite a *jolly old cove*. He is, indeed, if you will
pardon the partiality of a daughter, a regular *brick*.
He says he will help us if we can't get on, and I make
no doubt will in due time *fork out the tin*. I am busy
working a cap for you, dear aunty ; it is from a pretty
German pattern, and I think when finished will be
quite a *stunner*. There is a shop in Regent Street where
I hire patterns, and can get six of them for five *bob*. I
then return them without buying them, which I think
a capital *dodge*. I hope you will sport it for my sake at
your first *tea and turn out*.

" I have nothing more to say particular, but am
always

" Your affectionate niece,
" ELIZA DINGWALL."

"*P.S.*—I am trying to break Willie off his horrid habit of taking snuff. I had rather see him take his cigar when we are walking. You will be told, I daresay, that I sometimes take a *weed* myself. It is not true, dear aunty."

Before leaving the question of change in Scottish expressions, it may be proper to add a few words on the subject of Scottish *dialects, i.e.*, on the differences which exist in different counties or localities in the Scottish tongue itself. These differences used to be as marked as different languages; of course they still exist amongst the peasantry as before. The change consists in their gradual vanishing from the conversation of the educated and refined. The dialects with which I am most conversant are the two which present the greatest contrast, viz., the Angus and the Aberdeen, or the slow and broad Scotch—the quick and sharp Scotch. Whilst the one talks of " Buuts and shoon," the other calls the same articles " beets and sheen." With the Aberdonian " what " is always " fat " or " fatten "; " music " is " meesic "; " brutes " are " breets "; " What are ye duin'? " of southern Scotch, in Aberdeen would be " Fat are ye deein'? " Fergusson, nearly a century ago, noted this peculiarity of dialect in his poem of the Leith Races :—

> " The Buchan bodies through the beach,
>   Their bunch of Findrams cry ;
> And skirl out bauld in Norland speech,
>   Gude speldans *fa* will buy ? "

" Findon," or " Finnan haddies," are split, smoked, and partially dried haddocks. Fergusson, in using the word " *Findrams*," which is not found in our glossaries, has been thought to be in error, but his accuracy has been verified singularly enough, within the last few days, by a worthy octogenarian Newhaven fisherman, bearing the characteristic name of Flucker, who remarked "that it was a word commonly used in his youth; and, above all," he added, "when Leith Races were held on the sands, he was like to be deeved wi' the lang-tongued hizzies skirling out, '*Aell a Findram Speldrains*,' and they jist ca'ed it that to get a better grip o't wi' their tongues."

In Galloway, in 1684, Symson, afterwards an ousted Episcopalian minister (of Kirkinner), notes some peculiarities in the speech of the people in that district. " Some of the countrey people, especially those of the elder sort, do very often omit the letter ' h ' after ' t ' as ting for thing; tree for three; tatch for thatch; wit for with; fait for faith; mout for mouth, etc.; and also, contrary to some north countrey people, they oftentimes pronounce ' w ' for ' v,' as serwant for servant; and so they call the months of February, March, and April, the *ware* quarter, from *ver*.[1] Hence their common proverb, speaking of the storms in February, ' *winter never comes till ware comes*.' " These peculiarities of language have almost disappeared— the immense influx of Irish emigrants during late years has exercised a perceptible influence over the dialect of Wigtownshire.

When a southerner mentioned the death of a friend to a lady of the granite city, she asked, "Fat dee'd he o'?" which being utterly incomprehensible to the person asked, another Aberdonian lady kindly explained the question, and put it into language which she supposed *could* not be mistaken, as thus, "Fat did he dee o'?" If there was this difference between the Aberdeen and the Forfar dialect, how much greater

---

[1] *Ver*, the spring months.—*e.g.*,
"This was in *ver* quhen wynter tid."—*Barbour*.

must be that difference when contrasted with the *ore rotundo* language of an English southern dignitary. Such a one being present at a school examination in Aberdeen wished to put some questions on Scripture history himself, and asked an intelligent boy, " What was the ultimate fate of Pharaoh ? " This the boy not understanding, the master put the same question Aberdonicé, " Jemmy, fat was the hinner end o' Pharaoh ? " which called forth the ready reply, " He was drouned i' the Red Sea." A Forfarshire parent, dissatisfied with his son's English pronunciation, remonstrated with him, " What for div' ye say *why* ? Why canna ye say ' what for ' ? "

The power of Scottish phraseology, or rather of Scottish *language*, could not be better displayed than in the following Aberdonian description of London theatricals :—Mr Taylor, at one time well known in London as having the management of the opera-house, had his father up from Aberdeen to visit him and see the wonders of the capital. When the old man returned home, his friends, anxious to know the impressions produced on his mind by scenes and characters so different from what he had been accustomed to at home, inquired what sort of business his son carried on. " Ou," said he (in reference to the operatic singers and the corps de ballet), " he just keeps a curn [1] o' quainies [2] and a wheen widdyfous,[3] and gars them fissle,[4] and loup, and mak' murgeons,[5] to please the great fowk."

Another ludicrous interrogatory occurred regarding the death of a Mr Thomas Thomson. It appeared there were two cousins of this name, both corpulent men. When it was announced that Mr Thomas

---

[1] A number.   [2] Young girls.   [3] Gallows birds.
[4] Make whistling noises.   [5] Distorted gestures.

Thomson was dead, an Aberdeen friend of the family asked, "Fatten Thamas Thamson?" He was informed that it was a fat Thomas Thomson, upon which the Aberdeen query naturally arose, "Ay, but fatten fat Thamas Thamson?" Another illustration of the Aberdeen dialect is thus given: "The Pope o' Rome requires a bull to do his wark, but the Emperor o' France made a coo dee't a'"—a cow do it all—a pun on *coup d'état*. A young lady from Aberdeen had been on a visit to Montrose, and was disappointed at finding there a great lack of beaux, and balls, and concerts. This lack was not made up to her by the invitations which she had received to dinner parties. And she thus expressed her feelings on the subject in her native dialect, when asked how she liked Montrose: "Indeed there's neither men nor meesic, and fat care I for meat?" There is no male society and no concerts, and what do I care for dinners? The dialect and the local feelings of Aberdeen were said to have produced some amusement in London, as displayed by the lady of the Provost of Aberdeen when accompanying her husband going up officially to the capital. Some persons to whom she had been introduced recommended her going to the opera as one of the sights worthy the attention of a stranger. The good lady, full of the greatness of her situation as wife of the provost, and knowing the sensation her appearance in public occasioned when in her own city, and supposing that a little excitement would accompany her with the London public, rather declined, under the modest plea, "Fat for should I gang to the opera, just to creat' a confeesion?" An aunt of mine, who knew Aberdeen well, used to tell a traditionary story of two Aberdonian ladies, who by their insinuations against each other, finely illustrated the force of the dialect then in common

use. They had both of them been very attentive to a
sick lady in declining health, and on her death each
had felt a distrust of the perfect disinterestedness of
the other's attention. This created more than a coolness between them, and the bad feeling came out on
their passing in the street. The one insinuated her
suspicions of unfair dealing with the property of the
deceased by ejaculating, as the other passed her,
" Henny pig [1] and green tea," to which the other
retorted, in the same spirit, " Silk coat and negligée." [2]
Aberdonian pronunciation produced on one occasion
a curious equivoque between the minister and a mother
of a family with whom he was conversing in a pastoral
way. The minister had said, " Weel, Margaret, I hope
you're thoroughly ashamed of your *sins*." Now, in
Aberdeenshire *sons* are pronounced sins; accordingly,
to the minister's surprise, Margaret burst forth,
" Ashamed o' ma sins! na, na, I'm proud o' ma sins.
Indeed, gin it werna for thae cutties o' dauchters, I
should be *ower* proud o' ma sins."

Any of my readers who are not much conversant
with Aberdeen dialect will find the following a good
specimen:—A lady who resided in Aberdeen, being
on a visit to some friends in the country, joined an
excursion on horseback. Not being much of an
equestrian, she was mounted upon a Highland pony
as being the *canniest baste*. He, however, had a trick
of standing still in crossing a stream. A burn had to
be crossed—the rest of the party passed on, while
" Paddy " remained, pretending to drink. Miss More,
in great desperation, called out to one of her friends:
" Bell, 'oman, turn back an gie me your bit fuppie,
for the breet's stannin' i' the peel wi' ma."

A rich specimen of Aberdeen dialect, under peculiar

[1] Honey jar.   [2] A kind of loose gown formerly worn.

207

circumstances, was supplied by an Aberdonian lady who had risen in the world from selling fruit at a stall to be the wife of the Lord Provost. Driving along in her own carriage, she ordered it to stop, and called to her a poor woman whom she saw following her old occupation. After some colloquy, she dismissed her very coolly, remarking, "Deed, freet's dear sin' I sauld freet in streets o' Aberdeen." This anecdote of reference to a good lady's more humble occupation than riding in her carriage may introduce a somewhat analogous anecdote, in which a more distinguished personage than the wife of the Provost of Aberdeen takes a prominent part. The present Archbishop of Canterbury tells the story himself, with that admixture of humour and of true dignity by which his Grace's manner is so happily distinguished. The Archbishop's father in early life lived much at Dollar, where, I believe, he had some legal and official appointment. His sons, the Archbishop and his brother, attended the grammar school, rather celebrated in the country; they ran about and played like other lads, and were known as schoolboys to the peasantry. In after days, when the Archbishop had arrived at his present place of dignity as Primate of all England, he was attending a great confirmation service at Croydon—the church-wardens, clergy, mayors, etc., of the place in attendance upon the Archbishop, and a great congregation of spectators. On going up the centre of the church, a Dollar man, who had got into the crowd in a side aisle, said, loud enough for the Archbishop to hear, "There wasna muckle o' this at Dollar, my Lord."

I have not had leisure to pursue, as I had intended, a further consideration of Scottish Dialect, and their differences from each other in the north, south, east, and west of Scotland. I merely remark now, that the dialect of one district is considered quite barbarous, and laughed at by the inhabitants of another district where a different form of language is adopted. I have spoken of the essential difference between Aberdeen and Southern Scotch. An English gentleman had been visiting the Lord Provost of Edinburgh, and accompanied him to Aberdeen. His lordship of Edinburgh introduced his English friend to the Provost of Aberdeen, and they both attended a great dinner given by the latter. After grace had been said, the Provost kindly and hospitably addressed the company, Aberdonicé : " Now, gentlemen, fah tee, fah tee." The Englishman whispered to his friend, and asked what was meant by " fah tee, fah tee "; to which his lordship replied, " Hout, he canna speak ; he means fau too, fau too." Thus one Scotticism was held in terror by those who used a different Scotticism ; as at Inveraray, the wife of the chief writer of the place, seeking to secure her guest from the taint of inferior society, intimated to him, but somewhat confidentially, that Mrs W. (the rival writer's wife) was quite a vulgar body, so much so as to ask any one leaving the room to " *snib the door*," instead of bidding them, as she triumphantly observed, " *sneck* the door."

Now, to every one who follows these anecdotes of a past time, it must be obvious how much peculiarities of Scottish wit and humour depend upon the language in which they are clothed. As I have before remarked, much of the point depends upon the *broad Scotch* with which they are accompanied. As a type and representative of that phraseology, we would specially recommend a study of our Scottish proverbs. In fact, in Scottish proverbs will be found an epitome of the Scottish phraseology, which is peculiar and characteristic. I think it quite clear that there are proverbs exclusively Scottish, and as we find embodied in them traits of Scottish character, and many peculiar forms of Scottish thought and Scottish language, sayings of this kind, once so familiar, should have a place in our Scottish Reminiscences. Proverbs are literally, in many instances, becoming *reminiscences*. They now seem to belong to that older generation whom we recollect, and who used them in conversation freely and constantly. To strengthen an argument or illustrate a remark by a proverb was then a common practice in conversation. Their use, however, is now considered vulgar, and their formal application is almost prohibited by the rules of polite society. Lord Chesterfield denounced the practice of quoting proverbs as a palpable violation of all polite refinement in conversation. Notwithstanding all this, we acknowledge having much pleasure in recalling our national proverbial expressions. They are full of character, and we find amongst them important truths, expressed forcibly, wisely, and gracefully. The expression of Bacon has often been quoted : " The genius, wit, and wisdom of a nation, are discovered by their proverbs."

All nations have their proverbs, and a vast number of books have been written on the subject. We find, accordingly, that collections have been made of proverbs considered as belonging peculiarly to Scotland. The collections to which I have had access are the following :—

1. The fifth edition, by Balfour, of " Ray's Complete Collection of English Proverbs," in which is a separate collection of those which are considered Scottish Proverbs—1813; Ray professes to have taken these from Fergusson's work mentioned below.

2. A Complete Collection of Scottish Proverbs, explained and made intelligible to the English reader,

by James Kelly, M.A., published in London 1721.

3. Scottish Proverbs gathered together by David Fergusson, sometime minister at Dunfermline, and put *ordine alphabetico* when he departed this life anno 1598. Edinburgh, 1641.

4. A collection of Scots Proverbs, dedicated to the Tenantry of Scotland, by Allan Ramsay. This collection is found in the edition of his Poetical Works, 3 vols. post 8vo, Edin. 1818, but is not in the handsome edition of 1800. London, 2 vols. 8vo.

5. Scottish Proverbs, collected and arranged by Andrew Henderson, with an introductory Essay by W. Motherwell. Edin. 1832.

6. The Proverbial Philosophy of Scotland, an address to the School of Arts, by William Stirling of Keir, M.P. Stirling and Edin. 1855.

The collection of Ray, the great English naturalist, is well known. The first two editions, published at Cambridge in 1670 and 1678, were by the author; subsequent editions were by other editors.

The work by James Kelly professes to collect Scottish proverbs only. It is a volume of nearly 400 pages, and contains a short explanation or commentary attached to each, and often parallel sayings from other languages.[1] Mr Kelly bears ample testimony to the extraordinary free use made of proverbs in his time by his countrymen and by himself. He says that "there were current in society upwards of 3000 proverbs, exclusively Scottish." He adds, "The Scots are wonderfully given to this way of speaking, and, as the consequence of that, abound with proverbs,

[1] Amongst many acts of kindness and essential assistance which I have received and am constantly receiving from my friend, Mr Hugh James Rollo, I owe my introduction to this interesting Scottish volume, now, I believe, rather scarce.

many of which are very expressive, quick, and home to the purpose; and, indeed, this humour prevails universally over the whole nation, especially among the better sort of the commonalty, none of whom will discourse with you any considerable time but he will affirm every assertion and observation with a Scottish proverb. To that nation I owe my birth and education; and to that manner of speaking I was used from my infancy, to such a degree that I became in some measure remarkable for it." This was written in 1721, and we may see from Mr Kelly's account what a change has taken place in society as regards this mode of intercourse. Our author states that he has " omitted in his collection many popular proverbs which are very pat and expressive," and adds as his reason, that " since it does not become a man of manners to use them, it does not become a man of my age and profession to write them." What was Mr Kelly's profession or what his age does not appear from any statements in this volume; but, judging by many proverbs which he has *retained*, those which consideration of years and of profession induced him to omit must have been bad indeed, and unbecoming for *any* age or *any* profession.[1] The third collection by Mr Fergusson is mentioned by Kelly as the only one which had been made before his time, and that he had not met with it till he had made considerable progress in his own collection. The book is now extremely rare, and fetches a high price. By the great kindness of the learned librarian, I have been permitted to see the copy belonging to the library of the Writers to the Signet. It is the first edition, and very rare. A quaint little thin volume, such as delights the eyes of true

[1] Kelly's book is constantly quoted by Jamieson, and is, indeed, an excellent work for the study of good old Scotch.

bibliomaniacs, unpaged, and published at Edinburgh, 1641—although on the title-page the proverbs are said to have been collected at Mr Fergusson's death, 1598.[1] There is no preface or notice by the author, but an address from the printer, " to the merrie, judicious, and discreet reader."

The proverbs, amounting to 945, are given without any comment or explanation. Many of them are of a very antique cast of language; indeed some would be to most persons quite unintelligible without a lexicon. The printer, in his address " to the merrie, judicious, and discreet reader," refers in the following quaint expressions to the author :—" Therefore manie in this realme that hath hard of David Fergusson, sometime minister at Dunfermline, and of his quick answers and speeches, both to great persons and others inferiours, and hath hard of his proverbs which hee gathered together in his time, and now we put downe according to the order of the alphabet; and manie, of all ranks of persons, being verie desirous to have the said proverbs, I have thought good to put them to the presse for thy better satisfaction. . . . I know that there may be some that will say and marvell that a minister should have taken pains to gather such proverbs together; but they that knew his forme of powerfull preaching the word, and his ordinar talking, ever almost using proverbiall speeches, will not finde fault with this that he hath done. And whereas there are some old Scottish words not in use now, bear with that, because if ye alter those words, the proverb will have no grace; and so, recommending these proverbs to thy good use, I bid thee farewell."

I now subjoin a few of Fergusson's Proverbs,

[1] This probably throws back the collection to about the middle of the century.

verbatim, which are of a more obsolete character, and have appended explanations, of the correctness of which, however, I am not quite confident :—

A year a nurish,[1] *seven year a da.*[2] Refers, I presume, to fulfilling the maternal office.

Anes payit never cravit. Debts once paid give no more trouble.

All wald[3] *have all, all wald forgie.*[4] Those who exact much should be ready to concede.

A gangang[5] *fit*[6] *is aye*[7] *getting* (*gin*[8] *it were but a thorn*), or, as it sometimes runs, *gin it were but a broken tae, i.e., toe.* A man of industry will certainly get a living ; though the proverb is often applied to those who went abroad and got a mischief when they might safely have stayed at home—(Kelly).

All crakes,[9] *all bears.*[10] Spoken against bullies who kept a great hectoring, and yet, when put to it, tamely pocket an affront—(Kelly).

Bourd[11] *not wi' bawtie*[12] (*lest he bite you*). Do not jest too familiarly with your superiors (Kelly), or with dangerous characters.

Bread's house skailed never.[13] While people have bread they need not give up housekeeping. Spoken when one has bread and wishes something better—(Kelly).

Crabbit[14] *was and cause had.* Spoken ironically of persons put out of temper without adequate cause.

Dame deem[15] *warily, ye* (*watna*[16] *wha wytes*[17] *yersell*). Spoken to remind those who pass hard censures on others that they may themselves be censured.

---

[1] Nurse.
[2] Daw, a slut.
[3] Would.
[4] Forgive.
[5] Going or moving.
[6] Foot.
[7] Always.
[8] If.
[9] Boasters.
[10] Used as cowards (?).
[11] Jest.
[12] A dog's name.
[13] To skail house, to disfurnish.
[14] Being angry or cross.
[15] Judge.
[16] Know not.
[17] Blames.

Efter lang mint[1] *never dint.*[2] Spoken of long and painful labour producing little effect. Kelly's reading is " *Lang mint little dint.*" Spoken when men threaten much and dare not execute—(Kelly).

Fill fou[3] *and haud*[4] *fou maks a stark*[5] *man.* In Border language a *stark* man was one who takes and keeps boldly.

He that crabbs[6] *without cause should mease*[7] *without mends.*[8] Spoken to remind those who are angry without cause, that they should not be particular in requiring apologies from others.

He is worth na weill that may not bide na wae. He deserves not the sweet that will not taste the sour. He does not deserve prosperity who cannot meet adversity.

Kame[9] *sindle*[10] *kame sair.*[11] Applied to those who forbear for a while, but when once roused can act with severity.

Kamesters[12] *are aye creeshie.*[13] It is usual for men to look like their trade.

Let alane maks mony lurden.[14] Want of correction makes many a bad boy—(Kelly).

Mony tynes[15] *the half-mark*[16] *whinger*[17] (*for the halfe pennie whang*).[18] Another version of penny wise and pound foolish.

Na plie[19] *is best.*

[1] To aim at.

[2] A stroke.

[3] Full.   [4] Hold.

[5] Potent or strong.

[6] Is angry.

[7] Settle.

[8] Amends.

[9] Comb.

[10] Seldom.

[11] Painfully.

[12] Wool-combers.

[13] Greasy.

[14] Worthless fellow.

[15] Loses.

[16] Sixpenny.

[17] A sort of dagger or hanger which seems to have been used both at meals as a knife and in broils—
" And *whingers* now in friendship bare,
   The social meal to part and share,
   Had found a bloody sheath."—*Lay of the Last Minstrel.*

[18] Thong.   [19] No lawsuit.

Reavers [1] *should not be rewers.* [2] Those who are so fond of a thing as to snap at it, should not repent when they have got it—(Kelly).

Sok and seil is best. The interpretation of this proverb is not obvious, and later writers do not appear to have adopted it from Fergusson. It is quite clear that sok or sock is the ploughshare. Seil is happiness, as in Kelly. " Seil comes not till sorrow be o'er "; and in Aberdeen they say, " Seil o' your face," to express a blessing. My reading is " the plough and happiness the best lot." The happiest life is the healthy country one. See Robert Burns' spirited song with the chorus :

> " Up wi' my ploughman lad,
>   And hey my merry ploughman ;
> Of a' the trades that I do ken,
>   Commend me to the ploughman."

A somewhat different reading of this very obscure and now indeed obsolete proverb has been suggested by an esteemed and learned friend :—" I should say rather it meant that the ploughshare, or country life, accompanied with good luck or fortune was best; *i.e.*, that industry coupled with good fortune (good seasons and the like) was the combination that was most to be desired. *sæl*, in Anglo-Saxon, as a noun, means *opportunity*, and then good luck, happiness, etc.

There's mae [3] *madines* [4] *nor makines.* [5] Girls are more plentiful in the world than hares.

Ye bried [6] *of the gouk,* [7] *ye have not a rhyme* [8] *but ane.* Applied to persons who tire everybody by constantly harping on one subject.

The collection by Allan Ramsay is very good, and

[1] Robbers.
[2] Rue, to repent.
[3] More.
[4] Maidens.
[5] Hares.
[6] Take after.
[7] Cuckoo.
[8] Note.

professes to correct the errors of former collectors. I have now before me the *first edition*, Edinburgh, 1737, with the appropriate motto on the title-page, " That maun be true that a' men say." This edition contains proverbs only, the number being 2464. Some proverbs in this collection I do not find in others, and one quality it possesses in a remarkable degree—it is very Scotch. The language of the proverbial wisdom has the true Scottish flavour ; not only is this the case with the proverbs themselves, but the dedication to the tenantry of Scotland, prefixed to the collection, is written in pure Scottish dialect. From this dedication I make an extract, which falls in with our plan of recording Scotch reminiscences, as Allan Ramsay there states the great value set upon proverbs in his day, and the great importance which he attaches to them as teachers of moral wisdom, and as combining amusement with instruction. The prose of Allan Ramsay has, too, a spice of his poetry in its composition. His dedication is : To the tenantry of Scotland, farmers of the dales, and storemasters of the hills—

" Worthy friends—The following hoard of wise sayings and observations of our forefathers, which have been gathering through mony bygane ages, I have collected with great care, and restored to their proper sense. . . .

" As naething helps our happiness mair than to have the mind made up wi' right principles, I desire you, for the thriving and pleasure of you and yours, to use your een and lend your lugs to these guid *auld saws*, that shine wi' wail'd sense, and will as lang as the world wags. Gar your bairns get them by heart ; let them have a place among your family-books, and may never a window-sole through the country be without them. On a spare hour, when the day is clear, behind a ruck, or on the green howm, draw the treasure frae your pouch, an' enjoy the pleasant companion. Ye happy herds, while your hirdsell are feeding on the flowery braes, you may eithly make yoursells master of the haleware. How usefou' will it prove to you (wha hae sae few opportunities of common clattering) when ye forgather wi' your friends at kirk or market, banquet or bridal! By your proficiency you'll be able, in the proverbial way, to keep up the saul of a conversation that is baith blyth an usefou'."

Mr Henderson's work is a compilation from those already mentioned. It is very copious, and the introductory essay contains some excellent remarks upon the wisdom and wit of Scottish proverbial sayings.

Mr Stirling's (now Sir W. Stirling-Maxwell's) address, like everything he writes, indicates a minute and profound knowledge of his subject, and is full of picturesque and just views of human nature. He attaches much importance to the teaching conveyed in proverbial expressions, and recommends his readers even still to collect such proverbial expressions as may yet linger in conversation, because, as he observes, " If it is not yet registered, it is possible that it might have died with the tongue from which you took it, and so have been lost for ever. I believe," he adds, " the number of good old saws still floating as waifs and strays on the tide of popular talk to be much greater than might at first appear."

One remark is applicable to all these collections, viz., that out of so large a number there are many of them on which we have little grounds for deciding that they are *exclusively* Scottish. In fact, some are mere translations of proverbs adopted by many nations; some of universal adoption. Thus we have—

A burnt bairn fire dreads.
Ae swallow makes nae simmer.
Faint heart ne'er wan fair lady.
Ill weeds wax weel.
Mony sma's mak a muckle.
O' twa ills chuse the least.
Set a knave to grip a knave.
Twa wits are better than ane.
There's nae fule like an auld fule.
Ye canna mak' a silk purse o' a sow's lug.
Ae bird i' the hand is worth twa fleeing.
Mony cooks ne'er made gude kail.

Of numerous proverbs such as these, some may or may not be original in the Scottish. Sir William remarks that many of the best and oldest proverbs may be common to all people—may have occurred to all. In our national collections, therefore, some of the proverbs recorded may be simply translations into Scotch of what have been long considered the property of other nations. Still, I hope it is not a mere national partiality to say that many of the common proverbs *gain* much by such translation from other tongues. All that I would attempt now is, to select some of our more popular proverbial sayings, which many of us can remember as current amongst us, and were much used by the late generation in society, and to add a few from the collections I have named, which bear a very decided Scottish stamp either in turn of thought or in turn of language.

I remember being much struck the first time I heard the application of that pretty Scottish saying regarding a fair bride. I was walking in Montrose, a day or two before her marriage, with a young lady, a connection of mine, who merited this description, when she was kindly accosted by an old friend, an honest fish-wife of the town, " Weel, Miss Elizabeth, hae ye gotten a' yer claes ready ? " to which the young lady modestly answered, " Oh, Janet, my claes are soon got ready " ; and Janet replied, in the old Scotch proverb, " Ay, weel, *a bonnie bride's sune buskit.*" [1]   In the old collecton, an addition less sentimental is made to this proverb, *A short horse is sune wispit.*[2]

To encourage strenuous exertions to meet difficult circumstances, is well expressed by *Setting a stout heart to a stey brae.*

The mode of expressing that the worth of a handsome woman outweighs even her beauty, has a very Scottish character—*She's better than she's bonnie.* The opposite of this was expressed by a Highlander of his own wife, when he somewhat ungrammatically said of her, " *She's bonnier than she's better.*"

The frequent evil to harvest operations from autumnal rains and fogs in Scotland is well told in the saying, *A dry summer ne'er made a dear peck.*

There can be no question as to country in the following, which seems to express generally that persons may have the name and appearance of greatness without the reality—*A' Stuarts are na sib*[3] *to the king.*

There is an excellent Scottish version of the common proverb, " He that's born to be hanged will never be drowned."—*The water will never warr,*[4] *the widdie, i.e.,* never cheat the gallows. This saying received a very naïve practical application during the anxiety and alarm of a storm. One of the passengers, a good simpleminded minister, was sharing the alarm that was felt around him, until spying one of his parishioners, of whose ignominious end he had long felt persuaded, he exclaimed to himself, " Oh, we are all safe now," and accordingly accosted the poor man with strong assurances of the great pleasure he had in seeing him on board.

[1] Attired.   [2] Curried.   [3] Related.   [4] Outrun.

It's ill getting the breeks aff the Highlandman is a proverb that savours very strong of a Lowland Scotch
origin. Having suffered loss at the hands of their
neighbours from the hills, this was a mode of expressing the painful truth that there was little hope of
obtaining redress from those who had no *means* at
their disposal.

Proverbs connected with the bagpipes I set down
as legitimate Scotch, as thus—*Ye are as lang in tuning
your pipes as anither wad play a spring.*[1] You are as long
of setting about a thing as another would be in doing
it.

There is a set of Scottish proverbs which we may
group together as containing one quality in common,
and that in reference to the Evil Spirit, and to his
agency in the world. This is a reference often, I fear,
too lightly made; but I am not conscious of anything
deliberately profane or irreverent in the following :—

The deil's nae sae ill as he's caa'd. The most of people
may be found to have some redeeming good point :
applied in *Guy Mannering* by the Deacon to Gilbert
Glossin, upon his intimating his intention to come to
his shop soon for the purpose of laying in his winter
stock of groceries.

To the same effect, *It's a sin to lee on the deil.* Even
of the worst people, *truth* at least should be spoken.

*He should hae a lang-shafted spune that sups kail wi' the
deil.* He should be well guarded and well protected
that has to do with cunning and unprincipled men.

Lang ere the deil dee by the dyke-side. Spoken when
the improbable death of some powerful and ill-
disposed person is talked of.

Let ae deil ding anither. Spoken when too bad persons
are at variance over some evil work.

[1] Tune.

The deil's bairns hae deil's luck. Spoken enviously when ill people prosper.

The deil's a busy bishop in his ain diocie. Bad men are sure to be active in promoting their own bad ends. A quaint proverb of this class I have been told of as coming from the reminiscences of an old lady of quality, to recommend a courteous manner to every one: *It's aye gude to be ceevill as the auld wife said when she beckit* [1] *to the deevil.*

Raise nae mair deils than ye are able to lay. Provoke no strifes which you may be unable to appease.

The deil's aye gude to his ain. A malicious proverb, spoken as if those whom we disparage were deriving their success from bad causes.

Ye wad do little for God an the deevil was dead. A sarcastic mode of telling a person that fear, rather than love or principle, is the motive to his good conduct.

In the old collection already referred to is a proverb which, although somewhat *personal*, is too good to omit. It is doubtful how it took its origin, whether as a satire against the decanal order in general, or against some obnoxious dean in particular. These are the terms of it: *The deil an' the dean begin wi' ae letter. When the deil has the dean the kirk will be the better.*

The deil's gane ower Jock Wabster is a saying which I have been accustomed to in my part of the country from early years. It expresses generally misfortune or confusion, but I am not quite sure of the *exact* meaning, or who is represented by " Jock Wabster." It was a great favourite with Sir Walter Scott, who quotes it twice in *Rob Roy*. Allan Ramsay introduces it in the *Gentle Shepherd* to express the misery of married life when the first dream of love has passed away :—

[1] Curtsied.

"The 'Deil gaes ower Jock Wabster,' hame grows hell,
When Pate misca's ye waur than tongue can tell."

There are two very pithy Scottish proverbial expressions for describing the case of young women losing their chance of good marriages by setting their aims too high. Thus an old lady, speaking of her grand-daughter having made what she considered a poor match, described her as having "*lookit at the moon, and lichtit*[1] *in the midden.*"

It is recorded again of a celebrated beauty, Becky Monteith, that being asked how she had not made a good marriage, she replied, "*Ye see, I wadna hae the walkers, and the riders gaed by.*"

It's ill to wauken sleeping dogs. It is a bad policy to rouse dangerous and mischievous people, who are for the present quiet.

It is nae mair ferly[2] *to see a woman greit than to see a goose go barefit.* A harsh and ungallent reference to the facility with which the softer sex can avail themselves of tears to carry a point.

A Scots mist will weet an Englishman to the skin. A proverb, evidently of Caledonian origin, arising from the frequent complaints made by English visitors of the heavy mists which hang about our hills, and which are found to annoy the southern traveller as it were downright rain.

Keep your ain fish-guts to your ain sea-maws. This was a favourite proverb with Sir Walter Scott, when he meant to express the policy of first considering the interests that are nearest home. The saying savours of the fishing population of the east cost.

A Yule feast may be done at Pasch. Festivities, although usually practised at Christmas, need not, on suitable occasions, be confined to any season.

[1] Fallen.   [2] Surprise.

It's better to sup wi' a cutty than want a spune. Cutty means anything short, stumpy, and not of full growth; frequently applied to a short-handled horn spoon. As Meg Merrilies says to the bewildered Dominie, " If ye dinna eat instantly, by the bread and salt, I'll put it down your throat wi' the *cutty spune.*"

" *Fules mak feasts and wise men eat 'em,* my Lord." This was said to a Scottish nobleman on his giving a great entertainment, and who readily answered, " Ay, and *Wise men make proverbs and fools repeat 'em.*"

A green Yule [1] *and a white Pays* [2] *mak a fat kirkyard.* A very coarse proverb, but may express a general truth as regards the effects of season on the human frame. Another of a similar character is, *An air* [3] *winter maks a sair* [4] *winter.*

Wha will bell the cat? The proverb is used in reference to a proposal for accomplishing a difficult or dangerous task, and alludes to the fable of the poor mice proposing to put a bell about the cat's neck, that they might be apprised of his coming. The historical application is well known. When the nobles of Scotland proposed to go in a body to Stirling to take Cochrane, the favourite of James the Third, and hang him, the Lord Gray asked, " It is well said, but wha will bell the cat? " The Earl of Angus accepted the challenge, and effected the object. To his dying day he was called Archibald Bell-the-Cat.

Ye hae tint the tongue o' the trump. " Trump " is a Jew's harp. To lose the tongue of it is to lose what is essential to its sound.

Meat and mass hinders nae man. Needful food, and suitable religious exercises, should not be spared under greatest haste.

Ye fand it whar the Highlandman fand the tangs (i.e., at

---

[1] Christmas.　　[2] Pasch or Easter.　　[3] Early.　　[4] Severe.

the fireside). A hit at our mountain neighbours, who occasionally took from the Lowlands—as having found—something that was never lost.

His head will ne'er rive (i.e., tear) his father's bonnet. A picturesque way of expressing that the son will never equal the influence and ability of his sire.

His bark is waur nor his bite. A good-natured apology for one who is good-hearted and rough in speech.

Do as the cow of Forfar did, tak a standing drink. This proverb relates to an occurrence which gave rise to a lawsuit and a whimsical legal decision. A woman in Forfar, who was brewing, set out her tub of beer to cool. A cow came by and drank it up. The owner of the cow was sued for compensation, but the bailies of Forfar, who tried the case, acquitted the owner of the cow, on the ground that the farewell drink, called in the Highlands the *dochan doris*,[1] or stirrup-cup, taken by the guest standing by the door, was never charged; and as the cow had taken but a standing drink outside, it could not, according to the Scottish usage, be chargeable. Sir Walter Scott has humorously alluded to this circumstance in the notes to *Waverley*, but has not mentioned it as the subject of an old Scotch proverb.

Bannocks are better nor nae kind o' bread. Evidently Scottish. Better have oatmeal cakes to eat than be in want of wheaten loaves.

Folly is a bonny dog. Meaning, I suppose, that many are imposed upon by the false appearances and attractions of vicious pleasures.

The e'ening brings a' hame is an interesting saying, meaning, that the evening of life, or the approach of

---

[1] The proper orthography of this expression is deoch-an-doruis (or dorais). *Deoch*, a drink; *an*, of the; *doruis* or *dorais*, possessive case of dorus or doras a door.

death, softens many of our political and religious differences. I do not find this proverb in the older collections, but Sir William Maxwell justly calls it " a beautiful proverb, which, lending itself to various uses, may be taken as an expression of faith in the gradual growth and spread of large-hearted Christian charity, the noblest result of our happy freedom of thought and discussion." The literal idea of the " e'ening bringing a' hame," has a high and illustrious antiquity, as in the fragment of Sappho, Ἑσπερε, παντα φὲρεις—φὲρεις ὄιν (or οἶνον) φὲρεις αἶγα, φὲρεις μητὲρι παῖδα —which is thus paraphrased by Lord Byron in " Don Juan," iii. 107 :—

> " O Hesperus, thou bringest all good things—
> Home to the weary, to the hungry cheer ;
> To the young birds the parent's brooding wings,
> The welcome stall to the o'erlaboured steer, etc.
> Thou bring'st the child, too, to the mother's breast."

A similar graceful and moral saying inculcates an acknowledgment of gratitude for the past favours which we have enjoyed when we come to the close of the day or the close of life—

Ruse[1] *the fair day at e'en.*

But a very learned and esteemed friend has suggested another reading of this proverb, in accordance with the celebrated saying of Solon (Arist. Eth. N. I. 10): Κατὰ Σόλωνα χρεών τέλος ὁξᾶν—Do not praise the fairness of the day *till* evening ; do not call the life happy *till* you have seen the close ; or, in other matters, do not boast that all is well till you have conducted your undertaking to a prosperous end.

Let him tak a spring on his ain fiddle. Spoken of a foolish and unreasonable person ; as if to say, " We

[1] Praise.

will for the present allow him to have his own way." Bailie Nicol Jarvie quotes the proverb with great bitterness, when he warns his opponent that *his* time for triumph will come ere long—" Aweel, aweel, sir, you're welcome to a tune on your ain fiddle; but see if I dinna gar ye dance till't afore its dune."

The kirk is meikle, but ye may say mass in ae end o't; or, as I have received it in another form, " If we canna preach in the kirk, we can sing mass in the quire." This intimates, where something is alleged to be too much, that you need take no more than what you have need for. I heard the proverb used in this sense by Sir Walter Scott at his own table. His son had complained of some quaighs which Sir Walter had produced for a dram after dinner, that they were too large. His answer was, " Well, Walter, as my good mother used to say, if the kirk is ower big, just sing mass in the quire." Here is another reference to kirk and quire—*He rives* [1] *the kirk to theik* [2] *the quire.* Spoken of unprofitable persons, who in the English proverb, " rob Peter to pay Paul."

The king's errand may come the cadger's gate yet. A great man may need the service of a very mean one.

The maut is aboon the meal. His liquor has done more for him than his meat. The man is drunk.

Mak a kirk and a mill o't. Turn a thing to any purpose you like; or rather, spoken sarcastically, Take it, and make the best of it.

Like a sow playing on a trump. No image could be well more incongruous than a pig performing on a Jew's harp.

Mair by luck than gude guiding. His success is due to his fortunate circumstances, rather than to his own discretion.

[1] Tears.   [2] Thatch.

He's not a man to ride the water wi'. A common Scottish saying to express you cannot trust such an one in trying times. May have arisen from the districts where fords abounded, and the crossing them was dangerous.

He rides on the riggin' o' the kirk. The rigging being the top of the roof, the proverb used to be applied to those who carried their zeal for church matters to the extreme point.

Leal heart never lee'd, well expresses that an honest, loyal disposition will scorn, under all circumstances, to tell a falsehood.

A common Scottish proverb, *Let that flee stick to the wa',* has an obvious meaning—" Say nothing more on that subject." But the derivation is not obvious.[1] In like manner, the meaning of *He that will to Cupar maun to Cupar,* is clearly that if a man is obstinate, and bent upon his own dangerous course, he must take it. But why Cupar? and whether is it the Cupar of Angus or the Cupar of Fife?

Kindness creeps where it canna gang prettily expresses that where love can do little, it will do that little, though it cannot do more.

In my part of the country a ridiculous addition used to be made to the common Scottish saying. *Mony a thing's made for the pennie, i.e.,* Many contrivances are thought of to get money. The addition is, " As the old woman said when she saw a black man," taking it for granted that he was an ingenious and curious piece of mechanism made for profit.

Bluid is thicker than water is a proverb which has a marked Scottish aspect, as meant to vindicate those

---

[1] It has been suggested, and with much reason, that the reference is to a fly sticking on a wet or a newly painted wall; this is corroborated by the addition in Rob Roy, " When the dirt's dry, it will rub out," which seems to point out the meaning and derivation of the proverb.

family predilections to which, as a nation, we are supposed to be rather strongly inclined.

There's aye water where the stirkie [1] *drouns*. Where certain effects are produced, there must be some causes at work—a proverb used to show that a universal popular suspicion as to an obvious effect must be laid in truth.

Better a finger aff than aye waggin'. This proverb I remember as a great favourite with many Scotch people. Better experience the worst, than have an evil always pending.

Cadgers are aye cracking o' crook saddles [2] has a very Scottish aspect, and signifies that professional men are very apt to talk too much of their profession.

The following is purely Scotch, for in no country but Scotland are singed sheep-heads to be met with : *He's like a sheep head in a pair o' tangs*.

As sure's deeth. A common Scotch proverbial expression to signify either the truth or certainty of a fact, or to pledge the speaker to a performance of his promise. In the latter sense an amusing illustration of faith in the superior obligation of this asseveration to any other, is recorded in the *Eglinton Papers*. [3] The Earl one day found a boy climbing up a tree, and called him to come down. The boy declined, because, he said, the Earl would thrash him. His Lordship pledged his honour that he would not do so. The boy replied, " I dinna ken onything about your honour, but if you say as sure's deeth I'll come doun."

Proverbs are sometimes local in their application.

The men o' the Mearns canna do mair than they may. Even the men of Kincardineshire can only do their utmost—a proverb intended to be highly compli-

[1] A young bullock.   [2] Saddle for supporting panniers.
[3] Vol. i., p. 134.

mentary to the powers of the men of that county.

I'll mak Cathkin's covenant wi' you, Let abee for let abee.
This is a local saying quoted often in Hamilton. The laird of that property had—very unlike the excellent family who have now possessed it for more than a century—been addicted to intemperance. One of his neighbours, in order to frighten him on his way home from his evening potations, disguised himself, on a very wet night, and, personating the devil, claimed a title to carry him off as his rightful property. Contrary to all expectation, however, the laird showed fight, and was about to commence the onslaught, when a parley was proposed, and the issue was, " Cathkin's covenant, Let abee for let abee."

When the castle of Stirling gets a hat, the Carse of Corntown pays for that. This is a local proverbial saying; the meaning is, that when the clouds descend so low as to envelop Stirling Castle, a deluge of rain may be expected in the adjacent country.

I will conclude this notice of our proverbial reminiscences, by adding a cluster of Scottish proverbs, selected from an excellent article on the general subject in the *North British Review* of February 1858. The reviewer designates these as " broader in their mirth, and more caustic in their tone," than the moral proverbial expressions of the Spanish and Italian:—

A blate [1] *cat maks a proud mouse.*
Better a toom [2] *house than an ill tenant.*
Jouk [3] *and let the jaw* [4] *gang by.*
Mony ane speirs the gate [5] *he kens fu' weel.*
The tod [6] *ne'er sped better than when he gaed his ain errand.*
A wilfu' man should be unco wise.
He that has a meikle nose thinks ilka ane speaks o't.
He that teaches himsell has a fule for his maister.

[1] Shy.	[3] Stoop down.	[5] The way
[2] Empty.	[4] Wave.	[6] Fox.

It's an ill cause that the lawyer thinks shame o'.
Lippen [1] to me, but look to yoursell.
Mair whistle than woo, as the souter said when shearing the soo.
Ye gae far about seeking the nearest.
Ye'll no sell your hen on a rainy day.
Ye'll mend when ye grow better.
Ye're nae chicken for a' your cheepin'. [2]

I have now adduced quite sufficient specimens to convince those who may not have given attention to the subject, how much of wisdom, knowledge of life, and good feeling are contained in these aphorisms which compose the mass of our Scottish proverbial sayings. No doubt, to many of my younger readers proverbs are little known, and to all they are becoming more and more matters of reminiscence. I am quite convinced that much of the old quaint and characteristic Scottish talk which we are now endeavouring to recall depended on a happy use of those abstracts of moral sentiment. And this feeling will be confirmed when we call to mind how often those of the old Scottish school of character, whose conversation we have ourselves admired, had most largely availed themselves of the use of its *proverbial* philosophy.

I have already spoken of (p. 9) a Scottish peculiarity, viz., that of naming individuals from lands which have been possessed long by the family, or frequently from the landed estates which they acquire. The use of this mode of discriminating individuals in the Highland districts is sufficiently obvious. Where the inhabitants of a whole countryside are Campbells, or Frasers, or Gordons, nothing could be more convenient than addressing the individuals of each clan by the name of his estate. Indeed, some years ago, any other designation, as Mr Campbell, Mr Fraser, would

---

[1] Trust to.   [2] Chirping.

have been resented as an indignity. Their consequence sprang from their possession.[1] But all this is fast wearing away. The estates of old families have often changed hands, and Highlanders are most unwilling to give the names of old properties to new proprietors. The custom, however, lingers amongst us, in the northern districts especially. Farms also used to give their names to the tenants.[2] I can recall an amusing instance of this practice belonging to my early days. The oldest recollections I have are connected with the name, the figure, the sayings and doings, of the old cow-herd at Fasque in my father's time; his name was Boggy, *i.e.*, his ordinary appellation; his true name was Sandy Anderson. But he was called Boggy from the circumstance of having once held a wretched farm on Deeside named Boggendreep. He had long left it, and been unfortunate in it, but the name never left him—he was Boggy to his grave. The territorial appellation used to be reckoned complimentary, and more respectful than Mr or any higher title to which the individual might be entitled. I recollect, in my brother's time, at Fasque, his showing off some of his home stock to Mr Williamson, the Aberdeen butcher. They came to a fine stot, and Sir Alexander said, with some appearance of boast, " I was offered twenty guineas for that ox." " Indeed, Fasque," said Williamson, " ye should hae steekit your neive upo' that."

Sir Walter Scott had marked in his diary a territorial greeting of two proprietors which had amused him much. The laird of Kilspindie had met the laird of Tannachy-Tulloch, and the following compliments

---

[1] Even in Forfarshire, where Carnegies abound, we had Craigo, Balnamoon, Pitarrow, etc.

[2] This custom is still in use in Galloway; and " Challoch," " Eschonchan," " Tonderghie," " Balsalloch," and " Drummorral," etc., appear regularly at kirk and market.

passed between them:—" Yer maist obedient hummil servant, Tannachy-Tulloch." To which the reply was, " Yer nain man, Kilspindie."

In proportion as we advance towards the Highland district this custom of distinguishing clans or races, and marking them out according to the district they occupied, became more apparent. There was the Glengarry country, the Fraser country, the Gordon country, etc., etc. These names carried also with them certain moral features as characteristic of each division. Hence the following anecdote:—The morning litany of an old laird of Cultoquhey, when he took his morning draught at the cauld well, was in these terms: " Frae the ire o' the Drummonds, the pride o' the Graemes, the greed o' the Campbells, and the wind o' the Murrays, guid Lord deliver us."

The Duke of Athole, having learned that Cultoquhey was in the habit of mentioning his Grace's family in such uncomplimentary terms, invited the humorist to Dunkeld, for the purpose of giving him a hint to desist from the reference. After dinner, the Duke asked his guest what were the precise terms in which he was in the habit of alluding to his powerful neighbours. Cultoquhey repeated his liturgy without a moment's hesitation. " I recommend you," said his Grace, looking very angry, " in future to omit my name from your morning devotions." All he got from Cultoquhey was, " Thank ye, my Lord Duke," taking off his glass with the utmost sangfroid.

CHAPTER VII

ON SCOTTISH STORIES OF WIT
AND HUMOUR

THE portion of our subject which we proposed under the head of "Reminiscences of Scottish Stories of Wit or Humour," yet remains to be considered. This is closely connected with the questions of Scottish dialect and expressions; indeed, on some points hardly separable, as the wit, to a great extent, proceeds from the quaint and picturesque modes of expressing it. But here we are met by a difficulty. On high authority it has been declared that no such thing as wit exists amongst us. What has no existence can have no change. We cannot be said to have lost a quality which we never possessed. Many of my readers are no doubt familiar with what Sydney Smith declared on this point, and certainly on the question of wit he must be considered an authority. He used to say (I am almost ashamed to repeat it), "It requires a surgical operation to get a joke well into a Scotch understanding. Their only idea of wit, which prevails occasionally in the north, and which, under the name of WUT, is so infinitely distressing to people of good taste, is laughing immoderately at stated intervals." Strange language to use of a country which has produced Smollet, Burns, Scott, Galt, and Wilson—all remarkable for the humour diffused through their writings! Indeed, we may fairly ask, have they equals in this respect amongst English writers? Charles Lamb had the same notion, or, I should rather say, the same prejudice, about Scottish people not being accessible to wit; and he tells a story of what happened

234

to himself, in corroboration of the opinion. He had been asked to a party, and one object of the invitation had been to meet a son of Burns. When he arrived, Mr Burns had not made his appearance, and in the course of conversation regarding the family of the poet, Lamb, in his lackadaisical kind of manner, said, " I wish it had been the father instead of the son " ; upon which four Scotsmen present with one voice exclaimed, " That's impossible, for *he's dead*." [1] Now, there will be dull men and matter-of-fact men everywhere, who do not take a joke, or enter into a jocular allusion; but surely, as a general remark, this is far from being a natural quality of our country. Sydney Smith and Charles Lamb say so. But, at the risk of being considered presumptuous, I will say I think them entirely mistaken. I should say that there was, on the contrary, a strong *connection* between the Scottish temperament and, call it if you like, humour, if it is not wit. And what is the difference? My readers need not be afraid that they are to be led through a labyrinth of metaphysical distinctions between wit and humour. I have read Dr Campbell's dissertation on the difference, in his Philosophy of Rhetoric; I have read Sydney Smith's own two lectures; but I confess I am not much the wiser. Professors of rhetoric, no doubt, must have such discussions; but when you wish to be amused by the thing itself, it is somewhat disappointing to be presented with metaphysical analysis. It is like instituting an examination of the glass and cork of a champagne bottle, and a chemical testing of the wine. In the very process the volatile and sparkling draught which was to delight the palate

---

[1] After all, the remark may not have been so absurd then as it appears now. Burns had not been long dead, nor was he then so noted a character as he is now. The Scotsmen might really have supposed a Southerner unacquainted with the *fact* of the poet's death.

has become like ditch water, vapid and dead. What I mean is, that, call it wit or humour, or what you please, there is a school of Scottish pleasantry, amusing and characteristic beyond all other. Don't think of *analysing* its nature, or the qualities of which it is composed; enjoy its quaint and amusing flow of oddity and fun; as we may, for instance, suppose it to have flowed on that eventful night so joyously described by Burns :—

> " The souter tauld his queerest stories,
> The landlord's laugh was ready chorus."

Or we may think of the delight it gave the good Mr Balwhidder, when he tells, in his Annals of the Parish, of some such story, that it was a " jocosity that was just a kittle to hear." When I speak of changes in such Scottish humour which have taken place, I refer to a particular sort of humour, and I speak of the sort of feeling that belongs to Scottish pleasantry—which is sly, and cheery, and pawky. It is undoubtedly a humour that depends a good deal upon the vehicle in which the story is conveyed. If, as we have said, our quaint dialect is passing away, and our national eccentric points of character, we must expect to find much of the peculiar humour allied with them to have passed away also. In other departments of wit and repartee, and acute hits at men and things, Scotsmen (whatever Sydney Smith may have said to the contrary) are equal to their neighbours, and, so far as I know, may have gained rather than lost. But this peculiar humour of which I now speak has not, in our day, the scope and development which were permitted to it by the former generation. Where the tendency exists, the exercise of it is kept down by the usages and feelings of society. For examples of it (in its full force at any rate) we must go back to a race who are departed. One remark, however, has occurred to me in regard to the specimens we have of this kind of humour, viz., that they do not always proceed from the personal wit or cleverness of any of the individuals concerned in them. The amusement comes from the circumstances, from the concurrence or combination of the ideas, and in many cases from the mere expressions which describe the facts. The humour of the narrative is unquestionable, and yet no one has tried to be humorous. In short, it is the *Scottishness* that gives the zest. The same ideas differently expounded might have no point at all. There is, for example, something highly original in the notions of celestial mechanics entertained by an honest Scottish Fife lass regarding the theory of comets. Having occasion to go out after dark, and having observed the brilliant comet then visible (1858), she ran in with breathless haste to the house, calling on her fellow-servants to " Come oot and see a new star that hasna got its tail cuttit aff yet ! " Exquisite astronomical speculation ! Stars, like puppies, are born with tails, and in due time have them docked. Take an example of a story where there is no display of any one's wit or humour, and yet it is a good story, and one can't exactly say why :—An English traveller had gone on a fine Highland road so long, without having seen an indication of fellow-travellers, that he became astonished at the solitude of the country; and no doubt before the Highlands were so much frequented as they are in our time, the roads sometimes bore a very striking aspect of solitariness. Our traveller, at last coming up to an old man breaking stones, asked him if there was *any* traffic on this road—was it at *all* frequented ? " Ay," he said, coolly, " it's no' ill at that; there was

a cadger body yestreen, and there's yoursell the day."
No English version of the story could have half such
amusement, or have so quaint a character. An answer
even still more characteristic is recorded to have been
given by a countryman to a traveller. Being doubtful
of his way, he inquired if he were on the right road to
Dunkeld. With some of his national inquisitiveness
about strangers, the countryman asked his inquirer
where he came from. Offended at the liberty, as he
considered it, he sharply reminded the man that where
he came from was nothing to him; but all the answer
he got was the quiet rejoinder, " Indeed, it's just as
little to me whar ye're gaen." A friend has told me of
an answer highly characteristic of this dry and uncon-
cerned quality which he heard given to a fellow-
traveller. A gentleman sitting opposite to him in the
stagecoach at Berwick complained bitterly that the
cushion on which he sat was quite wet. On looking
up to the roof he saw a hole through which the rain
descended copiously, and at once accounted for the
mischief. He called for the coachman, and in great
wrath reproached him with the evil under which he
suffered, and pointed to the hole which was the cause
of it. All the satisfaction, however, that he got was
the quiet unmoved reply, " Ay, mony a ane has complained o' *that* hole." Another anecdote I heard from
a gentleman who vouched for the truth, which is just
a case where the narrative has its humour not from
the wit which is displayed but from that dry matter-of-
fact view of things peculiar to some of our countrymen. The friend of my informant was walking in a
street of Perth, when, to his horror, he saw a workman
fall from a roof where he was mending slates, right
upon the pavement. By extraordinary good fortune
he was not killed, and on the gentleman going up to

his assistance, and exclaiming, with much excitement, "God bless me, are you much hurt?" all the answer he got was the cool rejoinder, "On the contrary, sir." A similar matter-of-fact answer was made by one of the old race of Montrose humorists. He was coming out of church, and in the press of the kirk *skailing*, a young man thoughtlessly trod on the old gentleman's toe, which was tender with corns. He hastened to apologise, saying, "I am very sorry, sir; I beg your pardon." The only acknowledgment of which was the dry answer, "And ye've as muckle need, sir." An old man marrying a very young wife, his friends rallied him on the inequality of their ages. "She will be near me," he replied, "to close my een." "Weel," remarked another of the party, "I've had twa wives, and they *opened my een*."

One of the best specimens of cool Scottish matter-of-fact view of things has been supplied by a kind correspondent, who narrates it from his own personal recollection.

The back windows of the house where he was brought up looked upon the Greyfriars Church that was burnt down. On the Sunday morning in which that event took place, as they were all preparing to go to church, the flames began to burst forth; the young people screamed from the back part of the house, "A fire! A fire!" and all was in a state of confusion and alarm. The housemaid was not at home, it being her turn for the Sunday "out." Kitty, the cook, was taking her place, and performing her duties. The old woman was always very particular on the subject of her responsibility on such occasions, and came panting and hobbling upstairs from the lower regions, and exclaimed, "Oh, what is't, what is't?" "O Kitty, look here, the Greyfriars Church is on fire!" "Is that a', Miss? What a fricht ye geed me! I thought ye said the parlour fire was out."

In connection with the subject of Scottish *toasts* I am supplied by a first-rate Highland authority of one of the most graceful and crushing replies of a lady to what was intended as a sarcastic compliment and smart saying at her expense.

About the beginning of the present century the then Campbell of Combie, on Loch Awe side, in Argyleshire, was a man of extraordinary character, and of great physical strength, and such swiftness of foot that it is said he could "catch the best *tup* on the hill." He also looked upon himself as a "pretty man," though in this he was singular; also, it was more than whispered that the laird was not remarkable for his principles of honesty. There also lived in the same district a Miss MacNabb of Bar-a'-Chaistril, a lady who, before she had passed the zenith of life, had never been remarkable for her beauty—the contrary even had passed into a proverb, while she was in her teens; but, to counterbalance this defect in external qualities, nature had endowed her with great benevolence, while she was renowned for her probity. One day the laird of Combie, who piqued himself on his *bon-mots*, was, as frequently happened, a guest of Miss MacNabb's, and after dinner several toasts had gone round as usual, Combie rose with great solemnity and addressing the lady of the house requested an especial bumper, insisting on all the guests to fill to the brim. He then rose and said, addressing himself to Miss MacNabb, "I propose the old Scottish toast of 'Honest men and *bonnie* lassies,'" and bowing to the hostess, he resumed his seat. The lady returned his bow with her usual amiable smile, and taking up her glass, replied, "Weel, Combie, I am sure *we* may drink that, for it will neither apply to *you* nor *me*.

An amusing example of a quiet cool view of a pecuniary transaction happened to my father whilst doing the business of the rent-day. He was receiving sums of money from the tenants in succession. After looking over a bundle of notes which he had just received from one of them, a well-known character, he said in banter, " James, the notes are not correct." To which the farmer, who was much of a humorist, drily answered, " I dinna ken what they may be *noo* ; but they were a' richt afore ye had your fingers in amang 'em." An English farmer would hardly have spoken thus to his landlord. The Duke of Buccleuch told me an answer very quaintly Scotch, given to his grandmother by a farmer of the old school. A dinner was given to some tenantry of the vast estates of the family, in the time of Duke Henry. His Duchess (the last descendant of the Dukes of Montague) always appeared at table on such occasions, and did the honours with that mixture of dignity and of affable kindness for which she was so remarkable. Abundant hospitality was shown to all the guests. The Duchess, having observed one of the tenants supplied with boiled beef from a noble round, proposed that he should add a supply of cabbage : on his declining, the Duchess good-humouredly remarked, " Why, boiled beef and ' greens ' seem so naturally to go together, I wonder you don't take it." To which the honest farmer objected, " Ah, but your Grace maun alloo it's a vary *windy* vegetable," in delicate allusion to the flatulent quality of the esculent. Similar to this was the naïve answer of a farmer on the occasion of a rent-day. The lady of the house asked him if he would take some " rhubarb-tart," to which he innocently answered, " Thank ye, mem, I dinna *need* it."

A Highland minister, dining with the patroness of his parish, ventured to say, " I'll thank your leddyship for a little more of that apple-tart " ; " It's not apple-tart, it's rhubarb," replied the lady. " Rhubarb ! " repeated the other, with a look of surprise and alarm, and immediately called out to the attendant, " Freend, I'll thank you for a dram."

A characteristic *table* anecdote I can recall amongst Deeside reminiscences. My aunt, Mrs Forbes, had entertained an honest Scotch farmer at Banchory Lodge ; a draught of ale had been offered to him, which he had quickly despatched. My aunt observing that the glass had no head or effervescence, observed, that she feared it had not been a good bottle, " Oh, verra gude, ma'am, it's just some strong o' the aaple," an expression which indicates the beer to be somewhat sharp or pungent. It turned out to have been a bottle of *vinegar* decanted by mistake.

An amusing instance of an old Scottish farmer being unacquainted with table refinements occurred at a tenant's dinner in the north. The servant had put down beside him a dessert spoon when he had been helped to pudding. This seemed quite superfluous to the honest man, who exclaimed, " Tak' it awa', my man ; my mou's as big for puddin' as it is for kail."

Amongst the lower orders in Scotland humour is found, occasionally, very rich in mere children, and I recollect a remarkable illustration of this early native humour occurring in a family in Forfarshire, where I used in former days to be very intimate. A wretched woman, who used to traverse the country as a beggar or tramp, left a poor, half-starved little girl by the roadside, near the house of my friends. Always ready to assist the unfortunate, they took charge of the child, and as she grew a little older they began to give her some education, and taught her to read. She soon made some progress in reading the Bible, and the native odd humour of which we speak began soon to show itself. On reading the passage, which began, " Then David rose," etc., the child stopped, and looked up knowingly, to say, " I ken wha that was," and on being asked what she could mean, she confidently said, " That's David Rowse the pleuchman." And again, reading the passage where the words occur, " He took Paul's girdle," the child said, with much confidence, " I ken what he took that for," and on being asked to explain, replied at once, " To bake 's bannocks on "; " girdle " being in the north the name for the iron plate hung over the fire for baking oatcakes or bannocks.

To a distinguished member of the Church of Scotland I am indebted for an excellent story of quaint child humour, which he had from the lips of an old woman who related the story of herself :—When a girl of eight years of age she was taken by her grandmother to church. The parish minister was not only a long preacher, but, as the custom was, delivered two sermons on the Sabbath day without any interval, and thus saved the parishioners the two journeys to church. Elizabeth was sufficiently wearied before the close of the first discourse ; but when, after singing and prayer, the good minister opened the Bible, read a second text, and prepared to give a second sermon, the young girl, being both tired and hungry, lost all patience, and cried out to her grandmother, to the no small amusement of those who were so near as to hear her, " Come awa', granny, and gang hame ; this is a lang grace, and nae meat."

A most amusing account of child humour used to be narrated by an old Mr Campbell of Jura, who told the story of his own son. It seems the boy was much spoilt by indulgence. In fact, the parents were scarce able to refuse him anything he demanded. He was in the drawing-room on one occasion when dinner was announced, and on being ordered up to the nursery he insisted on going down to dinner with the company. His mother was for refusal, but the child persevered, and kept saying, " If I dinna gang, I'll tell thon." His father then, for peace sake, let him go. So he went and sat at table by his mother. When he found every one getting soup and himself omitted, he demanded soup, and repeated, " If I dinna get it, I'll tell thon." Well, soup was given, and various other things yielded to his importunities, to which he always added the usual threat of " telling thon." At last, when it came to wine, his mother stood firm, and positively refused, as " a bad thing for little boys," and so on. He then became more vociferous than ever about " telling thon " ; and as still he was refused, he declared, " Now, I will tell thon," and at last roared out, " *Ma new breeks were made oot o' the auld curtains !* "

The Rev. Mr Agnew has kindly sent me an anecdote which supplies an example of cleverness in a Scottish boy, and which rivals, as he observes, the smartness of the London boy, termed by *Punch* the " Street boy." It has also a touch of quiet, sly Scottish *humour*. A gentleman, editor of a Glasgow paper, well known as a bon-vivant and epicure, and by no means a popular character, was returning one day from his office, and met near his own house a boy carrying a splendid salmon. The gentleman looked at it with longing eyes, and addressed the boy : " Where are you taking that salmon, my boy ? " Boy : " Do you ken gin ae Mr —— (giving the gentleman's name) lives hereabout ? " Mr —— : " Yes, oh yes ; his house is here

just by." Boy (looking sly) : " Weel, it's no' for him."
Of this same Scottish *boy cleverness*, the Rev. Mr M'Lure
of Marykirk kindly supplies a capital specimen, in an
instance which occurred at what is called the market,
at Fettercairn, where there is always a hiring of servants. A boy was asked by a farmer if he wished to
be engaged. " Ou ay," said the youth. " Wha was your
last maister ? " was the next question. " Oh, yonder
him," said the boy ; and then agreeing to wait where
he was standing with some other servants till the inquirer should return from examination of the boy's
late employer. The farmer returned and accosted the
boy, " Weel, lathie, I've been speerin' about ye, an'
I'm tae tak' ye." " Ou ay," was the prompt reply,
" an' I've been speerin' about *ye tae*, an' I'm nae
gaen."

We could not have had a better specimen of the cool
self-sufficiency of these young domestics of the Scottish type than the following :—I heard of a boy making
a very cool and determined exit from the house into
which he had very lately been introduced. He had
been told that he should be dismissed if he broke any
of the china that was under his charge. On the morning of a great dinner-party he was entrusted (rather
rashly) with a great load of plates, which he was to
carry upstairs from the kitchen to the dining-room,
and which were piled up, and rested upon his two
hands. In going upstairs his foot slipped, and the
plates were broken to atoms. He at once went up to
the drawing-room, put his head in at the door, and
shouted : " The plates are a' smashed, and I'm awa'."

A facetious and acute friend, who rather leans to
the Sydney Smith view of Scottish wit, declares that
all our humorous stories are about lairds, and lairds
that are drunk. Of such stories there are certainly not

a few. The following is one of the best belonging to my part of the country, and to many persons I should perhaps apologise for introducing it at all. The story has been told of various parties and localities, but no doubt the genuine laird was a laird of Balnamoon (pronounced in the country Bonnymoon), and that the locality was a wild tract of land, not far from his place, called Munrimmon Moor. Balnamoon had been dining out in the neighbourhood, where, by mistake, they had put down to him after dinner, cherry brandy, instead of port wine, his usual beverage. The rich flavour and strength so pleased him that, having tasted it, he would have nothing else. On rising from table, therefore, the laird would be more affected by his drink than if he had taken his ordinary allowance of port. His servant Harry or Hairy was to drive him home in a gig, or whisky as it was called, the usual open carriage of the time. On crossing the moor, however, whether from greater exposure to the blast, or from the laird's unsteadiness of head, his hat and wig came off and fell upon the ground. Harry got out to pick them up and restore them to his master. The laird was satisfied with the hat, but demurred at the wig. " It's no' my wig, Hairy, lad ; it's no' my wig," and refused to have anything to do with it. Hairy lost his patience, and, anxious to get home, remonstrated with his master, " Ye'd better tak' it, sir, for there's nae *waile* [1] o' wigs on Munrimmon Moor." The humour of the agrument is exquisite, putting to the laird in his unreasonable objection the sly insinuation that in such a locality, if he did not take *this* wig, he was not likely to find another. Then, what a rich expression, " waile o' wigs." In English what is it ? " A choice of perukes " ; which is nothing compar-

[1] Choice.

able to the "waile o' wigs." I ought to mention also an amusing sequel to the story, viz., in what happened after the affair of the wig had been settled, and the laird had consented to return home. When the whisky drove up to the door, Hairy, sitting in front, told the servant who came "to tak' out the laird." No laird was to be seen; and it appeared that he had fallen out on the moor without Hairy observing it. Of course, they went back, and, picking him up, brought him safe home. A neighbouring laird having called a few days after, and having referred to the accident, Balnamoon quietly added, "Indeed, I maun hae a lume [1] that'll *haud in.*"

The laird of Balnamoon was a truly eccentric character. He joined with his drinking propensities a great zeal for the Episcopal church, the service of which he read to his own family with much solemnity and earnestness of manner. Two gentlemen, one of them a stranger to the country, having called pretty early one Sunday morning, Balnamoon invited them to dinner, and as they accepted the invitation, they remained and joined in the forenoon devotional exercises conducted by Balnamoon himself. The stranger was much impressed with the laird's performance of the service, and during a walk which they took before dinner, mentioned to his friend how highly he esteemed the religious deportment of their host. The gentleman said nothing, but smiled to himself at the scene which he anticipated was to follow. After dinner, Balnamoon set himself, according to the custom of old hospitable Scottish hosts, to make his guests as drunk as possible. The result was, that the party spent the evening in a riotous debauch, and were carried to bed by the servants at a late hour. Next day, when they

[1] A vessel.

had taken leave and left the house, the gentleman who had introduced his friend asked him what he thought of their entertainer—" Why, really," he replied, with evident astonishment, " sic a speat o' praying, and sic a speat o' drinking, I never knew in the whole course o' my life."

Lady Dalhousie, mother, I mean, of the late distinguished Marquis of Dalhousie, used to tell a characteristic anecdote of her day. But here, on mention of the name Christian, Countess of Dalhousie, may I pause a moment to recall the memory of one who was a very remarkable person. She was for many years, to me and mine, a sincere, and true and valuable friend. By an awful dispensation of God's providence her death happened *instantaneously* under my roof in 1839. Lady Dalhousie was eminently distinguished for a fund of the most varied knowledge, for a clear and powerful judgment, for acute observation, a kind heart, a brilliant wit. Her story was thus :—A Scottish judge, somewhat in the predicament of the Laird of Balnamoon, had dined at Coalstoun with her father Charles Brown, an advocate, and son of George Brown, who sat in the Supreme Court as a judge with the title of Lord Coalstoun. The party had been convivial, as we know parties of the highest legal characters often were in those days. When breaking up and going to the drawing-room, one of them, not seeing his way very clearly, stepped out of the dining-room window, which was open to the summer air. The ground at Coalstoun sloping off from the house behind, the worthy judge got a great fall, and rolled down the bank. He contrived, however, as tipsy men generally do, to regain his legs, and was able to reach the drawing-room. The first remark he made was an innocent remonstrance with his friend the host, " Od,

Charlie Brown, what gars ye hae sic lang steps, to your *front door* ? "

On Deeside, where many original stories had their origin, I recollect hearing several of an excellent and worthy, but very simple-minded man, the Laird of Craigmyle. On one occasion, when the beautiful and clever Jane, Duchess of Gordon, was scouring through the country, intent upon some of those electioneering schemes which often occupied her fertile imagination and active energies, she came to call at Craigmyle, and having heard that the laird was making bricks on the property, for the purpose of building a new garden wall, with her usual tact she opened the subject, and kindly asked, " Well, Mr Gordon, and how do your bricks come on ? " Good Craigmyle's thoughts were much occupied with a new leather portion of his dress which had been lately constructed, so, looking down on his nether garments, he said in pure Aberdeen dialect, " Muckle obleeged to yer Grace, the breeks war sum ticht at first, but they are deeing weel eneuch noo."

The last Laird of Macnab, before the clan finally broke up and emigrated to Canada, was a well-known character in the country, and being poor, used to ride about on a most wretched horse, which gave occasion to many jibes at his expense. The laird was in the constant habit of riding up from the country to attend the Musselburgh races. A young wit, by way of play-ing him off on the racecourse, asked him, in a con-temptuous tone, " Is that the same horse you had last year, laird ? " " Na," said the laird, brandishing his whip in the interrogator's face in so emphatic a manner as to preclude further questioning, " na ; but it's the same *whup*." In those days, as might be expected, people were not nice in expressions of their dislike of persons and measures. If there be not more charity in society than of old, there is certainly more courtesy. I have, from a friend, an anecdote illustrative of this remark, in regard to feelings exercised towards an unpopular laird. In the neighbourhood of Banff, in Forfarshire, the seat of a very ancient branch of the Ramsays, lived a proprietor who bore the appellation of Corb, from the name of his estate. This family has passed away, and its property merged in Banff. The laird was intensely disliked in the neighbourhood. Sir George Ramsay was, on the other hand, universally popular and respected. On one occasion, Sir George, in passing a morass in his own neighbourhood, had missed the road and fallen into a bog to an alarming depth. To his great relief, he saw a passenger coming along the path, which was at no great distance. He called loudly for his help, but the man took no notice. Poor Sir George felt himself sinking, and redoubled his cries for assistance; all at once the passenger rushed forward, carefully extricated him from his perilous position, and politely apologised for his first neglect of his appeal, adding, as his reason, " Indeed, Sir George, I thought it was Corb ! " evidently meaning that *had* it been Corb, he must have taken his chance for him.

In Lanarkshire there lived a sma' sma' laird named Hamilton, who was noted for his eccentricity. On one occasion, a neighbour waited on him, and requested his name as an accommodation to a " bit bill " for twenty pounds at three months' date, which led to the following characteristic and truly Scottish colloquy :—" Na, na, I canna do that." " What for no, laird ? ye hae dune the same thing for ithers." " Ay, ay, Tammas, but there's wheels within wheels ye ken naething about; I canna do't." " It's a sma' affair to refuse me, laird." " Weel, ye see, Tammas, if I was to pit my name till't, ye wad get the siller frae the bank, and when the time came round, ye wadna be ready, and I wad hae to pay't; sae then you and me wad quarrel; sae we may just as weel quarrel *the noo*, as lang's the siller's in ma pouch." On one occasion, Hamilton having business with the late Duke of Hamilton at Hamilton Palace, the Duke politely asked him to lunch. A liveried servant waited upon them, and was most assiduous in his attentions to the Duke and his guest. At last our eccentric friend lost patience, and looking at the servant, addressed him thus, " What the deil for are ye dance, dancing, about the room that gait? can ye no' draw in your chair and sit down? I'm sure there's *plenty on the table for three.*"

As a specimen of the old-fashioned laird, now be-come a Reminiscence, who adhered pertinaciously to old Scottish usages, and to the old Scottish dialect, I cannot, I am sure, adduce a better specimen than Mr Fergusson of Pitfour, to whose servant I have already referred. He was always called Pitfour, from the name of his property in Aberdeenshire. He must have died fifty years ago. He was for many years M.P. for the county of Aberdeen, and I have reason to believe that he made the enlightened parliamentary declaration which has been given to others : He said " he had often heard speeches in the *House*, which had changed his opinion, but none that had ever changed his vote." I recollect hearing of his dining in London sixty years ago, at the house of a Scottish friend, where there was a swell party, and Pitfour was introduced as a great northern proprietor, and county M.P. A fashionable lady patronised him graciously, and took great charge of him, and asked him about his estates. Pitfour was very dry and sparing in his communications, as for example, " What does

your home farm chiefly produce, Mr Fergusson?"
Answer, " Girss." " I beg your pardon, Mr Fergusson, what does your home farm produce?" All she
could extract was, " Girss."

Of another laird, whom I heard often spoken of in
old times, an anecdote was told strongly Scottish.
Our friend had much difficulty (as many worthy
lairds have had) in meeting the claims of those two
woeful periods of the year called with us in Scotland
the " tarmes." He had been employing for some time
as workman a stranger from the south on some house
repairs, of the not uncommon name in England of
Christmas. His servant early one morning called out
at the laird's door in great excitement that " Christmas
had run away, and nobody knew where he had
gone." He coolly turned in his bed with the ejacula-
tion, " I only wish he had taken Whitsunday and
Martinmas along with him." I do not know a better
illustration of quiet, shrewd, and acute Scottish
humour than the following little story, which an
esteemed correspondent mentions having heard from
his father when a boy, relating to a former Duke of
Athole, who had *no family of his own*, and whom he
mentions as having remembered very well :—He met
one morning, one of his cottars or gardeners, whose
wife he knew to be in the *hopeful way*. Asking him
" how Marget was the day," the man replied that she
had that morning given him twins. Upon which the
Duke said : " Weel, Donald ; ye ken the Almighty
never sends bairns without the meat." " That may
be, your Grace," said Donald ; " but whiles I think
that Providence maks a mistak in thae matters, and
sends the bairns to ae hoose and the meat to anither ! "
The Duke took the hint, and sent him a cow with
calf in the following morning.

I have heard of an amusing scene between a laird, noted for his meanness, and a wandering sort of Edie Ochiltree, a well-known itinerant who lived by his wits and what he could pick up in his rounds amongst the houses through the country. The laird, having seen the beggar sit down near his gate to examine the contents of his pock or wallet, conjectured that he had come from his house, and so drew near to see what he had carried off. As the laird was keenly investigating the mendicant's spoils, his quick eye detected some bones on which there remained more meat than should have been allowed to leave his kitchen. Accordingly he pounced upon the bones, declaring he had been robbed, and insisted on the beggar returning to the house and giving back the spoil. He was, however, prepared for the attack, and sturdily defended his property, boldly asserting, " Na, na, laird, thae are no Tod-brae banes ; they are Inchbyre banes, and nane o' your honour's "—meaning that he had received these bones at the house of a neighbour of a more liberal character. The beggar's professional discrimination between the merits of the bones of the two mansions, and his pertinacious defence of his own property, would have been most amusing to a bystander.

I have, however, a reverse story, in which the beggar is quietly silenced by the proprietor. A noble lord, some generations back, well known for his frugal habits, had just picked up a small copper coin in his own avenue, and had been observed by one of the itinerating mendicant race, who, grudging the transfer of the piece into the peer's pocket, exclaimed, " O, gie't to me, my lord " ; to which the quiet answer was, " Na, na ; fin' a fardin' for yersell, puir body."

There are always pointed anecdotes against houses

wanting in a liberal and hospitable expenditure in Scotland. Thus, we have heard of a master leaving such a mansion, and taxing his servant with being drunk, which he had too often been after other country visits. On this occasion, however, he was innocent of the charge, for he had not the *opportunity* to transgress. So, when his master asserted, " Jemmy, you are drunk ! " Jemmy very quietly answered, " Indeed, sir, I wish I wur." At another mansion, notorious for scanty fare, a gentleman was inquiring of the gardener about a dog which some time ago he had given to the laird. The gardener showed him a lank greyhound, on which the gentleman said, " No, no ; the dog I gave your master was a mastiff, not a greyhound " ; to which the gardener quietly answered, " Indeed, ony dog micht sune become a greyhound by stopping here."

From a friend and relative, a minister of the Established Church of Scotland, I used to hear many characteristic stories. He had a curious vein of this sort of humour in himself, besides what he brought out from others. One of his peculiarities was a mortal antipathy to the whole French nation, whom he frequently abused in no measured terms. At the same time he had great relish of a glass of claret, which he considered the prince of all social beverages. So he usually finished off his anti-gallican tirades with the reservation, " But the bodies brew the braw drink." He lived amongst his own people, and knew well the habits and peculiarities of a race gone by. He had many stories connected with the pastoral relation between minister and people, and all such stories are curious, not merely for their amusement, but from the illustration they afford us of that peculiar Scottish humour which we are now describing. He had himself, when a very young boy, before he came up to the Edinburgh High School, been at the parochial school where he resided, and which, like many others, at that period, had a considerable reputation for the skill and scholarship of the master. He used to describe school scenes rather different, I suspect, from school scenes in our day. One boy, on coming late, explained that the cause had been a regular pitched battle between his parents, with the details of which he amused his school-fellows; and he described the battle in vivid and Scottish Homeric terms: " And eh, as they faucht, and they faucht," adding, however, with much complacency, " but my minnie dang, she did tho'."

There was a style of conversation and quaint modes of expression between ministers and their people at that time, which, I suppose, would seem strange to the present generation; as for example, I recollect a conversation between this relative and one of his parishioners of this description—It had been a very wet and unpromising autumn. The minister met a certain Janet of his flock, and accosted her very kindly. He remarked, " Bad prospect for the har'st (harvest), Janet, this wet." *Janet:* " Indeed, sir, I've seen as muckle as that there'll be nae har'st the year." *Minister:* " Na, Janet, deil as muckle as that 't ever you saw."

As I have said, he was a clergyman of the Established Church, and had many stories about ministers and people, arising out of his own pastoral experience, or the experience of friends and neighbours. He was much delighted with the not very refined rebuke which one of his own farmers had given to a young minister who had for some Sundays occupied his pulpit. The young man had dined with the farmer in the afternoon when services were over, and his appetite was so sharp, that he thought it necessary to apologise to his host for eating so substantial a dinner. "You see," he said, "I am always very hungry after preaching." The old gentleman, not much admiring the youth's pulpit ministrations, having heard this apology two or three times, at last replied sarcastically, "Indeed, sir, I'm no' surprised at it, considering the *trash* that comes aff your stamach in the morning."

What I wish to keep in view is, to distinguish anecdotes which are amusing on account merely of the expressions used, from those which have real wit and humour *combined*, with the purely Scottish vehicle in which they are conveyed.

Of this class I could not have a better specimen to commence with than the defence of the liturgy of his church, by John Skinner of Langside, of whom previous mention has been made. It is witty and clever.

Being present at a party (I think at Lord Forbes's), where were also several ministers of the Establishment, the conversation over their wine turned, among other things, on the Prayer Book. Skinner took no part in it, till one minister remarked to him, "The great fau't I hae' to your prayer book is that ye use the Lord's Prayer sae aften—ye juist mak' a dishclout o't." Skinner's rejoinder was, "Verra true! Ay, man, we mak' a dishclout o't, an' we wring't, an' we wring't, an' we wring't, an' the bree [1] o't washes a' the lave o' our prayers."

No one, I think, could deny the wit of the two following rejoinders.

A ruling elder of a country parish in the west of Scotland was well known in the district as a shrewd and ready-witted man. He received many a visit from persons who liked a banter, or to hear a good joke.

[1] Juice.

Three young students gave him a call in order to have a little amusement at the elder's expense. On approaching him, one of them saluted him, " Well, Father Abraham, how are you to-day ? " " You are wrong," said the other, " this is old Father Isaac." " Tuts," said the third, " you are both mistaken ; this is old Father Jacob." David looked at the young men, and in his own way replied, " I am neither old Father Abraham, nor old Father Isaac, nor old Father Jacob ; but I am Saul the son of Kish, seeking his father's asses, and lo ! I've found three o' them."

For many years the Baptist community of Dunfermline was presided over by brothers David Dewar and James Inglis, the latter of whom has just recently gone to his reward. Brother David was a plain, honest, straightforward man, who never hesitated to express his convictions, however unpalatable they might be to others. Being elected a member of the Prison Board, he was called upon to give his vote in the choice of a chaplain from the licentiates of the Established Kirk. The party who had gained the confidence of the Board had proved rather an indifferent preacher in a charge to which he had previously been appointed ; and on David being asked to signify his assent to the choice of the Board, he said, " Weel, I've no objections to the man, for I understand he has preached a kirk toom (empty) already, and if he be as successful in the jail, he'll maybe preach it vawcant as weel."

From Mr Inglis, clerk of the Court of Session, I have the following Scottish rejoinder :—

" I recollect my father relating a conversation between a Perthshire laird and one of his tenants. The laird's eldest son was rather a simpleton. Laird says, ' I am going to send the young laird abroad.' ' What for ? ' asks the tenant ; answered, ' To see the world ' ;

tenant replies, 'But, lord-sake, laird, will no' the world see *him*?'"

An admirably humorous reply is recorded of a Scotch officer, well known and esteemed in his day for mirth and humour. Captain Innes of the Guards (usually called Jock Innes by his contemporaries) was with others getting ready for Flushing or some of those expeditions of the beginning of the great war. His commanding officer (Lord Huntly, my correspondent thinks) remonstrated about the badness of his hat, and recommended a new one. " Na, na! bide a wee," said Jock; " where we're gain' faith there'll soon be mair hats nor *heads*."

I recollect being much amused with a Scottish reference of this kind in the heart of London. Many years ago a Scotch party had dined at Simpson's famous beef-steak house in the Strand. On coming away some of the party could not find their hats, and my uncle was jocularly asking the waiter, whom he knew to be a *Deeside* man, " Whar are our bonnets, Jeems ? " To which he replied, " 'Deed, I mind the day when I had neither hat nor bonnet."

There is an odd and original way of putting a matter sometimes in Scotch people, which is irresistibly comic, although by the persons nothing comic is intended; as for example, when in 1786 Edinburgh was illuminated on account of the recovery of George III. from severe illness. In a house where great preparation was going on for the occasion, by getting the candles fixed in tin sconces, an old nurse of the family, looking on, exclaimed, " Ay, it's a braw time for the cannel-makers when the king is sick, honest man ! "

Scottish farmers of the old school were a shrewd and humorous race, sometimes not indisposed to look with a little jealousy upon their younger brethren, who, on their part, perhaps, showed their contempt for the old-fashioned ways. I take the following example from the columns of the *Peterhead Sentinel*, just as it appeared—June 14, 1861 :—

"AN ANECDOTE FOR DEAN RAMSAY.—The following characteristic and amusing anecdote was communicated to us the other day by a gentleman who happened to be a party to the conversation detailed below. This gentleman was passing along a road not a hundred miles from Peterhead one day this week. Two different farms skirt the separate sides of the turnpike, one of which is rented by a farmer who cultivates his land according to the most advanced system of agriculture, and the other of which is farmed by a gentleman of the old school. Our informant met the latter worthy at the side of the turnpike opposite his neighbour's farm, and seeing a fine crop of wheat upon what appeared to be (and really was) very thin and poor land, asked, ' When was that wheat sown ? ' ' O I dinna ken,' replied the gentleman of the old school, with a sort of half-indifference, half-contempt. ' But isn't it strange that such a fine crop should be reared on such bad land ? ' asked our informant. ' O, na—nae at a'—deevil thank it ; a gravesteen wad gie guid bree [1] gin ye gied it plenty o' butter ! ' "

But perhaps the best anecdote illustrative of the keen shrewdness of the Scottish farmer is related by Mr Boyd [2] in one of his charming series of papers, reprinted from *Fraser's Magazine*. " A friend of mine, a country parson, on first going to his parish, resolved to farm his glebe for himself. A neighbouring farmer kindly offered the parson to plough one of his fields. The farmer said that he would send his man John with a plough and a pair of horses on a certain day

[1] Broth.   [2] Rev. A. K. H. Boyd.

'If ye're goin' about,' said the farmer to the clergyman, ' John will be unco weel pleased if you speak to
him, and say it's a fine day, or the like o' that; but
dinna,' said the farmer, with much solemnity, ' dinna
say onything to him about ploughin' and sawin'; for
John,' he added, ' is a stupid body, but he has been
ploughin' and sawin' a' his life, and he'll see in a
minute that *ye* ken naething aboot ploughin' and sawin'.
And then,' said the sagacious old farmer, with much
earnestness, ' if he comes to think that ye ken naething
aboot ploughin' and sawin', he'll think that ye ken
naething about onything ! ' ''

The following is rather an original commentary, by
a layman, upon clerical incomes :—A relative of mine
going to church with a Forfarshire farmer, one of the
old school, asked him the amount of the minister's
stipend. He said, " Od, it's a gude ane—the maist
part of £300 a year." " Well," said my relative, " many
of these Scotch ministers are but poorly off." " They've
eneuch, sir, they've eneuch; if they'd mair, it would
want a' their time to the spendin' o't."

Scotch gamekeepers had often much dry quiet
humour. I was much amused by the answer of one
of those under the following circumstances :—An
Ayrshire gentleman, who was from the first a very
bad shot, or rather no shot at all, when out on 1st of
September, having failed, time after time, in bringing
down a single bird, had at last pointed out to him by
his attendant bag-carrier a large covey, thick and close
on the stubbles. " Noo, Mr Jeems, let drive at them,
just as they are ! " Mr Jeems did let drive, as advised,
but not a feather remained to testify the shot. All
flew off, safe and sound. " Hech, sir " remarks his
friend, " but ye've made thae yins *shift their quarters*."

The two following anecdotes of rejoinders from

Scottish guidwives, and for which I am indebted, as for many other kind communications, to the Rev. Mr Blair of Dunblane, appear to me as good examples of the peculiar Scottish pithy phraseology which we refer to, as any that I have met with.

An old lady from whom the "Great Unknown" had derived many an ancient tale, was waited upon one day by the author of "Waverley." On his endeavouring to give the authorship the go-by, the old dame protested, "D'ye think, sir, I dinna ken my ain groats in ither folk's kail?"[1]

A conceited packman called at a farmhouse in the west of Scotland, in order to dispose of some of his wares. The goodwife was offended by his southern accent, and his high talk about York, London, and other big places. "An' whaur come ye frae yersell?" was the question of the guidwife. "Ou, I am from the Border." "The Border—oh! I thocht that; for we aye think the *selvidge* is the wakest bit o' the wab!"

The following is a good specimen of ready Scotch humorous reply, by a master to his discontented workman, and in which he turned the tables upon him, in his reference to Scripture. In a town of one of the central counties a Mr J—— carried on, about a century ago, a very extensive business in the linen manufacture. Although *strikes* were then unknown among the labouring classes, the spirit from which these take their rise has no doubt at all times existed. Among Mr J——'s many workmen, one had given him constant annoyance for years, from his discontented and argumentative spirit. Insisting one day on getting something or other which his master thought most unreasonable, and refused to give in to, he at last sub-

[1] I believe the lady was Mrs Murray Keith of Ravelston, with whom Sir Walter had in early life much intercourse.

mitted, with a bad grace, saying, " You're nae better than *Pharaoh*, sir, forcin' puir folk to mak' bricks without straw." " Well, Saunders," quietly rejoined his master, " if I'm nae better than Pharaoh in one respect, I'll be better in another, for *I'll no' hinder ye going to the wilderness whenever you choose*."

Persons who are curious in Scottish stories of wit and humour speak much of the sayings of a certain " Laird of Logan," who was a well-known character in the West of Scotland. This same Laird of Logan was at a meeting of the heritors of Cumnock, where a proposal was made to erect a new churchyard wall. He met the proposition with the dry remark, " I never big dykes till the *tenants* complain." Calling one day for a gill of whisky in a public-house, the laird was asked if he would take any water with the spirit. " Na, na," replied he, " I would rather ye would tak' the water out o't."

The laird sold a horse to an Englishman, saying, " You buy him as you see him; but he's an *honest* beast." The purchaser took him home. In a few days he stumbled and fell, to the damage of his own knees and his rider's head. On this the angry purchaser re-monstrated with the laird, whose reply was, " Well, sir, I told ye he was an honest beast; many a time has he threatened to come down with me, and I kenned he would keep his word some day."

At the time of the threatened invasion, the laird had been taunted at a meeting at Ayr with want of loyal spirit at Cumnock, as at that place no volunteer corps had been raised to meet the coming danger; Cumnock, it should be recollected, being on a high situation, and ten or twelve miles from the coast. " What sort of people are you up at Cumnock? " said an Ayr gentleman; " you have not a single volunteer!" "Never you heed," says Logan, very quietly; "if the French land at Ayr, there will soon be plenty of volunteers up at Cumnock."

A pendant to the story of candid admission on the part of the minister, that the people might be *weary* after his sermon, has been given on the authority of the narrator, a Fife gentleman, ninety years of age when he told it. He had been to church at Elie, and listening to a young and perhaps bombastic preacher, who happened to be officiating for the Rev. Dr Milligan, who was in church. After service, meeting the Doctor in the passage, he introduced the young clergyman, who, on being asked by the old man how he did, elevated his shirt collar, and complained of fatigue, and being very much "*tired*." "Tired, did ye say, my man?" said the old satirist, who was slightly deaf; "Lord, man! if you're *half* as tired as I am, I pity ye!"

I have been much pleased with an offering from Carluke, containing two very pithy anecdotes. Mr Rankin very kindly writes:—"Your 'Reminiscences' are most refreshing. I am very little of a story-collector, but I have recorded some of an old schoolmaster, who was a story-teller. As a sort of payment for the amusement I have derived from your book, I shall give one or two."

He sends the two following :—

"Shortly after Mr Kay had been inducted school-master of Carluke (1790), the bederal called at the school, verbally announcing, proclamation-ways, that Mrs So-and-So's funeral would be on Fuirsday. 'At what hour?' asked the dominie. 'Ou, ony time atween ten and twa.' At two o'clock of the day fixed, Mr Kay —quite a stranger to the customs of the district— arrived at the place, and was astonished to find a crowd

263

of men and lads, standing here and there, some smoking, and all *arglebargling*,[1] as if at the end of a fair. He was instantly, but mysteriously, approached, and touched on the arm by a red-faced bareheaded man, who seemed to be in authority, and was beckoned to follow. On entering the barn, which was seated all round, he found numbers sitting, each with the head bent down, and each with his hat between his knees—all gravity and silence. Anon a voice was heard issuing from the far end, and a long prayer was uttered. They had worked at this—what was called ' *a service* '— during three previous hours, one party succeeding another, and many taking advantage of every service, which consisted of a prayer by way of grace, a glass of *white* wine, a glass of *red* wine, a glass of *rum*, and a prayer by way of thanksgiving. After the long invocation, bread and wine passed round. Silence prevailed. Most partook of both *rounds* of wine, but when the rum came, many nodded refusal, and by and by the nodding seemed to be universal, and the trays passed on so much the more quickly. A sumphish weather-beaten man, with a large flat blue bonnet on his knee, who had nodded unwittingly, and was about to lose the last chance of a glass of rum, raised his head, saying, amid the deep silence, ' Od, I daursay I *wull* tak' anither glass,' and in a sort of vengeful, yet apologetic tone, added, ' The auld jaud yince cheated me wi' a cauve ' (calf).''

At a farmer's funeral in the country, an undertaker was in charge of the ceremonial, and directing how it was to proceed, when he noticed a little man giving orders, and, as he thought, rather encroaching upon the duties and privileges of his own office. He asked him, '' And wha are ye, mi man, that tak' sae muckle

---

[1] Disputing or bandying words backwards and forwards.

on ye?" "Oh, dinna ye ken?" said the man, under a strong sense of his own importance, "I'm the corp's brither."[1]

Curious scenes took place at funerals where there was, in times gone by, an unfortunate tendency to join with such solemnities more attention to festal entertainment than was becoming. A farmer, at the interment of his second wife, exercised a liberal hospitality to his friends at the inn near the church. On looking over the bill, the master defended the charge as moderate. But he reminded him, "Ye forget, man, that it's no' ilka ane that brings a *second* funeral to your house."

"Dr Scott, minister of Carluke (1770), was a fine graceful kindly man, always stepping about in his bag-wig and cane in hand, with a kind and ready word to every one. He was officiating at a bridal in his parish, where there was a goodly company, had partaken of the good cheer, and waited till the young people were fairly warmed in the dance. A dissenting body had sprung up in the parish, which he tried to think was beneath him even to notice, when he could help it, yet never seemed to feel at all keenly when the dissenters were alluded to. One of the chief leaders of this body was at the bridal, and felt it to be his bounden duty to call upon the minister for his reasons for sanctioning by his presence so sinful an enjoyment. 'Weel, minister, what think ye o' this dancin'?' 'Why, John,' said the minister, blithely, 'I think it an excellent exercise for young people, and, I dare say, so do you.' 'Ah, sir, I'm no sure about it; I see nae authority for't in the Scriptures.' 'Umph, indeed, John; you cannot forget David.' 'Ah, sir, Dauvid; gif they were a' to dance as Dauvid did, it would be

---

[1] In Scotland the remains of the deceased person is called the "corp."

a different thing a'thegither.' ' Hoot-o-fie, hoot-o-fie, John; would you have the young folk strip to the sark?' "

Reference has been made to the eccentric Laird of Balnamoon, his wig, and his " speats o' drinking and praying." A story of this laird is recorded, which I do think is well named, by a correspondent who communicates it, as a " quintessential phasis of dry Scotch humour," and the explanation of which would perhaps be thrown away upon any one who *needed* the explanation. The story is this :—The laird riding past a high steep bank, stopped opposite a hole in it, and said, " Hairy, I saw a brock gang in there." " Did ye?" said Hairy; " wull ye haud my horse, sir?" " Certainly," said the laird, and away rushed Hairy for a spade. After digging for half-an-hour, he came back, quite done, to the laird, who had regarded him musingly. " I canna find him, sir," said Hairy. " 'Deed," said the laird, very coolly, " I wad ha wondered if ye had, for it's ten years sin' I saw him gang in there."

Amongst many humorous colloquies between Balnamoon and his servant, the following must have been very racy and very original. The laird, accompanied by Hairy, after a dinner-party, was riding on his way home, through a ford, when he fell off into the water. " Whae's that fau'n?" he inquired. " 'Deed," quoth Hairy, " I witna an it be na your honour."

There is a peculiarity connected with what we have considered Scotch humour. It is more common for Scotsmen to associate their own feelings with *national* events and national history than for Englishmen. Take as illustrations the following, as being perhaps as good as any :—The Rev. Robert Scott, a Scotsman who forgets not Scotland in his southern vicarage, and whom I have named before as having sent me some good reminiscences, tells me that, at Inveraray, some thirty years ago, he could not help overhearing the conversation of some Lowland cattle-dealers in the public room in which he was. The subject of the bravery of our navy being started, one of the inter-locutors expressed his surprise that Nelson should have issued his signal at Trafalgar in the terms, "*England expects*," etc. He was met with the answer (which seemed highly satisfactory to the rest), "Ah, Nelson only said '*expects*' of the English; he said naething of Scotland, for he *kent* the *Scotch* would do theirs."

I am assured the following manifestation of national feeling against the memory of a Scottish character actually took place within a few years :—Williamson (the Duke of Buccleuch's huntsman) was one afternoon riding home from hunting through Haddington; and as he passed the old Abbey, he saw an ancient woman looking through the iron grating in front of the burial-place of the Lauderdale family, holding by the bars, and grinning and dancing with rage. "Eh, gudewife," said Williamson, "what ails ye?" "It's the Duke of Lauderdale," cried she. "Eh, if I could win at him, I wud rax the banes o' him."

To this class belongs the following complacent Scottish remark upon Bannockburn. A splenetic Englishman said to a Scottish countryman, something of a wag, that no man of taste would think of remain-ing any time in such a country as Scotland. To which the canny Sco treplied, "Tastes differ; I'se tak ye to a place no' far frae Stirling, whaur thretty thousand o' your countrymen ha' been for five hunder years, and they've nae thocht o' leavin' yet."

In a similar spirit, an honest Scotch farmer, who had sent some sheep to compete at a great English agricultural cattle-show, and was much disgusted at not getting a prize, consoled himself for the disappointment, by insinuating that the judges could hardly act quite impartially by a Scottish competitor, complacently remarking, " It's aye been the same since Bannockburn."

Then, again, take the story told in Lockhart's Life of Sir Walter Scott, of the blacksmith whom Sir Walter had formerly known as a horse-doctor, and whom he found at a small country town south of the Border, practising medicine with a reckless use of " laudamy and calomy," [1] apologising at the same time for the mischief he might do, by the assurance that it " *would be lang before it made up for Flodden.*" How graphically it describes the interest felt by Scotchmen of his rank in the incidents of their national history. A similar example has been recorded in connection with Bannockburn. Two Englishmen visited the field of that great battle, and a country blacksmith pointed out the positions of the two armies, the stone on which was fixed the Bruce's standard, etc. The gentlemen, pleased with the intelligence of their guide, on leaving pressed his acceptance of a crown-piece. " Na, na," replied the Scotsman, with much pride, " it has cost ye eneuch already." Such an example of self-denial on the part of a Scottish cicerone is, we fear, now rather a " reminiscence."

A north country drover had, however, a more *tangible* opportunity of gratifying his national animosity against the Southron, and of which he availed himself. Returning homewards, after a somewhat unsuccessful journey, and not in very good humour

[1] Laudanum and calomel.

with the Englishers, when passing through Carlisle he saw a notice stuck up, offering a reward of £50 for any one who would do a piece of service to the community, by officiating as executioner of the law on a noted criminal then under sentence of death. Seeing a chance to make up for his bad market, and comforted with the assurance that he was unknown there, he undertook the office, executed the condemned, and got the fee. When moving off with the money, he was twitted at as a " mean beggarly Scot," doing for money what no *Englishman* would. With a grin and quiet glee, he only replied, " I'll hang ye a' at the price."

Some Scotsmen, no doubt, have a very complacent feeling regarding the superiority of their countrymen, and make no hesitation in proclaiming their opinion, I have always admired the quaint expression of such belief in a case which has recently been reported to me. A young Englishman had taken a Scottish shooting-ground, and enjoyed his mountain sport so much as to imbibe a strong partiality for his northern residence and all its accompaniments. At a German watering-place he encountered, next year, an original character, a Scotsman of the old school, very national, and somewhat bigoted in his nationality: he determined to pass himself off to him as a genuine Scottish native; and, accordingly, he talked of Scotland and haggis, and sheep's head, and whisky; he boasted of Bannockburn, and admired Queen Mary; looked upon Scott and Burns as superior to all English writers; and staggered, although he did not convince, the old gentleman. On going away he took leave of his Scottish friend, and said, " Well, sir, next time we meet, I hope you will receive me as a real countryman." " Weel," he said, " I'm jest thinkin', my lad, ye're nae Scotsman; but I'll tell ye what ye are—ye're juist an *impruived* Englishman."

I am afraid we must allow that Scottish people have a *leetle* national vanity, and may be too ready sometimes to press the claim of their country to an extravagantly assumed pre-eminence in the annals of genius and celebrities. An extreme case of such pretension I heard of lately, which is amusing. A Scotsman, in reference to the distinction awarded to Sir Walter Scott, on occasion of his centenary, had roundly asserted, " But *all* who have been eminent men were Scotsmen." An Englishman, offended at such assumption of national pre-eminence, asked indignantly, " What do you say to Shakspeare? " To which the other quietly replied, " Weel, his tawlent wad justifee the inference." This is rich, as an example of an *à priori* argument in favour of a man being a Scotsman.

We find in the conversation of old people frequent mention of a class of beings well-known in country parishes, now either become commonplace, like the rest of the world, or removed altogether, and shut up in poorhouses or madhouses—I mean the individuals frequently called parochial *idiots*; but who were rather of the order of naturals. They were eccentric, or somewhat crazy, useless, idle creatures, who used to wander about from house to house, and sometimes made very shrewd sarcastic remarks upon what was going on in the parish. I heard such a person once described as one who was " wanting in twopence of change for a shilling." They used to take great liberty of speech regarding the conduct and disposition of those with whom they came in contact, and many odd sayings which emanated from them were traditionary in country localities. I have a kindly feeling towards these imperfectly intelligent, but often perfectly cunning beings; partly, I believe, from recollections of early associations in boyish days with some of those Davy Gellatleys. I have therefore preserved several anecdotes with which I have been favoured, where their odd sayings and indications of a degree of mental activity have been recorded. These persons seem to have had a partiality for getting near the pulpit in church, and their presence there was accordingly sometimes annoying to the preacher and the congregation; as at Maybole, when Dr Paul, now of St Cuthbert's, was minister in 1823, John M'Lymont, an individual of this class, had been in the habit of standing so close to the pulpit door as to overlook the Bible and pulpit board. When required, however, by the clergyman to keep at a greater distance, and not *look in upon the minister*, he got intensely angry and violent. He threatened the minister: " Sir, bæby (maybe) I'll come farther"; meaning to intimate that perhaps he would, if much provoked, come into the pulpit altogether. This, indeed, actually took place on another occasion, and the tenure of the ministerial position was justified by an argument of a most amusing nature. The circumstance, I am assured, happened in a parish in the north. The clergyman, on coming into church, found the pulpit occupied by the parish natural. The authorities had been unable to remove him without more violence than was seemly, and therefore waited for the minister to dispossess Tam of the place he had assumed. " Come down, sir, immediately!" was the peremptory and indignant call; and on Tam being unmoved, it was repeated with still greater energy. Tam, however, replied, looking down confidentially from his elevation, " Na, na, minister! juist ye come up wi' me. This is a perverse generation, and faith they need us baith." It is curious to mark the sort of glimmering of sense, and even of discriminating thought, displayed by persons of this class. As an example, take a conversation held by this same John M'Lymont, with Dr Paul, whom he met some time after. He seemed to have recovered his good humour, as he stopped him and said, " Sir, I would like to speer a question at ye on a subject that's troubling me." " Well, Johnnie, what is the question ? " To which he replied, " Sir, is it lawful at ony time to tell a lee ? " The minister desired to know what Johnnie himself thought upon the point. " Weel, sir," said he, " I'll no' say but in every case it's wrang to tell a lee ; but," added he, looking archly and giving a knowing wink, " I think there are *waur lees than ithers*." " How, Johnnie ? " and then he instantly replied, with all the simplicity of a fool, " *To keep down a din, for instance.* I'll no' say but a man does wrang in telling a lee to keep down a din, but I'm sure he does not do half sae muckle wrang as a man who tells a lee to kick up a deevilment o' a din." This opened a question not likely to occur to such a mind. Mr Asher, minister of Inveraven, in Morayshire, narrated to Dr Paul a curious example of want of intelligence combined with a power of cunning to redress a fancied wrong, shown by a poor natural of the parish, who had been seized with a violent inflammatory attack, and was in great danger. The medical attendant saw it necessary to bleed him, but he resisted, and would not submit to it. At last the case became so hopeless that they were obliged to use force, and, holding his hands and feet, the doctor opened a vein and drew blood, upon which the poor creature, struggling violently, bawled out, " O doctor, doctor ! you'll kill me ! you'll kill me ! and depend upon it the first thing I'll do when I get to the other world will be to *report you to the board of Supervision there, and get you dismissed.*" A most extraordinary sensation was once produced on a congregation by Rab Hamilton, a well-remembered crazy creature of the west country, on the occasion of his attendance at the parish kirk of " Auld Ayr, wham ne'er a toun surpasses," the minister of which, in the opinion of Rab's own minister, Mr Peebles, had a tendency to Socinian doctrines. Miss Kirkwood, Bothwell, relates the story from the recollection of her aunt, who was present. Rab had put his head between some iron rails, the first intimation of which to the congregation was a stentorian voice crying out, " Murder! my heed'll hae to be cuttit aff! Holy minister! congregation! Oh, my heed maun be cuttit aff. It's a judgment for leaving my godlie Mr Peebles at the Newton." After he had been extricated and quieted, when asked why he put his head there, he said, " It was juist to look on [1] wi' *anither woman.*"

The following anecdote of this same Rab Hamilton from a kind correspondent at Ayr sanctions the opinion that he must have occasionally said such clever things as made some think him more rogue than fool. Dr Auld often showed him kindness, but being once addressed by him when in a hurry and out of humour, he said, " Get away, Rab; I have nothing for you to-day." " Whaw, whew," cried Rab, in a half-howl, half-whining tone, " I dinna want onything the day, Maister Auld; I wanted to tell you an awsome dream I hae had. I dreamt I was deed." " Weel, what then?" said Dr Auld. " Ou, I was carried far, far, and up, up, up, till I cam' to heeven's yett, where I chappit, and chappit, and chappit, till at last an angel keekit out, and said ' Wha are ye?' ' A'm puir Rab

---

[1] Read from the same book.

Hamilton.' ' Whaur are ye frae ? ' ' Frae the wicked toun o' Ayr.' ' I dinna ken ony sic place,' said the angel. ' Oh, but A'm juist frae there.' Weel, the angel sends for the Apostle Peter, and Peter comes wi' his key and opens the yett, and says to me, ' Honest man, do you come frae the auld toun o' Ayr ? ' ' 'Deed do I,' says I. ' Weel,' says Peter, ' I ken the place, but naebody's cam' frae the toun o'Ayr, no' since the year' " so-and-so—mentioning the year when Dr Auld was inducted into the parish. Dr Auld could not resist giving him his answer, and telling him to go about his business.

The pathetic complaint of one of this class, residing at a farmhouse, has often been narrated, and forms a good illustration of idiot life and feelings. He was living in the greatest comfort, and every want provided. But, like the rest of mankind, he had his own trials, and his own cause for anxiety and annoyance. In this poor fellow's case it was the *great turkey-cock* at the farm, of which he stood so terribly in awe that he was afraid to come within a great distance of his enemy. Some of his friends, coming to visit him, reminded him how comfortable he was, and how grateful he ought to be for the great care taken of him. He admitted the truth of the remark generally, but still, like others, he had his unknown grief which sorely beset his path in life. There was a secret grievance which embittered his lot; and to his friend he thus opened his heart : " Ae, ae, but oh, I'm sair hadden doun wi' the bubbly jock." [1]

I have received two anecdotes illustrative both of the occasional acuteness of mind, and of the sensitiveness of feeling occasionally indicated by persons thus situated. A well-known idiot, Jamie Fraser, belonging

[1] Sorely kept under by the turkey-cock.

to the parish of Lunan, in Forfarshire, quite surprised people sometimes by his replies. The congregation of his parish church had for some time distressed the minister by their habit of sleeping in church. He had often endeavoured to impress them with a sense of the impropriety of such conduct, and one day Jamie was sitting in the front gallery, wide awake, when many were slumbering round him. The clergyman endeavoured to draw the attention of his hearers to his discourse by stating the fact, saying, "You see, even Jamie Fraser, the idiot, does not fall asleep, as so many of you are doing." Jamie, not liking, perhaps, to be thus designated, coolly replied, "An I hadna been an idiot, I micht ha' been sleepin' too." Another of these imbeciles, belonging to Peebles, had been sitting at church for some time listening attentively to a strong representation from the pulpit of the guilt of deceit and falsehood in Christian characters. He was observed to turn red, and grow very uneasy, until at last, as if wincing under the supposed attack upon himself personally, he roared out, "Indeed, minister, there's mair leears in Peebles than me." As examples of this class of persons possessing much of the dry humour of their more sane countrymen, and of their facility to utter sly and ready-witted sayings, I have received the two following from Mr W. Chambers:—Daft Jock Gray, the supposed original of David Gellatley, was one day assailed by the minister of a south-country parish on the subject of his idleness. "John," said the minister, rather pompously, "you are a very idle fellow; you might surely herd a few cows." "Me hird!" replied Jock; "I dinna ken corn frae gerss."

"There was a carrier named Davie Loch who was reputed to be rather light of wits, but at the same time

not without a sense of his worldly interests. His
mother, finding her end approaching, addressed her
son in the presence of a number of the neighbours.
'The house will be Davie's and the furniture too.'
'Eh, hear her,' quoth Davie; 'sensible to the last,
sensible to the last.' 'The lyin' siller——' 'Eh yes;
how clear she is about everything!' 'The lyin' siller
is to be divided between my twa dauchters.' 'Steek
the bed doors, steek the bed doors,'[1] interposed
Davie; 'she's ravin' now'; and the old dying
woman was shut up accordingly."

In the *Memorials of the Montgomeries*, Earls of
Eglinton, vol. i., p. 134, occurs an anecdote illustrative
of the peculiar acuteness and quaint humour which
occasionally mark the sayings of persons considered
as imbeciles. There was a certain "Daft Will Speir,"
who was a privileged haunter of Eglinton Castle and
grounds. He was discovered by the Earl one day
taking a near cut, and crossing a fence in the demesne.
The Earl called out, "Come back, sir, that's not the
road." "Do you ken," said Will, "whaur I'm gaun'?"
"No," replied his lordship. "Weel, hoo the deil do
ye ken whether this be the road or no'?"

This same "Daft Will Speir" was passing the
minister's glebe, where haymaking was in progress.
The minister asked Will if he thought the weather
would keep up, as it looked rather like rain. "Weel,"
said Will, "I canna be very sure, but I'll be passin'
this way the nicht, an' I'll ca' in and tell ye." "Well,
Will," said his master one day to him, seeing that he
had just finished his dinner, "have you had a good
dinner to-day?" (Will had been grumbling some
time before.) "Ou, verra gude," answered Will;

---

[1] Close the doors. The old woman was lying in a "box-bed." See *Life
of Robert Chambers*, p. 12.

"but gin onybody asks if I got a dram after't, what
will I say?" This poor creature had a high sense of
duty. It appears he had been given the charge of the
coal-stores at the Earl of Eglinton's. Having on one
occasion been reprimanded for allowing the supplies
to run out before further supplies were ordered, he
was ever afterwards most careful to fulfil his duty.
In course of time poor Will became "sick unto death,"
and the minister came to see him. Thinking him in
really a good frame of mind, the minister asked him,
in presence of the laird and others, if there were not
one *great* thought which was ever to him the highest
consolation in his hour of trouble. "Ou ay," gasped
the sufferer, "Lord be thankit, a' the bunkers are fu'!"

The following anecdote is told regarding the late
Lord Dundrennan:—A half-silly basket-woman passing down his avenue at Compstone one day, he met
her, and said, "My good woman, there's no road this
way." "Na, sir," she said, "I think ye're wrang there;
I think it's a most beautifu' road."

These poor creatures have invariably a great delight
in attending funerals. In many country places hardly
a funeral ever took place without the attendance of
the parochial idiot. It seemed almost a necessary
association; and such attendance seemed to constitute
the great delight of those creatures. I have myself
witnessed again and again the sort of funeral scene
portrayed by Sir Walter Scott, who no doubt took
his description from what was common in his day:
"The funeral pomp set forth—saulies with their batons
and gumphions of tarnished white crape. Six starved
horses, themselves the very emblems of mortality,
well cloaked and plumed, lugging along the hearse
with its dismal emblazonry, crept in slow pace towards
the place of interment, preceded by Jamie Duff, an

idiot, who, with weepers and cravat made of white paper, *attended on every funeral,* and followed by six mourning coaches filled with the company."—*Guy Mannering.*

The following anecdote, supplied by Mr Blair, is an amusing illustration both of the funeral propensity, and of the working of a defective brain, in a half-witted carle, who used to range the province of Galloway armed with a huge pike-staff, and who one day met a funeral procession a few miles from Wigtown. A long train of carriages, and farmers riding on horseback, suggested the propriety of his bestriding his staff, and following after the funeral. The procession marched at a brisk pace, and on reaching the kirkyard stile, as each rider dismounted, " Daft Jock " descended from his wooden steed, besmeared with mire and perspiration, exclaiming, " Hech, sirs, had it no' been for the fashion o' the thing, I micht as weel hae been on my ain feet."

The withdrawal of these characters from public view, and the loss of importance which they once enjoyed in Scottish society, seem to me inexplicable. Have they ceased to exist, or are they removed from our sight to different scenes? The fool was, in early times, a very important personage in most Scottish households of any distinction. Indeed this had been so common as to be a public nuisance.

It seemed that persons *assumed* the character, for we find a Scottish Act of Parliament, dated 19th January 1449, with this title :—" Act for the way-putting of *Fenyent* Fules," etc. (Thomson's Acts of Parliament of Scotland, vol. i.); and it enacts very stringent measures against such persons. They seem to have formed a link between the helpless idiot and the boisterous madman, sharing the eccentricity of the latter and the stupidity of the former, generally adding, however, a good deal of the sharp-wittedness of the *knave*.. Up to the middle of the eighteenth century this appears to have been still an appendage to some families. I have before me a little publication with the title, " The Life and Death of Jamie Fleeman, the Laird of Udny's Fool. Tenth edition. Aberdeen, 1810." With portrait. Also twenty-sixth edition, of 1829. I should suppose this account of a family fool was a fair representation of a good specimen of the class. He was evidently of defective intellect, but at times showed the odd humour and quick conclusion which so often mark the disordered brain. I can only now give two examples taken from his history :— Having found a horse-shoe on the road, he met Mr Craigie, the minister of St Fergus, and showed it to him, asking, in pretended ignorance, what it was. " Why, Jamie," said Mr Craigie, good humouredly, " anybody that was not a fool would know that it is a horse-shoe." " Ah ! " said Jamie, with affected simplicity, " what it is to be wise—to ken it's no' a meer's shoe ! "

On another occasion, when all the countryside were hastening to the Perth races, Jamie had cut across the fields and reached a bridge near the town, and sat down upon the parapet. He commenced munching away at a large portion of a leg of mutton which he had somehow become possessed of, and of which he was amazingly proud. The laird came riding past, and seeing Jamie sitting on the bridge, accosted him :— " Ay, Fleeman, are ye here already? " " Ou ay," quoth Fleeman, with an air of assumed dignity and archness not easy to describe, while his eye glanced significantly towards the mutton, " Ou ay, ye ken a body when he *has onything*."

Of witty retorts by half-witted creatures of this class, I do not know of one more pointed than what is recorded of such a character who used to hang about the residence of a late Lord Fife. It would appear that some parts of his lordship's estates were barren, and in a very unproductive condition. Under the improved system of agriculture and of draining, great preparations had been made for securing a good crop in a certain field, where Lord Fife, his factor, and others interested in the subject, were collected together. There was much discussion, and some difference of opinion, as to the crop with which the field had best be sown. The idiot retainer, who had been listening unnoticed to all that was said, at last cried out, " Saw't wi' factors, ma lord; they are sure to thrive everywhere."

There was an idiot who lived long in Lauder, and seems to have had a great resemblance to the jester of old times. He was a staunch supporter of the Established Church. One day some one gave him a bad shilling. On Sunday he went to the Seceders' meeting-house, and when the ladle was taken round he put in his bad shilling and took out elevenpence halfpenny. Afterwards he went in high glee to the late Lord Lauderdale, calling out, " I've cheated the Seceders the day, my lord; I've cheated the Seceders."

Jemmy had long harboured a dislike to the steward on the property, which he made manifest in the following manner :—Lord Lauderdale and Sir Anthony Maitland used to take him out shooting; and one day Lord Maitland (he was then), on having to cross the Leader, said, " Now, Jemmy, you shall carry me through the water," which Jemmy duly did. The steward, who was shooting with them, expected the same service, and accordingly said, " Now, Jemmy, you must carry *me* over." "Verra weel," said Jemmy. He took the steward on his back, and when he had carefully carried him half-way across the river he paid off his grudge by dropping him quietly into the water.

A daft individual used to frequent the same district, about whom a variety of opinions were entertained, some people thinking him not so foolish as he sometimes seemed. On one occasion a person, wishing to test whether he knew the value of money, held out a sixpence and a penny, and offered him his choice. "I'll tak' the wee ane," he said, giving as his modest reason, "I'se no' be greedy." At another time, a miller laughing at him for his witlessness, he said, "Some things I ken, and some I dinna ken." On being asked what he knew, he said, "I ken a miller has aye a gey fat sou." "An' what d'ye no' ken?" said the miller. "Ou," he returned, "I dinna ken wha's expense she's fed at."

A very amusing collision of one of those penurious lairds, already referred to, a certain Mr Gordon of Rothie, with a half-daft beggar wanderer of the name of Jock Muilton, has been recorded. The laird was very shabby, as usual, and, meeting Jock, began to banter him on the subject of his dress:—"Ye're very grand, Jock. Thae's fine claes ye hae gotten; whaur did ye get that coat?" Jock told him who had given him his coat, and then, looking slily at the laird, he inquired, as with great simplicity, "And whaur did ye get *yours*, laird?"

For another admirable story of a rencontre between a penurious laird and the parish natural I am indebted to the *Scotsman*, June 16, 1871. Once on a time there was a Highland laird renowned for his caution in money matters, and his precise keeping of books. His charities were there; but that department of his

bookkeeping was not believed to be heavy. On examination, a sum of half-a-crown was unexpectedly
discovered in it; but this was accounted for in a
manner creditable to his intentions, if not to his success in executing them. It had been given in mistake
instead of a coin of a different denomination, to " the
natural " of the parish for holding his shelty while he
transacted business at the bank. A gleam in the boy's
eye drew his attention to a gleam of white as the metal
dropped into his pocket. In vain the laird assured him
it was not a good bawbee—if he would give it up he
would get another—it was " guid eneuch " for the
like of him. And when the laird in his extremity swore
a great oath that unless it was given up he would
never give another halfpenny, the answer was—" Ech,
laird, it wad be lang or ye gied me saxty."

Another example of shrewd and ready humour in
one of that class is the following :—In this case the
idiot was musical, and earned a few stray pence by
playing Scottish airs on a flute. He resided at Stirling,
and used to hang about the doors of the inn to watch
the arrival and departure of travellers. A lady, who
used to give him something occasionally, was just
starting, and said to Jamie that she had only a fourpenny
piece, and that he must be content with that, for she
could not stay to get more. Jamie was not satisfied,
and as the lady drove out, he expressed his feelings by
playing with all his might, " O wearie o' the *toom
pouch*." [1]

The spirit in Jamie Fraser before mentioned, and
which had kept him awake, shows itself in idiots occasionally by making them restless and troublesome.
One of this character had annoyed the clergyman
where he attended church by fidgeting, and by un-

[1] Empty pocket.

couth sounds which he uttered during divine service. Accordingly, one day before church began, he was cautioned against moving, or "making a whisht," under the penalty of being turned out. The poor creature sat quite still and silent, till, in a very important part of the sermon, he felt an inclination to cough. So he shouted out, "Minister, may a puir body like me noo gie a hoast?"[1]

I have two anecdotes of two peers, who might be said to come under the description of half-witted. In their case the same sort of dry Scotch humour came out under the cloak of mental disease. The first is of a Scottish nobleman of the last century who had been a soldier the greater part of his life, but was obliged to come home on account of aberration of mind, superinduced by hereditary propensity. Desirous of putting him under due restraint, and at the same time of engaging his mind in his favourite pursuit, his friends secured a Sergeant Briggs to be his companion, and, in fact, keeper. To render the sergeant acceptable as a companion they introduced him to the old earl as *Colonel* Briggs. Being asked how he liked "the colonel," the earl showed how acute he still was by his answer, "Oh, very well; he is a sensible man, and a good soldier, but he *smells damnably of the halbert.*"

The second anecdote relates also to a Scottish nobleman labouring under aberration of mind, and is, I believe, a traditionary one. In Scotland, some hundred years ago, madhouses did not exist, or were on a very limited scale; and there was often great difficulty in procuring suitable accommodation for patients who required special treatment and seclusion from the world. The gentleman in question had been

[1] A cough.

consigned to the Canongate prison, and his position there was far from comfortable. An old friend called to see him, and asked how it had happened that he was placed in so unpleasant a situation. His reply was, "Sir, it was more the kind interest and patronage of my friends than my own merits that have placed me here." "But have you not remonstrated or complained?" asked his visitor. "I told them" said his lordship, "that they were a pack of infernal villains." "Did you?" said his friend; "that was bold language; and what did they say to that?" "Oh," said the peer, "I took care not to tell them till they were fairly out of the place, and weel up the Canongate."

In Peebles there was a crazy being of this kind called "Daft Yedie." On one occasion he saw a gentleman, a stranger in the town, who had a club foot. Yedie contemplated this phenomenon with some interest, and, addressing the gentleman, said compassionately, "It's a great pity—it spoils the boot." There is a story of one of those half-witted creatures of a different character from the humorous ones already recorded; I think it is exceedingly affecting. The story is traditionary in a country district, and I am not aware of its being ever printed.

A poor boy, of this class, who had evidently manifested a tendency towards religious and devotional feelings, asked permission from the clergyman to attend the Lord's Table and partake of the holy communion with the other members of the congregation (whether Episcopalian or Presbyterian I do not know). The clergyman demurred for some time, under the impression of his mind being incapable of a right and due understanding of the sacred ordinance. But observing the extreme earnestness of the poor boy, he at last gave consent, and he was allowed to come. He was much affected, and all the way home was heard to exclaim, "Oh! I hae seen the pretty man." This referred to his seeing the Lord Jesus whom he had approached in the sacrament. He kept repeating the words, and went with them on his lips to rest for the night. Not appearing at the usual hour for breakfast, when they went to his bedside they found him dead! The excitement had been too much—mind and body had given away—and the half-idiot of earth awoke to the glories and the bliss of his Redeemer's presence.

Analogous with the language of the *defective* intellect is the language of the imperfectly formed intellect, and I have often thought there was something very touching and very fresh in the expression of feelings and notions by children. I have given examples before, but the following is, to my taste, a charming specimen :—A little boy had lived for some time with a very penurious uncle, who took good care that the child's health should not be injured by over-feeding. The uncle was one day walking out, the child at his side, when a friend accosted him, accompanied by a greyhound. While the elders were talking, the little fellow, never having seen a dog so slim and slight of form, clasped the creature round the neck with the impassioned cry, "Oh, doggie, doggie, and div ye live wi' your uncle tae, that ye are so thin?"

In connection with funerals, I am indebted to the kindness of Lord Kinloch for a characteristic anecdote of cautious Scottish character in the west country. It was the old fashion, still practised in some districts, to carry the coffin to the grave on long poles, or "spokes," as they were commonly termed. There were usually two bearers abreast on each side. On a certain occasion one of the two said to his companion, "I'm awfu' tired wi' carryin'." "Do you *carry*?"

was the interrogatory in reply. " Yes; what do you do ? " " Oh," said the other, " I aye *lean*." His friend's fatigue was at once accounted for.

I am strongly tempted to give an account of a parish functionary in the words of a kind correspondent from Kilmarnock, although communicated in the following very flattering terms :—" In common with every Scottish man worthy of the name, I have been delighted with your book, and have the ambition to add a pebble to the cairn, and accordingly send you a *bellman story* ; it has, at least, the merit of being unprinted and unedited."

The incumbent of Craigie parish, in this district of Ayrshire, had asked a Mr Wood, tutor in the Cairnhill family, to officiate for him on a particular Sunday. Mr Wood, however, between the time of being asked and the appointed day, got intimation of the dangerous illness of his father; in the hurry of setting out to see him, he forgot to arrange for the pulpit being filled. The bellman of Craigie parish, by name Matthew Dinning, and at this time about eighty years of age, was a very little " crined "[1] old man, and always wore a broad Scottish blue bonnet, with a red " bob " on the top. The parish is a small rural one, so that Matthew knew every inhabitant in it, and had seen most of them grow up. On this particular day, after the congregation had waited for some time, Matthew was seen to walk very slowly up the middle of the church, with the large Bible and psalm-book under his arm, to mount the pulpit stair; and after taking his bonnet off, and smoothing down his forehead with his " loof," thus addressed the audience :—

" My freens, there was ane Wuds tae hae preached here the day, but he has nayther comed himsell, nor

[1] Shrivelled.

had the ceevility tae sen' us the scart o' a pen. Ye'll bide here for ten meenonts, and gin naebody comes forrit in that time, ye can gang awa' hame. Some say his feyther's dead; as for that I kenna."

The following is another illustration of the character of the old Scottish betheral. One of those worthies, who was parochial grave-digger, had been missing for two days or so, and the minister had in vain sent to discover him at most likely places. He bethought, at last, to make inquiry at a "public" at some distance from the village, and on entering the door he met his man in the trance, quite fou', staggering out, supporting himself with a hand on each wa'. To the minister's sharp rebuke and rising wrath for his indecent and shameful behaviour, John, a wag in his way, and emboldened by liquor, made answer, "'Deed, sir, sin' I ca'd at the manse, I hae buried an auld wife, and I've just drucken her, hough an' horn." Such was his candid admission of the manner in which he had disposed of the church fees paid for the interment.

An encounter of wits between a laird and an elder:—A certain laird in Fife, well-known for his parsimonious habits, and who, although his substance largely increased, did not increase his liberality in his weekly contribution to the church collection, which never exceeded the sum of one penny, one day by mistake dropped into the plate at the door half-a-crown; but discovering his error before he was seated in his pew, he hurried back, and was about to replace the coin by his customary penny, when the elder in attendance cried out, "Stop, laird; ye may put *in* what ye like, but ye maun tak naething *oot*!" The laird, finding his explanations went for nothing, at last said, "Aweel, I suppose I'll get credit for it in heaven." "Na, na, laird," said the elder, sarcastically; "ye'll only get credit for the *penny*."

The following is not a bad specimen of sly *piper* wit :—

The Rev. Mr Johnstone of Monquhitter, a very grandiloquent pulpit orator in his day, accosting a travelling piper, well known in the district, with the question, "Well, John, how does the wind pay?" received from John, with a low bow, the answer, "Your Reverence has the advantage of me."

Apropos to stories connected with ministers and pipers, there cannot be a better specimen than the famous one preserved by Sir Walter Scott, in his notes to *Waverley*, which I am tempted to reproduce, as possibly some of my readers may have forgotten it. The gudewife of the inn at Greenlaw had received four clerical guests into her house, a father and three sons. The father took an early opportunity of calling the attention of the landlady to the subject of his visit, and, introducing himself, commenced in rather a pompous manner: "Now, confess, Luckie Buchan, you never remember having such a party in your house before. Here am I, a placed minister, with my three sons, who are themselves *all* placed ministers." The landlady, accustomed to a good deal of deference and attention from the county families, not quite liking the high tone assumed by the minister on the occasion, and being well aware that all the four were reckoned very poor and uninteresting preachers, answered rather drily, " 'Deed, minister, I canna just say that I ever had sic a party before in the hoose, except it were in the '45, when I had a piper and his three sons—*a'* pipers. But," she added quietly, as if aside, " deil a spring could they play amang them."

I have received from Rev. William Blair, A.M.,

U.P. minister at Dunblane, many kind communications. I have made a selection, which I now group together, and they have this character in common, that they are all anecdotes of ministers :—

Rev. Walter Dunlop of Dumfries was well known for pithy and facetious replies : he was kindly known under the appellation of our " Watty Dunlop." On one occasion two irreverent young fellows determined, as they said, to " taigle " [1] the minister. Coming up to him in the High Street of Dumfries, they accosted him with much solemnity —" Maister Dunlop, dae ye hear the news ? " " What news ? " " Oh, the deil's deed." " Is he ? " said Mr Dunlop, " then I maun pray for twa faitherless bairns." On another occasion Mr Dunlop met, with characteristic humour, an attempt to play off a trick against him. It was known that he was to dine with a minister whose house was close to the church, so that his return back must be through the churchyard. Accordingly some idle and mischievous youths waited for him in the dark night, and one of them came up to him, dressed as a ghost, in hopes of putting him in a fright. Watty's cool accost speedily upset the plan : " Weel, Maister Ghaist, is this a general rising, or are ye juist takin' a daunder frae yer grave by yersell ? " I have received from a correspondent another specimen of Watty's acute rejoinders. Some years ago the celebrated Edward Irving had been lecturing at Dumfries, and a man who passed as a wag in that locality had been to hear him. He met Watty Dunlop the following day, who said, " Weel, Willie, man, an' what do ye think of Mr Irving ? " " Oh," said Willie, contemptuously, " the man's crack't." Dunlop patted him on the shoulder, with a quiet remark, " Willie, ye'll aften see a light peeping through a crack ! "

He was accompanying a funeral one day, when he met a man driving a flock of geese. The wayward disposition of the bipeds at the moment was too much for the driver's temper, and he indignantly cried out, " Deevil choke

[1] Confound.

them!" Mr Dunlop walked a little farther on, and passed a farmstead, where a servant was driving out a number of swine, and banning them with "Deevil tak' them!" Upon which, Mr Dunlop stepped up to him, and said, "Ay, ay, my man: your gentleman 'll be wi' ye i' the noo; he's juist back the road there a bit, choking some geese till a man."

Shortly after the Disruption, Dr Cook of St Andrews was introduced to Mr Dunlop, upon which occasion Mr Dunlop said, "Weel, sir, ye've been lang Cook, Cooking them, but ye've dished them at last."

Mr Clark of Dalreoch, whose head was vastly dispro-portioned to his body, met Mr Dunlop one day. "Weel, Mr Clark, that's a great head o' yours." "Indeed it is, Mr Dunlop: I could contain yours inside of my own." "Juist sae," quietly replied Mr Dunlop: "I was e'en thinkin' it was geyan *toom*." [1]

Mr Dunlop happened one day to be present in a church court of a neighbouring presbytery. A Rev. Doctor was asked to pray, and declined. On the meeting adjourning, Mr Dunlop stepped up to the Doctor, and asked how he did. The Doctor, never having been introduced, did not reply. Mr Dunlop withdrew, and said to his friend, "Eh! but isna he a queer man, that Doctor, he'll neither speak to God nor man."

The Rev. John Brown of Whitburn was riding out one day on an old pony, when he was accosted by a rude youth: "I say, Mr Broon, what gars your horse's tail wag that way?" "Oo, juist what gars your tongue wag: it's fashed wi' a *wakeness*."

About sixty years ago there were two ministers in Sanquhar of the name of Thomson, one of whom was father of the late Dr Andrew Thomson of Edinburgh, the other was father of Dr Thomson of Balfron. The domestic in the family of the latter was rather obtrusive with her secret devotions, sometimes kneeling on the stairs at night, and talking loud enough to be heard. On a communion season she was praying devoutly and exclusively for her

[1] Empty.

minister; "Remember Mr Tamson, no' him at the Green, but oor ain Mr Tamson."

Rev. Mr Leslie of Morayshire combined the duties of justice of peace with those of parochial clergyman. One day he was taken into confidence by a culprit who had been caught in the act of smuggling, and was threatened with a heavy fine. The culprit was a staunch Seceder, and owned a small farm. Mr Leslie, with an old-fashioned zeal for the Established Church, said to him, "The king will come in the cadger's road some day. Ye wadna come to the parish kirk, though it were to save your life, wad ye? Come noo, an' I'se mak' ye a' richt!" Next Sabbath the seceding smuggler appeared in the parish kirk, and as the paupers were receiving parochial allowance, Mr Leslie slipped a shilling into the smuggler's hand. When the J.P. Court was held, Mr Leslie was present, when a fine was proposed to be exacted from the smuggler. "Fine!" said Mr Leslie; "he's mair need o' something to get duds to his back. He's ane o' my *poor roll;* I gie'd him a shilling just last Sabbath."

A worthy old Seceder used to ride from Gargunnock to Buchlyvie every Sabbath to attend the Burgher kirk. One day as he rode past the parish kirk of Kippen, the elder at the plate accosted him, "I'm sure, John, it's no' like the thing to see you ridin' in sic a doonpour o' rain sae far by to thae Seceders. Ye ken the mercifu' man is mercifu' to his beast. Could ye no' step in by?" "Weel," said John, "I wadna care sae muckle about stablin' my beast inside, but it's anither thing mysel' gain' in."

The Rev. Dr George Lawson of Selkirk acted for many years as theological tutor to the Secession Church. One day, on entering Divinity Hall, he overheard a student remark that the professor's wig was uncombed. That same student, on that very day, had occasion to preach a sermon before the Doctor, for which he received a bit of severe criticism, the sting of which was in its tail: "You said my wig wasna kaimed this mornin', my lad, but I think I've redd your head to you."

The Rev. John Heugh of Stirling was one day admonishing one of his people of the sin of intemperance; "Man, John, you should never drink except when you're dry." "Weel, sir," quoth John, "that's what I'm aye doin', for I am never slocken'd."

The Rev. Mr M—— of Bathgate came up to a street-paviour one day, and addressed him, "Eh, John, what's this you're at?" "Oh! I'm mending the ways o' Bathgate!" "Ah, John, I've long been trying to mend the ways o' Bathgate, an' they're no' weel yet." "Weel, Mr M., if you had tried my plan, and come doon to your *knees*, ye wad maybe hae come mair speed!"

There once lived in Cupar a merchant whose store contained supplies of every character and description, so that he was commonly known by the sobriquet of Robbie A'Thing. One day a minister, who was well known for a servile use of MS. in the pulpit, called at the store, asking for a rope and pin to tether a young calf in the glebe. Robbie at once informed him that he could not furnish such articles to him. But the minister, being somewhat importunate, said, "Oh! I thought you were named Robbie A'Thing from the fact of your keeping all kinds of goods." "Weel a weel," said Robbie, "I keep a'thing in my shop but calf's tether-pins and paper sermons for ministers to read."

It was a somewhat whimsical advice, supported by whimsical argument, which used to be given by an old Scottish minister to young preachers, when they visited from home, to "sup well at the kail, for if they were good they were worth the supping, and if not they might be sure there was not much worth coming *after* them."

A good many families in and around Dunblane rejoice in the patronymic of Dochart. This name, which sounds somewhat Irish, is derived from Loch Dochart, in Perthshire. The M'Gregors having been proscribed, were subjected to severe penalties, and a group of the clan having been hunted by their superiors, swam the stream which issues from Loch Dochart, and in gratitude to the river they afterwards assumed the family name of Dochart. A young lad of this name, on being sent to Glasgow College, presented a letter from his minister to Rev. Dr Heugh of Glasgow. He gave his name as Dochart, and the name in the letter was M'Gregor. "Oh," said the Doctor, "I fear there is some mistake about your identity, the names don't agree." "Weel, sir, that's the way they spell the name in our country."

The relative whom I have mentioned as supplying so many Scottish anecdotes had many stories of a parochial functionary whose eccentricities have, in a great measure, given way before the assimilating spirit of the times. I mean the old SCOTTISH BEADLE, or betheral, as he used to be called. Some classes of men are found to have that nameless but distinguishing characteristic of figure and aspect which marks out particular occupations and professions of mankind. This was so much the case in the betheral class, that an old lady, observing a well-known judge and advocate walking together in the street, remarked to a friend as they passed by, "Dear me, Lucy, wha are thae twa *beddle-looking* bodies?" They were often great originals, and, I suspect, must have been in past times somewhat given to convivial habits, from a remark I recollect of the late Baron Clerk Rattray, viz., that in his younger days he had hardly ever known a perfectly sober betheral. However, this may have been, they were, as a class, remarkable for quaint humour, and for being shrewd observers of what was going on. I have heard of an occasion where the betheral made his wit furnish an apology for his want of sobriety. He had been sent round the parish by the minister to deliver notices at all the houses, of the catechising which was to precede the preparation for receiving the communion. On his return it was quite

evident that he had partaken too largely of refreshment since he had been on his expedition. The minister
reproached him for this improper conduct. The
betheral pleaded the pressing *hospitality* of the parishioners. The clergyman did not admit the plea, and
added, " Now, John, I go through the parish, and you
don't see me return fou', as you have done." " Ay,
minister," rejoined the betheral, with much complacency, " but then aiblins ye're no' sae popular i'
the parish as me."

My relative used to tell of one of these officials receiving, with much ceremony, a brother betheral, from
a neighbouring parish, who had come with the minister
thereof for the purpose of preaching on some special
occasion. After service, the betheral of the stranger
clergyman felt proud of the performance of the appointed duty, and said in a triumphant tone to his
friend, " I think oor minister did weel ; ay, he gars
the stour flee oot o' the cushion." To which the other
rejoined, with a calm feeling of superiority, " Stour
oot o' the cushion ! hout, our minister, sin' he cam' wi'
us, has dung the guts oot o' twa Bibles." Another
description I have heard of an energetic preacher more
forcible than delicate—" Eh, oor minister had a great
power o' watter, for he grat, and spat, and swat like
mischeef." An obliging anonymous correspondent
has sent me a story of a functionary of this class whose
pride was centred not so much in the performance of
the minister as of the precentor. He states that he
remembers an old .beadle of the church which was
called " Haddo's Hole," and sometimes the " Little
Kirk," in Edinburgh, whose son occasionally officiated
as precentor. He was not very well qualified for the
duty, but the father had a high opinion of his son's
vocal powers. In those days there was always service

in the church on the Tuesday evenings; and when the father was asked on such occasions, "Who's to preach to-night?" his self-complacent reply used to be, "I divna ken wha's till preach, but my son's for till precent." The following is a more correct version of a betheral story than one which occupied this page in the last edition. The beadle had been asked to recommend a person for the same office, and his answer was, "If ye had wanted twa or three bits o' elder bodies, I cud hae gotten them for ye as easily as penny baps oot of Mr Rowan's shop," pointing to a baker's shop opposite to where the colloquy took place; "or even if ye had wanted a minister, I might hae helpit ye to get ane; but as for a gude *beadle*, that's about the maist difficult thing I ken o' just now."

Perhaps the following may seem to illustrate the self-importance of the betheral tribe. The Rev. Dr Hugh Blair was one Sunday absent from his pulpit and next morning meeting his beadle in the street he inquired how matters went in the High Church on Sabbath. "'Deed, I dare say no' very weel," was the answer; "I wasna there ony mair than yoursell."

Mr Turnbull of Dundee kindly sends me an excellent anecdote of the "Betheral" type, which illustrates the *esprit de corps* of the betheralian mind. The late Dr Robertson of Glasgow had, while in the parish of Mains, a quaint old church attendant of the name of Walter Nicoll, commonly called "Watty Nuckle," whom he invited to come and visit him after he had been removed to Glasgow. Watty accordingly ventured on the (to him) terrible journey, and was received by the Doctor with great kindness. The Doctor, amongst other sights, took him to see the Cathedral church, and showed him all through it, and after they were coming away the Doctor asked Watty what he thought of it, and if it was not better than the Mains church. Watty shook his head, and said, " Aweel, sir, you see she's bigger; but she has nae laft, and she's sair fashed wi' thae pillars."

On the same subject of beadle peculiarities, I have received from Mrs Mearns of Kineff Manse an exquisitely characteristic illustration of beadle *professional* habits being made to bear upon the tender passion :— A certain beadle had fancied the manse housemaid, but at a loss for an opportunity to declare himself, one day—a Sunday—when his duties were ended, he looked sheepish, and said, " Mary, wad *ye* tak a turn, Mary ? " He led her to the churchyard, and pointing with his finger, got out, " My fowk lie there, Mary; wad ye like to lie there ? " The *grave* hint was taken, and she became his wife, but does not yet lie *there*.

Here is another good example of betheral refinement or philosophy. He was carefully dressing up a grave, and adjusting the turf upon it. The clergyman, passing through the churchyard, observed, " That's beautiful sod, Jeems." " Indeed is't, minister, and I grudge it upon the grave o' sic a scamp."

This class of functionaries were very free in their remarks upon the preaching of strangers, who used occasionally to occupy the pulpit of their church— the city betherals speaking sometimes in a most condescending manner of clergy from the provincial parishes. As, for example, a betheral of one of the large churches in Glasgow, criticising the sermon of a minister from the country who had been preaching in the city church, characterised it as " gude coorse country wark." A betheral of one of the churches of St Giles, Edinburgh, used to call on the family of Mr Robert Stevenson, engineer, who was one of the elders. On one occasion they asked him what had been the text on such a night, when none of the family had been present.   The man of office, confused at the question, and unwilling to show anything like ignorance, poured forth, " Weel, ye see, the text last day was just entirely, sirs—yes—the text, sirs—what was it again?—ou ay, just entirely, ye see it was, ' What profiteth a man if he lose the world, and gain his own soul?' "   Most of such stories are usually of an old standing.   A more recent one has been told me of a betheral of a royal burgh much decayed from former importance, and governed by a feeble municipality of old men, who continued in office, and in fact constituted rather the shadow than the substance of a corporation.   A clergyman from a distance having come to officiate in the parish church, the betheral, knowing the terms on which it was usual for the minister officiating to pray for the efficiency of the local magistracy, quietly cautioned the clergyman before service that, in regard to the town-council there, it would be quite out of place for him to pray that they should be a " terror to evil-doers," because, as he said, " the puir auld bodies could be nae terror to onybody."   A minister of Easter Anstruther, during the last century, used to say of the magistrates of Wester Anstruther, that " instead of being a terror to evil-doers, evil-doers were a terror to them."

The " minister's man " was a functionary well known in many parishes, and who often evinced much Scottish humour and original character.   These men were (like the betheral) great critics of sermons, and often severe upon strangers, sometimes with a sly hit at their own minister.   One of these, David, a well-known character, complimenting a young minister who had preached, told him, " Your introduction, sir, is aye grand; its worth a' the rest o' the sermon —could ye no' mak' it a' introduction?"

David's criticisms of his master's sermons were sometimes sharp enough and shrewd. On one occasion, driving the minister home from a neighbouring church where he had been preaching, and who, as he thought, had acquitted himself pretty well, inquired of David what *he* thought of it. The subject of discourse had been the escape of the Israelites from Egypt. So David opened his criticism: "Thocht o't, sir? 'deed I thocht nocht o't ava. It was a vara imperfect discourse in ma opinion; ye did weel eneuch till ye took them through, but where did ye leave them? just daunerin' o' the sea-shore without a place to gang till. Had it no' been for Pharaoh they had been better on the other side, where they were comfortably encampit, than daunerin' where ye left them. It's painful to hear a sermon stoppit afore it's richt ended, just as it is to hear ane streekit out lang after it's dune. That's ma opinion o' the sermon ye gied us to-day." "Very freely given, David, very freely given; drive on a little faster, for I think ye're daunerin' noo yersell."

To another who had gone through a long course of parish official life a gentleman one day remarked: "John, ye hae been sae lang about the minister's hand that I dare say ye could preach a sermon yersell now." To which John modestly replied, "O na, sir, I couldna preach a sermon, but maybe I could draw an inference." "Well, John," said the gentleman, humouring the quiet vanity of the beadle, "what inference could ye draw frae this text, ' A wild ass snuffeth up the wind at her pleasure?'" (Jer. ii., 24). "Weel, sir, I wad draw this inference, he would snuff a lang time afore he would fatten upon't." I had an anecdote from a friend, of a reply from a betheral to the minister *in* church, which was quaint and amusing from the shrewd self-importance it indicated in his own acuteness. The clergyman had been annoyed during the course of his sermon by the restlessness and occasional whining of a dog, which at last began to bark outright. He looked out for the beadle, and directed him very peremptorily, "John, carry that dog out." John looked up to the pulpit and, with a very knowing expression, said, "Na, na, sir; I'se just mak' him gae out on his ain four legs." I have another story of canine misbehaviour in church. A dog was present during the service, and in the sermon the worthy minister was in the habit of speaking very loud, and, in fact, when he got warmed with his subject, of shouting almost at the top of his voice. The dog, who, in the early part, had been very quiet, became quite excited, as is not uncommon with some dogs when hearing a noise, and from whinging and whining, as the speaker's voice rose loud and strong, at last began to bark and howl. The minister, naturally much annoyed at the interruption, called upon the betheral to put out the dog, who at once expressed his readiness to obey the order, but could not resist the temptation to look up to the pulpit, and to say very significantly, "Ay, ay, sir; but indeed it was yersell began it." There is a dog story connected with Reminiscences of Glasgow (see *Chambers's Journal*, March 1855), which is full of meaning. The bowls of rum-punch which so remarkably characterised the Glasgow dinners of last century and the early part of the present, it is to be feared made some of the congregation given to somnolency on the Sundays following. The members of the town-council often adopted Saturday for such meetings; accordingly, the Rev. Mr Thom, an excellent clergyman,[1] took occasion to mark this propensity with some acerbity. A dog had been very troublesome, and disturbed the congregation for some time, when the minister at last gave orders to the beadle, "Take out that dog; he'd wauken a Glasgow magistrate."

The parochial grave-diggers had sometimes a very familiar professional style of dealing with the solemn subjects connected with their office. Thus I have heard of a grave-digger pointing out a large human bone to a lady who was looking at his work, of digging a grave, and asking her: 'D'ye ken wha's bane that is, mem?—that's Jenny Fraser's hench-bane"; adding with a serious aspect, "a weel-baned family thae Frasers."

It would be impossible in these Reminiscences to omit the well-known and often repeated anecdote connected with an eminent divine of our own country, whose works take a high place in our theological literature. The story to which I allude was rendered popular throughout the kingdom some years ago, by the inimitable mode in which it was told, or rather acted, by the late Charles Matthews. But Matthews was wrong in the person of whom he related the humorous address. I have assurance of the parties from a friend, whose father, a distinguished clergyman in the Scottish Church at the time, had accurate knowledge of the whole circumstances. The late celebrated Dr Macknight, a learned and profound scholar and commentator, was nevertheless, as a preacher, to a great degree heavy, unrelieved by fancy or imagination; an able writer, but a dull speaker. His colleague,

---

[1] It was of this minister, Mr Thom of Govan, that Sir Walter Scott remarked "that he had demolished all his own chances of a Glasgow benefice, by preaching before the town-council from a text in Hosea, 'Ephraim's drink is sour.'"

Dr Henry, well-known as the author of a History of England, was, on the other hand, a man of great humour, and could not resist a joke when the temptation came upon him. On one occasion when coming to church, Dr Macknight had been caught in a shower of rain, and entered the vestry soaked with wet. Every means were used to relieve him from his discomfort; but as the time drew on for divine service he became much distressed, and ejaculated over and over, " Oh, I wush that I was dry. Do you think I'm dry ? Do you think I'm dry eneuch noo ? " His jocose colleague could resist no longer, but, patting him on the shoulder, comforted him with the sly assurance, " Bide a wee, Doctor, and ye'se be *dry eneuch* when ye get into the pu'pit."

Another quaint remark of the facetious doctor to his more formal colleague has been preserved by friends of the family. Dr Henry, who with all his pleasantry and abilities, had himself as little popularity in the pulpit as his coadjutor, had been remarking to Dr Macknight what a blessing it was that they were two colleagues in one charge, and continued dwelling on the subject so long, that Dr Macknight, not quite pleased at the frequent reiteration of the remark, said that it certainly was a great pleasure to himself, but he did not see what great benefit it might be to the world. " Ah," said Dr Henry, " an it hadna been for that, there wad hae been *twa* toom [1] kirks this day." Lord Cockburn tells a characteristic anecdote of Dr Henry's behaviour the last day of his life. I am indebted to a gentleman, himself also a distinguished member of the Scottish Church, for an authentic anecdote of this learned divine, and which occurred whilst Dr Macknight was the minister of Maybole.

[1] Empty.

One of his parishioners, a well-known humorous blacksmith of the parish, who, no doubt, thought that the Doctor's learned books were rather a waste of time and labour for a country pastor, was asked if his minister was at home. The Doctor was then busy bringing out his laborious and valuable work, his *Harmony of the Four Gospels*. " Na, he's gane to Edinburgh on a verra useless job." On being asked what this useless work might be which engaged his pastor's time and attention, he answered, " He's gane to mak' four men agree wha ne'er cast oot." The good-humoured and candid answer of a learned and rather long-winded preacher of the old school always appeared to me quite charming. The good man was far from being a popular preacher, and yet he could not reduce his discourses below the hour and a half. On being asked, as a gentle hint of their possibly needless length, if he did not feel *tired* after preaching so long, he replied, " Na, na, I'm no' tired " ; adding, however, with much naïveté, " But, Lord, how tired the fowk whiles are."

The late good, kind-hearted Dr David Dickson was fond of telling a story of a Scottish termagant of the days before kirk-session discipline had passed away. A couple were brought before the court, and Janet, the wife, was charged with violent and undutiful conduct, and with wounding her husband by throwing a three-legged stool at his head. The minister rebuked her conduct, and pointed out its grievous character, by explaining that just as Christ was head of his Church, so the husband was head of the wife; and therefore in assaulting *him*, she had in fact injured her own body. " Weel," she replied, " it's come to a fine pass gin a wife canna kame her ain head " ; " Ay, but, Janet," rejoined the minister, " a three-legged stool is a thief-like bane-kame to scart yer ain head wi'!"

The following is a dry Scottish case, of a minister's wife quietly " kaming her husband's head." Mr Mair, a Scotch minister, was rather short-tempered, and had a wife named Rebecca, whom for brevity's sake he addressed as " Becky." He kept a diary, and among other entries, this one was very frequent—" Becky and I had a rippet, for which I desire to be humble." A gentleman who had been on a visit to the minister went to Edinburgh, and told the story to a minister and his wife there; when the lady replied " Weel, he must have been an excellent man, Mr Mair. My husband and I sometimes too have ' rippets,' but catch him if he's ever humble."

Our object in bringing up and recording anecdotes of this kind is to elucidate the sort of humour we refer to, and to show it as a humour of *past* times. A modern clergyman could hardly adopt the tone and manner of the older class of ministers—men not less useful and beloved, on account of their odd Scottish humour, which indeed suited their time. Could a clergyman, for instance, now come off from the trying position in which we have heard of a northern minister being placed, and by the same way through which he extricated himself with much good nature and quiet sarcasm? A young man, sitting opposite to him in the front of the gallery, had been up late on the previous night, and had stuffed the cards with which he had been occupied into his coat pocket. Forgetting the circumstance, he pulled out his handkerchief, and the cards all flew about. The minister simply looked at him, and remarked, " Eh, man, your psalm-buik has been ill bund."

An admirable story of a quiet pulpit rebuke is

traditionary in Fife, and is told of Mr Shirra, a Seceding minister of Kirkcaldy, a man still well-remembered by some of the older generation for many excellent and some eccentric qualities. A young officer of a volunteer corps on duty in the place, very proud of his fresh uniform, had come to Mr Shirra's church, and walked about as if looking for a seat, but in fact to show off his dress, which he saw was attracting attention from some of the less grave members of the congregation. He came to his place, however, rather quickly, on Mr Shirra quietly remonstrating, "O man, will ye sit doun, and we'll see your new breeks when the kirk's dune." This same Mr Shirra was well-known from his quaint, and, as it were, parenthetical comments which he introduced in his reading of Scripture; as, for example, on reading from the 116th Psalm, "I said in my haste all men are liars," he quietly observed, "Indeed, Dauvid, my man, an ye had been i' this parish ye might hae said it at your leisure."

There was something even still more pungent in the incidental remark of a good man, in the course of his sermon, who had in a country place taken to preaching out of doors in the summer afternoons. He used to collect the people as they were taking air by the side of a stream outside the village. On one occasion he had unfortunately taken his place on a bank, and fixed himself on an *ants' nest*. The active habits of those little creatures soon made the position of the intruder upon their domain very uncomfortable; and, afraid that his audience might observe something of this discomfort in his manner, he apologised by the remark: "Brethren, though I hope I have the Word of God in my mouth, I think the deil himself has gotten into my breeks."

There was often no doubt a sharp conflict of wits when some of these humorist ministers came into collision with members of their flocks who were *also* humorists. Of this nature is the following anecdote, which I am assured is genuine:—A minister in the north was taking to task one of his hearers who was a frequent defaulter, and was reproaching him as a habitual absentee from public worship. The accused vindicated himself on the plea of a dislike to long sermons. " 'Deed, man," said the reverend monitor, a little nettled at the insinuation thrown out against himself, " if ye dinna mend, ye may land yersell where ye'll no' be troubled wi' mony sermons either lang or short." " Weel, aiblins sae," retorted John, " but *that* mayna be for want o' ministers."

An answer to another clergyman, Mr Shireff, parochial minister of St Ninian's, is indicative of Scottish and really clever wit. One of the members of his church was John Henderson or Anderson—a very decent douce shoemaker—and who left the church and joined the Independents, who had a meeting in Stirling. Some time afterwards, when Mr Shireff met John on the road, he said, " And so, John, I understand you have become an Independent?" " 'Deed, sir," replied John, " that's true." " Oh, John," said the minister, " I'm sure you ken that a rowin' (rolling) stane gathers nae fog " (moss). " Ay," said John, " that's true too; but can ye tell me what guid the fog does to the stane?" Mr Shireff himself afterwards became a Baptist. The wit, however, was all in favour of the minister in the following:—

Dr Gilchrist, formerly of the East Parish of Green-ock, and who died minister of the Canongate, Edin-burgh, received an intimation of one of his hearers who had been exceedingly irregular in his attendance

U   305

that he had taken seats in an Episcopal chapel. One day soon after, he met his former parishioner, who told him candidly that he had " changed his religion." " Indeed," said the Doctor quietly ; " how's that ? I ne'er heard ye had ony." It was this same Dr Gilchrist who gave the well-known quiet but forcible rebuke to a young minister whom he considered rather conceited and fond of putting forward his own doings, and who was to officiate in the Doctor's church. He explained to him the mode in which he usually conducted the service, and stated that he always finished the prayer before the sermon with the Lord's Prayer. The young minister demurred at this, and asked if he " might not introduce any other short prayer ? " " Ou ay," was the Doctor's quiet reply, " gif ye can gie us onything *better*."

There is a story current of a sharp hit at the pretensions of a minister who required a little set-down. The scene was on a Monday by a burn near Inverness. A stranger is fishing by a burn side one Monday morning, when the parish minister accosts him from the other side of the stream thus :—" Good sport ? " " Not very." " I am also an angler," but, pompously, " I am a *fisher of men*." " Are you always successful ? " " Not very." " So I guessed, as I keeked into your creel [1] yesterday."

At Banchory, on Deeside, some of the criticisms and remarks on sermons were very quaint and characteristic. My cousin had asked the Leys grieve what he thought of a young man's preaching, who had been more successful in appropriating the words than the ideas of Dr Chalmers. He drily answered, " Ou, Sir Thomas, just a floorish o' the surface." But the same hearer bore this unequivocal testimony to another

---

[1] Basket for fish.

preacher whom he really admired. He was asked if he did not think the sermon long: " Na, I should nae hae thocht it lang an I'd been sitting on thorns."

I think the following is about as good a sample of what we call Scotch " pawky " as any I know:—A countryman had lost his wife and a favourite cow on the same day. His friends consoled him for the loss of the wife; and being highly respectable, several hints and offers were made towards getting another for him. " Ou ay," he at length replied; " you're a' keen eneuch to get me anither wife, but no' yin o' ye offers to gie me anither coo."

The following anecdotes, collected from different contributors, are fair samples of the quaint and original character of Scottish ways and expressions, now becoming more and more matters of reminiscence:— A poor man came to his minister for the purpose of intimating his intention of being married. As he expressed, however, some doubts on the subject, and seemed to hesitate, the minister asked him if there were any doubts about his being accepted. No, that was not the difficulty; but he expressed a fear that it might not be altogether suitable, and he asked whether, if he were once married, he could not (in case of unsuitability and unhappiness) get *un*married. The clergyman assured him that it was impossible; if he married, it must be for better and worse; that he could not go back upon the step. So thus instructed he went away. After a time he returned, and said he had made up his mind to try the experiment, and he came and was married. Ere long he came back very disconsolate, and declared it would not do at all; that he was quite miserable, and begged to be unmarried. The minister assured him that was out of the question, and urged him to put away the notion of anything so absurd. The man insisted that the marriage could not hold good, for the wife was " waur than the deevil." The minister demurred, saying that it was quite impossible. " 'Deed, sir," said the poor man, " the Bible tells ye that if ye resist the deil he flees frae ye, but if ye resist her she flees *at* ye."

A faithful minister of the gospel, being one day engaged in visiting some members of his flock, came to the door of a house where his gentle tapping could not be heard for the noise of contention within. After waiting a little he opened the door and walked in, saying, with an authoritative voice, " I should like to know who is the head of this house." " Weel, sir," said the husband and father, " if ye sit doun a wee, we'll maybe be able to tell ye, for we're just trying to settle that point."

I have received from my kind correspondent, Rev. Mr Hogg of Kirkmahoe, the following most amusing account of a passage-at-arms between a minister and " minister's man," both of them of the old school. The minister of a parish in Dumfriesshire had a man who had long and faithfully served at the manse. During the minister's absence, a ploughing match came off in the district, and the man, feeling the old spirit return with the force of former days, wished to enter the lists, and go in for a prize, which he did, and gained the *fifth* prize. The minister, on his return home, and glancing at the local newspaper, saw the report of the match, and the name of his own man in the prize-list. Being of a crusty temper, he rang the bell in fury, and summoned John, when the following colloquy took place :—" John, how is this ? Who gave you leave to go to the ploughing-match ? " " You were not at hame, sir." " Well, you should have written to me." " I didn't think it was worth while, sir, as we had our ain ploughing *forrit*."[1] "That may be; but why were you not higher in the prize-list? I'm ashamed of you, and you ought to be ashamed of yourself for being so far behind." John's patience had given way, and, in his haste he burst forth, "Indeed, I'm thinking, sir, that if ye were at a *preaching* match, and five-and-thirty in the field, ye wadna come in for *onything*, let a-be for a fift'."

Stories of humorous encounters between ministers and their hearers are numerous, and though often seasoned with dry and caustic humour, they never indicate appearance of bitterness or ill-feeling between the parties. As an example, a clergyman thought his people were making rather an unconscionable objection to his using a MS. in delivering his sermon. They urged, "What gars ye tak up your bit papers to the pu'pit?" He replied that it was best, for really he could not remember his sermon, and must have his papers. "Weel, weel, minister, then dinna expect that *we* can remember them."

Some of these encounters arise out of the old question of sleeping in church. For example: "I see, James, that you tak' a bit nap in the kirk," said a minister to one of his people; "can ye no tak a mull with you? and when you become heavy an extra pinch would keep you up." "Maybe it wad," said James, "but pit you the sneeshin intil your sermon, minister, and maybe that'll serve the same purpose." As a specimen of the matter-of-fact view of religious questions frequently recorded of older ministers, let me adduce a well-authenticated account of a minister in a far up-hill parish in Deeside. Returning thanks one Sabbath for the excellent harvest, he began as usual, "O Lord, we thank Thee," etc., and went on to men-

[1] Well advanced.

tion its abundance, and its safe ingathering; but, feeling anxious to be quite candid and scrupulously truthful, added, " all except a few sma' bitties at Birse no' worth o' mentioning."

A Scotch preacher, a man of large stature, being sent to officiate one Sunday at a country parish, was accommodated at night, in the manse, in a very diminutive closet—the usual best bedroom, appropriated to strangers, being otherwise occupied. " Is this the bedroom?" he said, starting back in amazement. " 'Deed ay, sir, this is the prophets' chalmer." " It maun be for the *minor* prophets, then," was the quiet reply.

Elders of the kirk, no doubt, frequently partook of the original and humorous character of ministers and others, their contemporaries; and amusing scenes must have passed, and good Scotch sayings been said, where they were concerned. Dr Chalmers used to repeat one of these sayings of an elder with great delight. The Doctor associated with the anecdote the name of Lady Glenorchy and the church which she endowed; but I am assured that the person was Lady Elizabeth Cunninghame, sister of Archibald, eleventh Earl of Eglinton, and wife of Sir John Cunninghame, Bart., of Caprington, near Kilmarnock. It seems her ladyship had, for some reason, taken offence at the proceedings of the Caprington parochial authorities, and a result of which was that she ceased putting her usual liberal offering into the plate at the door. This had gone on for some time, till one of the elders, of less forbearing character than the others, took his turn at the plate. Lady Elizabeth as usual passed by without a contribution, but made a formal curtsy to the elder at the plate, and sailed up the aisle. The good man was determined not to let her pass so easily, so

he quickly followed her, and urged the remonstrance:
" Gie us mair o' your siller and less o' your mainners,
my Lady Betty." My kind correspondent, Rev. Mr
Agnew, supplies me with an amusing pendant to this
anecdote :—At a great church meeting, Dr Chalmers
had told this story with much effect when Lord
Galloway was in the chair. After the meeting, Dr
Chalmers, and many who had been present, dined at
his lordship's hospitable table. After dinner, when
the morning meeting was discussed, Lord Galloway
addressed Dr Chalmers on the subject of this story
and, as if not quite pleased at its being introduced,
said, " Do you know, Doctor, the lady of whom you
told the story of the elder is a near relation of mine ? "
Dr Chalmers, with real or seeming simplicity, answered, " No, my lord, I did not ; but next time I
tell the story I can mention the fact." As a pendant to
the elder's disclaimer of " mainners " on the part of
a lady of rank, I may add an authentic anecdote of a
very blunt and unpolished Kincardineshire laird, expressing the same disclaimer of mainners on the part
of a servant, but in a far rougher form of speech. He
had been talking with a man who came to offer for
his service as a butler. But the laird soon found he
was far too grand a gentleman for his service, and became chafed with his requiring so many things as
conditions of coming ; till, on his dismissal, when the
man was bowing and scraping to show how genteel
he could be, he lost all patience, and roared out, " Get
out, ye fule ; gie us nane o' your mainners here."

Of an eccentric and eloquent professor and divine
of a northern Scottish university, there are numerous
and extraordinary traditionary anecdotes. I have
received an account of some of these anecdotes from
the kind communication of an eminent Scottish clergy-

man, who was himself in early days his frequent
hearer. The stories told of the strange observations
and allusions which he introduced into his pulpit
discourses almost surpass belief. For many reasons,
they are not suitable to the nature of this publication,
still less could they be tolerated in any pulpit administration now, although familiar with his contemporaries.
The remarkable circumstance, however, connected
with these eccentricities was, that he introduced them
with the utmost gravity, and oftentimes, after he had
delivered them, pursued his subject with great earnestness and eloquence, as if he had said nothing uncommon. One saying of the professor, however, *out*
of the pulpit, is too good to be omitted, and may be
recorded without violation of propriety. He happened
to meet at the house of a lawyer, whom he considered
rather a man of *sharp* practice, and for whom he had
no great favour, two of his own parishioners. The
lawyer jocularly and ungraciously put the question;
" Doctor, these are members of your flock; may I
ask, do you look upon them as white sheep or as
black sheep ? " " I don't know," answered the professor drily, " whether they are black or white sheep,
but I know that if they are long here they are pretty
sure to be fleeced."

It was a pungent answer given by a Free Kirk
member who had deserted his colours and returned to
the old faith. A short time after the Disruption, the
Free Church minister chanced to meet him who had
then left him and returned to the Established Church.
The minister bluntly accosted him : " Ay, man, John,
an' ye've left us ; what micht be your reason for that ?
Did ye think it wasna a guid road we was gaun ? "
" Ou, I daursay it was a guid eneuch road and a braw
road ; but, O minister, the tolls were unco high."

The following story I received from a member of the Penicuik family :—Dr Ritchie, who died minister of St Andrew's, Edinburgh, was, when a young man, tutor to Sir G. Clerk and his brothers. Whilst with them, the clergyman of the parish became unable, from infirmity and illness, to do his duty, and Mr Ritchie was appointed interim assistant. He was an active young man, and during his residence in the country had become fond of fishing, and was a good shot. When the grouse-shooting came round, his pupils happened to be laid up with a fever, so Mr Ritchie had all the shooting to himself. One day he walked over the moor so far that he became quite weary and footsore. On returning home he went into a cottage, where the good woman received him kindly, gave him water for his feet, and refreshment. In the course of conversation, he told her he was acting as assistant minister of the parish, and he explained how far he had travelled in pursuit of game, how weary he was, and how completely knocked up he was. " Weel, sir, I dinna doubt ye maun be sair travelled and tired wi' your walk." And then she added, with sly reference to his profession, " 'Deed, sir, I'm thinkin' ye micht hae travelled frae Genesis to Revelation and no' been sae forfauchten." [1]

Scotch people in general are, like this old woman, very jealous, as might be expected, of ministers joining the sportsman to their pastoral character. A proposal for the appointment of a minister to a particular parish, who was known in the country as a capital shot, called forth a rather neat Scottish *pun*, from an old woman of the parish, who significantly observed, " 'Deed, *Kilpatrick* would hae been a mair appropriate place for him." *Paatrick* is Scotch for partridge.

[1] Wearied.

I cannot do better in regard to the three following anecdotes of the late Professor Gillespie of St Andrews, than give them to my readers in the words with which Dr Lindsay Alexander kindly communicated them to me.

"In the *Cornhill Magazine* for March 1860, in an article on Student Life in Scotland, there is an anecdote of the late Professor Gillespie of St Andrews, which is told in such a way as to miss the point and humour of the story. The correct version, as I have heard it from the professor himself, is this : Having employed the village carpenter to put a frame round a dial at the manse of Cults, where he was a minister, he received from the man a bill to the following effect :— ' To fencing the *deil*, 5s. 6d.' ' When I paid him,' said the professor, ' I could not help saying, John, this is rather more than I counted on ; but I haven't a word to say. I get somewhere about two hundred a year for fencing the *deil*, and I'm afraid I don't do it half so effectually as you've done.'

" Whilst I am writing, another of the many stories of the learned and facetious professor rises in my mind. There was a worthy old woman at Cults whose place in church was what is commonly called the Lateran— a kind of small gallery at the top of the pulpit steps. She was a most regular attender, but as regularly fell asleep during sermon, of which fault the preacher had sometimes audible intimation. It was observed, however, that though Janet always slept during her own pastor's discourse, she could be attentive enough when she pleased, and especially was she alert when some young preacher occupied the pulpit. A little piqued, perhaps, at this, Mr Gillespie said to her one day, ' Janet, I think you hardly behave very respectfully to your own minister in one respect.' ' Me, sir ! ' exclaimed Janet, ' I wad like to see ony man, no' tae say

woman, by yoursell, say that o' me! What can you
mean, sir?' 'Weel, Janet, ye ken when I preach
you're almost always fast asleep before I've well given
out my text; but when any of these young men from
St Andrews preach for me, I see you never sleep a
wink. Now, that's what I call no' using me as you
should do.' 'Hoot, sir,' was the reply, 'is that a'?
I'll sune tell you the reason o' that. When you preach,
we a' ken the Word o' God's safe in your hands; but
when thae young birkies tak' it in haun', my certie,
but it taks us a' to look after them.' [1]

"I am tempted to subjoin another. In the Humanity
Class, one day, a youth who was rather fond of showing off his powers of language, translated Hor. Od.
iii., 3, 61, 62, somewhat thus:—' The fortunes of
Troy renascent under sorrowful omen shall be repeated with sad catastrophe.' 'Catastrophe!' cried
the professor. 'Catastrophe, Mr ——, that's Greek.
Give us it in plain English, if you please.' Thus
suddenly pulled down from his high horse, the student
effected his retreat with a rather lame and impotent
version. 'Now,' said the professor, his little sharp
eyes twinkling with fun, 'that brings to my recollection what once happened to a friend of mine, a minister
in the country. Being a scholarly man he was sometimes
betrayed into the use of words in the pulpit which the
people were not likely to understand; but being very
conscientious, he never detected himself in this, without pausing to give the meaning of the word he had
used, and sometimes his extempore explanations of
very fine words were a little like what we have just had
from Mr ——, rather too flat and commonplace. On

[1] I have abundant evidence to prove that a similar answer to that which
Dr Alexander records to have been made to Mr Gillespie has been given on
similar occasions by others.

one occasion he allowed this very word ' catastrophe '
to drop from him, on which he immediately added,
' that, you know, my friends, means the *end* of a thing.'
Next day, as he was riding through his parish, some
mischievous youth succeeded in fastening a bunch of
furze to his horse's tail—a trick which, had the animal
been skittish, might have exposed the worthy pastor's
horsemanship to too severe a trial, but which happily
had no effect whatever on the sober-minded and respectable quadruped which he bestrode. On, therefore, he quietly jogged, utterly unconscious of the
addition that had been made to his horse's caudal
region, until, as he was passing some cottages, he was
arrested by the shrill voice of an old woman exclaiming, ' Heh, sir ! Heh, sir ! there's a whun-buss at your
horse's catawstrophe ! ' "

I have several times adverted to the subject of
epigrams. A clever impromptu of this class has been
recorded as given by a judge's lady in reply to one
made by the witty Henry Erskine at a dinner-party at
Lord Armadale's. When a bottle of claret was called
for, port was brought in by mistake. A second time
claret was sent for, and a second time the same mistake
occurred. Henry Erskine addressed the host in an
impromptu, which was meant as a parody on the
well-known Scottish song, " My Jo, Janet "—

> " Kind sir, it's for your courtesie
>   When I come here to dine, sir,
> For the love ye bear to me,
>   Gie me the claret wine, sir."

To which Mrs Honeyman retorted—

> " Drink the port, the claret's dear,
>   Erskine, Erskine ;
> Ye'll get fou' on't, never fear,
>   My jo, Erskine."

Some of my younger readers may not be familiar with the epigram of John Home, author of the tragedy of " Douglas." The lines were great favourites with Sir Walter Scott, who delighted in repeating them. Home was very partial to claret, and could not bear port. He was exceedingly indignant when the Government laid a tax upon claret, having previously long connived at its introduction into Scotland under very mitigated duties. He embodied his anger in the following epigram :—

> " Firm and erect the Caledonian stood,
>   Old was his mutton, and his claret good ;
> ' Let him drink port,' an English statesman cried—
>   He drank the poison, and his spirit died."

There is a curious story traditionary in some families connected with the nobleman who is the subject of it, which, I am assured, is true, and further, that it has never yet appeared in print. The story is, therefore, a " Scottish reminiscence," and, as such, deserves a place here. The Earl of Lauderdale was so ill as to cause great alarm to his friends, and perplexity to his physicians. One distressing symptom was a total absence of sleep, and the medical men declared their opinion, that without sleep being induced he could not recover. His son, a queer eccentric-looking boy, who was considered not entirely right in his mind but somewhat " *daft*," and who accordingly had had little attention paid to his education, was sitting under the table, and cried out, " Sen' for that preachin' man frae Livingstone, for faither aye sleeps in the kirk." One of the doctors thought this hint worth attending to. The experiment of " getting a minister till him " succeeded, and, sleep coming on, he recovered. The Earl, out of gratitude for this benefit, took more notice of his son, paid attention to his education, and that boy became the Duke of Lauderdale, afterwards so famous or infamous in his country's history.

The following very amusing anecdote, although it belongs more properly to the division on peculiarities of Scottish phraseology, I give in the words of a correspondent who received it from the parties with whom it originated. About twenty years ago, he was paying a visit to a cousin, married to a Liverpool merchant of some standing. The husband had lately had a visit from his aged father, who formerly followed the occupation of farming in Stirlingshire, and who had probably never been out of Scotland before in his life. The son, finding his father rather *de trop* in his office, one day persuaded him to cross the ferry over the Mersey, and inspect the harvesting, then in full operation, on the Cheshire side. On landing, he approached a young woman reaping with the sickle in a field of oats, when the following dialogue ensued :—

Farmer.—Lassie, are yer aits muckle bookit[1] th' year?

Reaper.—What say'n yo?

Farmer.—I was speiring gif yer aits are muckle bookit th' year!

Reaper (in amazement).—I dunnot know what yo' say'n.

Farmer (in equal astonishment).—Gude—safe—us, —do ye no understaan gude plain English?—are—yer —aits—muckle—bookit?

Reaper decamps to her nearest companion, saying that was a madman, while he shouted in great wrath, " They were naething else than a set o' ignorant pock-puddings."

An English tourist visited Arran, and being a keen

[1] Oats heavy in bulk.

disciple of Izaak Walton, was arranging to have a day's good sport. Being told that the cleg, or horse-fly, would suit his purpose admirably for lure, he addressed himself to Christy, the Highland servant-girl :—" I say, my girl, can you get me some horse-flies ? " Christy looked stupid, and he repeated his question. Finding that she did not yet comprehend him, he exclaimed, " Why, girl, did you never see a horse-fly ? " " Naa, sir," said the girl, " but A wance saw a coo jump ower a preshipice."

The following anecdote is highly illustrative of the thoroughly attached old family serving-man. A correspondent sends it as told to him by an old schoolfellow of Sir Walter Scott's at Fraser and Adam's class, High School :—

One of the lairds of Abercairnie proposed *to go out*, on the occasion of one of the risings for the Stuarts, in the '15 or '45—but this was not with the will of his old serving-man, who, when Abercairnie was pulling on his boots, preparing to go, overturned a kettle of boiling water upon his legs, so as to disable him from joining his friends—saying, " Tak' that— let them fecht wha like; stay ye at hame and be laird o' Abercairnie."

A story illustrative of a union of polite courtesy with rough and violent ebullition of temper common in the old Scottish character, is well-known in the Lothian family. William Henry, fourth Marquis of Lothian, had for his guest at dinner an old countess to whom he wished to show particular respect and attention.[1] After a very complimentary reception, he put on his white gloves to hand her downstairs, led

---

[1] This Marquis of Lothian was aide-de-camp to the Duke of Cumberland at the battle of Culloden, who sullied his character as a soldier and a nobleman by the cruelties which he exercised on the vanquished.

her up to the upper end of the table, bowed, and retired to his own place. This I am assured was the usual custom with the chief lady guest by persons who themselves remember it. After all were seated, the Marquis addressed the lady, " Madam, may I have the honour and happiness of helping your ladyship to some fish ? " But he got no answer, for the poor woman was deaf as a post, and did not hear him. After a pause, but still in the most courteous accents, " Madam, have I your ladyship's permission to send you some fish ? " Then a little quicker, " Is your ladyship inclined to take fish ? " Very quick, and rather peremptory, " Madam, do ye choice fish ? " At last the thunder burst, to everybody's consternation, with a loud thump on the table and stamp on the floor : " Con—found ye, will ye have any fish ? " I am afraid the exclamation might have been even of a more pungent character.

A correspondent has kindly enabled me to add a reminiscence and anecdote of a type of Scottish character now nearly extinct—I mean the old Scottish *military* officer of the wars of Holland and the Low Countries. I give them in his own words :—" My father, the late Rev. Dr Bethune, minister of Dornoch, was on friendly terms with a fine old soldier, the late Colonel Alexander Sutherland of Calmaly and Brae-grudy, in Sutherlandshire, who was lieutenant-colonel of the ' Local Militia,' and who used occasionally, in his word of command, to break out with a Gaelic phrase to the men, much to the amusement of by-standers. He called his charger, a high-boned not overfed animal, Cadăver—a play upon accents, for he was a good classical scholar, and fond of quoting the Latin poets. But he had no relish nor respect for the ' Modern languages,' particularly for that of our

French neighbours, whom he looked upon as ' hereditary ' enemies ! My father and the colonel were both
politicians, as well as scholars. Reading a newspaper
article in his presence one day, my father stopped
short, handing the paper to him, and said, ' Colonel,
here is a *French* quotation, which you can translate
better than I can.' ' No, sir ! ' said the colonel, ' I
never learnt the language of the scoundrels ! ! ! ' The
colonel was known as ' Col. Sandy Sutherland,' and
the men always called him *Colonel Sandy*. He was a
splendid specimen of the hale veteran, with a stentorian
voice, and the last queue I remember to have seen."

A correspondent kindly sends me from Aberdeenshire a humorous story, very much of the same sort as
that of Colonel Erskine's servant, who considerately
suggested to his master that " maybe an aith might
relieve him." [1] My correspondent heard the story
from the late Bishop Skinner.

It was among the experiences of his father, Bishop
John Skinner. While making some pastoral visits in
the neighbourhood of the town (Aberdeen), the Bishop
took occasion to step into the cottage of two humble
parishioners, a man and his wife, who cultivated a
little croft. No one was within ; but as the door was
only on the latch, the Bishop knew that the worthy
couple could not be far distant. He therefore stepped
in the direction of the outhouses, and found them both
in the barn winnowing corn, in the primitive way,
with " riddles," betwixt two open doors. On the
Bishop making his appearance, the honest man ceased
his winnowing operations, and in the gladness of his
heart stepped briskly forward to welcome his pastor ;
but in his haste he trod upon the rim of the riddle,
which rebounded with great force against one of his

---

[1] Sir H. Moncreiff's *Life of Dr J. Erskine*.

shins. The accident made him suddenly pull up; and, instead of completing the reception, he stood vigorously rubbing the injured limb; and, not daring in such a venerable presence to give vent to the customary strong ejaculations, kept twisting his face into all sorts of grimaces. As was natural, the Bishop went forward, uttering the usual formulas of condolence and sympathy, the patient, meanwhile, continuing his rubbings and his silent but expressive contortions. At last Janet came to the rescue; and, clapping the Bishop coaxingly on the back, said, " Noo, Bishop, jist gang ye yir waas into the hoose, an' we'll follow fan he's had time to curse a fyllie, an' I'se warran' he'll seen be weel eneuch! "

The following might have been added as examples of the dry humorous manner in which our countrymen and countrywomen sometimes treat matters with which they have to deal, even when serious ones :—

An itinerant vendor of wood in Aberdeen having been asked how his wife was, replied, " Oh, she's fine; I hae ta'en her tae Banchory "; and on it being innocently remarked that the change of air would do her good, he looked up, and, with a half smile, said, " Hoot, she's i' the kirkyard."

The well-known aversion of the Scotch to hearing *read* sermons has often led to amusing occurrences. One pastor, in a country district, who was much respected by his people, but who, nevertheless, were never quite reconciled to his *paper* in the pulpit, found himself on one occasion in an awkward predicament, from this same paper question. One Sabbath afternoon, having exhausted both firstly and secondly, he came to the termination of his discourse; but, unfortunately, the manuscript was wanting. In vain efforts to seek the missing paper, he repeated " thirdly and lastly " *ad nauseam* to his hearers. At last one, cooler than the others, rose, and nodding to the minister, observed, " 'Deed, sir, If I'm no' mista'en, I saw ' thirdly and lastly ' fa' ower the poopit stairs " ; evidently enjoying the disappearance of so important a part of the obnoxious document.

This prejudice was indeed some years since in Scotland quite inveterate. The following anecdote has been kindly sent to me from *Memoirs of Charles Young*, lately published by his son :—

" I have a distinct recollection, one Sunday when I was living at Cults, and when a stranger was officiating for Dr Gillespie, observing that he had not proceeded five minutes with his ' discourse,' before there was a general commotion and stampede. The exodus at last became so serious, that, conceiving something to be wrong, probably a fire in the manse, I caught the infection, and eagerly inquired of the first person I encountered in the churchyard what was the matter, and was told, with an expression of sovereign scorn and disgust : ' Losh keep ye, young man ! Hae ye eyes, and see not ? Hae ye ears, and hear not ? *The man reads !* ' "

On one occasion, however, even this prejudice gave way before the power of the most eloquent preacher that Scotland ever heard, or perhaps that the world ever heard. A shrewd old Fife hearer of sermons had been objecting, in the usual exaggerated language, against reading sermons in the pulpit. A gentleman urged the case of Dr Chalmers, in defence of the practice. He used his paper in preaching rigidly, and yet with what an effect he read ! All the objector could reply to this was, " Ah, but it's *fell*[1] reading yon."

The two following are from a correspondent who

[1] Extraordinary.

heard them told by the late Dr Barclay the anatomist, well-known for his own dry Scottish humour.

A country laird, at his death, left his property in equal shares to his two sons, who continued to live very amicably together for many years. At length one said to the other, " Tam, we're gettin' auld now, you'll tak' a wife, and when I dee you'll get my share o' the grund." " Na, John, you're the youngest and maist active, you'll tak' a wife, and when I dee you'll get my share." " Od," says John, " Tam, that's jist the way wi' you when there's ony *fash or trouble*. The deevil a thing you'll do at a'."

A country clergyman, who was not on the most friendly terms with one of his heritors who resided in Stirling, and who had annoyed the minister by delay in paying him his teinds (or tithe), found it necessary to make the laird understand that his proportion of stipend must be paid so soon as it became due. The payment came next term punctual to the time. When the messenger was introduced to the minister, he asked who he was, remarking that he thought he had seen him before. " I am the hangman of Stirling, sir." " Oh, just so, take a seat till I write you a receipt." It was evident that the laird had chosen this medium of communication with the minister as an affront, and to show his spite. The minister, however, turned the tables upon him, sending back an acknowledgment for the payment in these terms :—" Received from Mr ——, by the hands of the hangman of Stirling, *his doer*,[1] the sum of," etc., etc.

The following story of pulpit criticism by a beadle used to be told, I am assured, by the late Rev. Dr Andrew Thomson :—

[1] In Scotland it is usual to term the law-agent or man of business of any person his " doer."

A clergyman in the country had a stranger preaching for him one day, and meeting his beadle, he said to him, " Well, Saunders, how did you like the sermon to-day ? " " I watna, sir ; it was rather ower plain and simple for me. I like thae sermons best that jumbles the joodgment and confoonds the sense. Od, sir, I never saw ane that could come up to yourself at that."

The epithet " canny " has frequently been applied to our countrymen, not in a severe or invidious spirit, but as indicating a due regard to personal interest and safety. In the larger edition of Jamieson (see edition of 1840) I find there are no fewer than eighteen meanings given of this word. The following extract from a provincial paper, which has been sent me, will furnish a good illustration. It is headed, the " PROPERTY QUALIFICATION," and goes on—" Give a Chartist a large estate, and a copious supply of ready money, and you make a Conservative of him. He can then see the other side of the moon, which he could never see before. Once, a determined Radical in Scotland, named Davy Armstrong, left his native village ; and many years afterwards, an old fellow grumbler met him, and commenced the old song. Davy shook his head. His friend was astonished, and soon perceived that Davy was no longer a grumbler, but a rank Tory. Wondering at the change, he was desirous of knowing the reason. Davy quietly and laconically replied : ' I've a coo (cow) noo.' "

But even still more " canny " was the eye to the main chance in an Aberdonian fellow-countryman, communicated in the following pleasant terms from a Nairn correspondent :—" I have just been reading your delightful ' Reminiscences,' which has brought to my recollection a story I used to hear my father tell. It was thus :—A countryman in a remote part of Aberdeenshire having got a newly coined sovereign in the days when such a thing was seldom seen in his part of the country, went about showing it to his friends and neighbours for the charge of one penny each sight. Evil days, however, unfortunately over-took him, and he was obliged to part with his loved coin. Soon after, a neighbour called on him, and asked a sight of his sovereign, at the same time tendering a penny. ' Ah, man,' says he, ' it's gane ; but I'll lat ye see *the cloutie it was rowt in* for a bawbee.' "

There was something very simple-minded in the manner in which a parishioner announced his canny care for his supposed interests when he became an elder of the kirk. The story is told of a man who had got himself installed in the eldership, and, in con-sequence, had for some time carried round the ladle for the collections. He had accepted the office of elder because some wag had made him believe that the re-muneration was sixpence each Sunday, with a boll of meal at New Year's Day. When the time arrived he claimed his meal, but was told he had been hoaxed. " It may be sae wi' the meal," he said coolly, " but I took care o' the saxpence mysell."

There was a good deal both of the *pawky* and the *canny* in the following anecdote, which I have from an honoured lady of the south of Scotland :—" There was an old man who always rode a donkey to his work, and tethered him while he worked on the roads, or whatever else it might be. It was suggested to him by my grandfather that he was suspected of putting it in to feed in the fields at other people's expense. ' Eh, laird, I could never be tempted to do that, for my cuddy winna eat onything but nettles and thristles.' One day my grandfather was riding along the road, when he saw Andrew Leslie at work, and his donkey up to the knees in one of his clover fields, feeding luxuriously. ' Hollo, Andrew,' said he; ' I thought you told me your cuddy would eat nothing but nettles and thistles.' ' Ay,' said he, ' but he misbehaved the day; he nearly kicket me ower his head, sae I pat him in there just to *punish* him.' "

There is a good deal of the same sort of simple character brought out in the two following. They were sent to me from Golspie, and are original, as they occurred in my correspondent's own experience. The one is a capital illustration of thrift, the other of kind feeling for the friendless, in the Highland character. I give the anecdotes in my correspondent's own words :—A little boy, some twelve years of age, came to me one day with the following message : " My mother wants a vomit from you, sir, and she bade me say if it will not be strong enough, she will send it back." " Oh, Mr Begg," said a woman to me, for whom I was weighing two grains of calomel for a child, " dinna be so mean wi' it; it is for a poor faitherless bairn."

The following, from a provincial paper, contains a very amusing recognition of a return which one of the itinerant race considered himself conscientiously bound to make to his clerical patron for an alms : " A beggar, while on his rounds one day this week, called on a clergyman (within two and a half miles of the Cross of Kilmarnock), who, obeying the biblical injunction of clothing the naked, offered the beggar an old top-coat. It was immediately rolled up, and the beggar, in going away with it under his arm, thoughtfully (!) remarked, ' I'll hae tae gie ye a day's *hearin'* for this na.' "

The natural and self-complacent manner in which

the following anecdote brings out in the Highlander an innate sense of the superiority of Celtic blood is highly characteristic:—A few years ago, when an English family were visiting in the Highlands, their attention was directed to a child crying; on their observing to the mother it was *cross*, she exclaimed: "Na, na, it's nae cross, for we're baith true Hieland."

The late Mr Grahame of Garsock, in Strathearn, whose grandson now " is laird himsel'," used to tell, with great *unction*, some thirty years ago, a story of a neighbour of his own of a still earlier generation, Drummond of Keltie, who, as it seems, had employed an itinerant tailor instead of a metropolitan artist. On one occasion a new pair of inexpressibles had been made for the laird; they were so tight that, after waxing hot and red in the attempt to try them on, he *let out* rather savagely at the tailor, who calmly assured him, " It's the fash'n; it's jist the fash'n." " Eh, ye haveril, is it the fashion for them *no to go on* ? "

An English gentleman writes to me—" We have all heard much of Scotch caution, and I met once with an instance of it which I think is worth recording, and which I tell as strictly original. About 1827, I fell into conversation, on board of a Stirling steamer, with a well-dressed middle-aged man, who told me he was a soldier of the 42nd, going on leave. He began to relate the campaigns he had gone through, and mentioned having been at the siege of St Sebastian. ' Ah! under Sir Thomas Graham?' ' Yes, sir; he commanded there.' ' Well,' I said, merely by way of carrying on the *crack*, ' and what do you think of *him* ? ' Instead of answering, he scanned me several times from head to foot, and from foot to head, and then said, in a tone of the most diplomatic caution, ' Ye'll perhaps be of the name of Grah'm yersel, sir? '

There could hardly be a better example, either of the circumspection of a real canny Scot, or of the lingering influence of the old patriarchal feeling, by which ' A name, a word, makes clansmen vassals to their lord.' "

Now when we linger over these old stories, we seem to live at another period, and in such reminiscences we converse with a generation different from our own. Changes are still going on around us. They have been going on for some time past. The changes are less striking as society advances, and we find fewer alterations for us to notice. Probably each generation will have less change to record than the generation that preceded; still every one who is tolerably advanced in life must feel that, comparing its beginning and its close, he has witnessed two epochs, and that in advanced life he looks on a different world from one which he can remember. To elucidate this fact has been my present object, and in attempting this task I cannot but feel how trifling and unsatisfactory my remarks must seem to many who have a more enlarged and minute acquaintance with Scottish life and manners than I have. But I shall be encouraged to hope for a favourable, or at least an indulgent, sentence upon these Reminiscences, if to any of my readers I shall have opened a fresh insight into the subject of social changes amongst us. Many causes have their effect upon the habits and customs of mankind, and of late years such causes have been greatly multiplied in number and activity. In many persons, and in some who have not altogether lost their national partialities, there is a general tendency to merge Scottish usages and Scottish expressions into the English forms, as being more correct and genteel. The facilities for moving, not merely from place to place in our own

country, but from one country to another; the spread
of knowledge and information by means of periodical
publications and newspapers; and the incredibly low
prices at which literary works are produced, must
have great effects. Then there is the improved taste
in art, which, together with literature, has been taken
up by young men who, fifty, sixty, seventy years ago,
or more, would have known no such sources of interest, or indeed who would have looked upon them as
unmanly and effeminate. When first these pursuits
were taken up by our Scottish young men, they excited
in the north much amazement, and, I fear, contempt,
as was evinced by a laird of the old school, who, the
first time he saw a young man at the pianoforte,
asked, with evident disgust, " Can the creature *sew*
ony ? " evidently putting the accomplishment of playing the pianoforte and the accomplishment of the
needle in the same category.

The greater facility of producing books, prints, and
other articles which tend to the comfort and embellishment of domestic life, must have considerable
influence upon the habits and tastes of a people. I
have often thought how much effect might be traced
to the single circumstances of the cheap production of
pianofortes. An increased facility of procuring the
means of acquaintance with good works of art and
literature acts both as cause and effect. A growing
and improved taste tends to stimulate the *production*
of the best works of art. These, in return, foster and
advance the power of forming a due *estimate* of art.
In the higher department of music, for example, the
cheap rate not only of *hearing* compositions of the first
class, but of *possessing* the works of the most eminent
composers, must have had influence upon thousands.
The principal oratorios of Handel may be purchased

for as many shillings each as they cost pounds years ago. Indeed, at that time the very names of these immortal works were known only to a few who were skilled to appreciate their high beauties. Now associations are formed for practising and studying the choral works of the great masters.

We might indeed adduce many more causes which seem to produce changes of habits, tastes, and associations amongst our people. For example, families do not vegetate for years in one retired spot as they used to do; young men are encouraged to attain accomplishments, and to have other sources of interest than the field or the bottle. Every one knows, or may know, everything that is going on through the whole world. There is a tendency in mankind to lose all that is peculiar, and in nations to part with all that distinguishes them from each other. We hear of wonderful changes in habits and customs where change seemed impossible. In India and Turkey even, peculiarities and prejudices are fading away under the influence of time. Amongst ourselves, no doubt, one circumstance tended greatly to call forth, and, as we may say, to *develop*, the peculiar Scotch humour of which we speak —and that was the familiarity of intercourse which took place between persons in different positions of life. This extended even to an occasional interchange of words between the minister and the members of his flock during time of service. I have two anecdotes in illustration of this fact, which I have reason to believe are quite authentic. In the church of Banchory on Deeside, to which I have referred, a former minister always preached without book, and being of an absent disposition, he sometimes forgot the head of discourse on which he was engaged, and got involved in confusion. On one occasion, being desirous of recalling

to his memory the division of his subject, he called
out to one of his elders, a farmer on the estate of Ley,
" Bush (the name of his farm), Bush, ye're sleeping."
" Na, sir, I'm no' sleeping—I'm listening." " Weel,
then, what had I begun to say?" " Oh, ye were
saying so-and-so." This was enough, and supplied
the minister with the thread of his discourse; and he
went on. The other anecdote related to the parish of
Cumbernauld, the minister of which was at the time
referred to noted for a very disjointed and rambling
style of preaching, without method or connection.
His principal heritor was the Lord Elphinstone of the
time, and unfortunately the minister and the peer were
not on good terms, and always ready to annoy each
other by sharp sayings or otherwise. The minister on
one occasion had somewhat in this spirit called upon
the beadle to " wauken my Lord Elphinstone," upon
which Lord Elphinstone said, " I'm no' sleeping,
minister." " Indeed you were, my lord." He again
disclaimed the sleeping. So as a test the preacher
asked him, " What had I been saying last then?"
" Oh, juist wauken Lord Elphinstone." " Ay, but
what did I say before that?" " Indeed," retorted
Lord Elphinstone, " I'll gie ye a guinea if ye'll tell that
yersell, minister." We can hardly imagine the *possibility*
of such scenes now taking place amongst us in church.
It seems as if all men were gradually approximating
to a common type or form in their manners and views
of life; oddities are sunk, prominences are rounded
off, sharp features are polished, and all things are becoming smooth and conventional. The remark, like
the effect, is general, and extends to other countries as
well as to our own. But as we have more recently
parted with our peculiarities of dialect, oddity, and
eccentricity, it becomes the more amusing to mark

our participation in this change, because a period of fifty years shows here a greater contrast than the same period would show in many other localities.

I have already referred to a custom which prevailed in all the rural parish churches, and which I remember in my early days at Fettercairn; the custom I mean, now quite obsolete, of the minister, after pronouncing the blessing, turning to the heritors, who always occupied the front seats of the gallery, and making low bows to each family. Another custom I recollect:— When the text had been given out, it was usual for the elder branches of the congregation to hand about their Bibles amongst the younger members, marking the place, and calling their attention to the passage. During service another handing about was frequent among the seniors, and that was a circulation of the sneeshin-mull or snuff-box. Indeed, I have heard of the same practice in an Episcopal church, and particularly in one case of an ordination, where the bishop took his pinch of snuff, and handed the mull to go round amongst the clergy assembled for the solemn occasion within the altar-rails.

Amongst Scottish reminiscences which do not extend beyond our own recollections we may mention the disappearance of Trinity Church in Edinburgh, which has taken place within the last quarter of a century. It was founded by Mary of Gueldres, queen of James II. of Scotland, in 1446, and liberally endowed for a provost, prebendaries, choristers, etc. It was never completed, but the portions built, viz., choir, transept, and central tower, were amongst the finest specimens of later Gothic work in Scotland. The pious founder had placed it at the east end of what was then the North Loch. She chose her own church for the resting-place of her remains as a sanc-

tuary of safety and repose. A railway parliamentary
bill, however, overrides founder's intentions and
Episcopal consecrations. Where once stood the beautiful church of the Holy Trinity, where once the
" pealing organ " and the " full-voiced choir " were
daily heard " in service high and anthems clear "—
where for 400 years slept the ashes of a Scottish Queen
—now resound the noise and turmoil of a railway
station.

But we have another example of the uncertainty of
all earthly concerns, and one which supplies a Scottish
reminiscence belonging to the last seventy years.
Wilhelmina, Viscountess Glenorchy, during her life-
time, built and endowed a church for two ministers,
who were provided with very handsome incomes.
She died 17th July 1786, and was buried on the 24th
July, aged forty-four. Her interment took place, by
her own direction, in the church she had founded,
immediately in front of the pulpit ; and she fixed upon
that spot as a place of security and safety, where her
mortal remains might rest in peace till the morning of
the resurrection. But alas for the uncertainty of all
earthly plans and projects for the future !—the iron
road came on its reckless course and swept the church
away. The site was required for the North British
Railway, which passed directly over the spot where
Lady Glenorchy had been buried. Her remains were
accordingly disinterred 24th December 1844 ; and
the trustees of the church, not having yet erected a
new one, deposited the body of their foundress in the
vaults beneath St John's Episcopal Church, and after
resting there for fifteen years, they were, in 1859,
removed to the building which is now Lady Glenorchy's Church.

In our reminiscences of many *changes* which have

taken place during fifty years in Scottish manners, it might form an interesting section to record some peculiarities which *remain*. I mean such peculiarities as yet linger amongst us, and still mark a difference in some of our social habits from those of England. Some Scottish usages die hard, and are found still to supply amusement for southern visitors. To give a few examples, persons still persist among us in calling the head of a family, or the host, the *landlord*, although he never charged his guests a halfpenny for the hospitality he exercises. In games, golf and curling still continue to mark the national character—cricket was long an exotic amongst us. In many of our educational institutions, however, it seems now fairly to have taken root. We continue to call our reception rooms "*public* rooms," although never used for any but domestic purposes. Military rank is attached to ladies, as we speak of Mrs Lieutenant Fraser, Mrs Captain Scott, Mrs Major Smith, Mrs Colonel Campbell. On the occasion of a death, we persist in sending circular notices to all the relatives, whether they know of it or not—a custom which, together with men wearing weepers at funeral solemnities, is unknown in England.[1] Announcing a married lady's death under her maiden name must seem strange to English ears —as, for example, we read of the demise of Mrs Jane Dickson, spouse of Thomas Morison. Scottish cookery retains its ground, and hotch-potch, minced collops, sheep's head singed, and occasionally haggis, are still marked peculiarities of the Scottish table. These social differences linger amongst us. But stronger points are worn away; eccentricities and oddities such as existed once will not do now. One does not see why eccentricity should be more developed in one

---

[1] And yet, even as we write, weepers seem to be passing into reminiscence.

age than in another, but we cannot avoid the conclusion that the day for real oddities is no more. Professors of colleges are those in whom one least expects oddity—grave and learned characters; and yet such *have* been in former times. We can scarcely now imagine such professors as we read of in a past generation. Take the case of no less distinguished a person than Adam Smith, author of the *Wealth of Nations*, who went about the streets talking and laughing to himself in such a manner as to make the market women think he was deranged; and he told of one himself who ejaculated, as he passed, " Hech, sirs, and he is weel pat on, too ! " expressing surprise that a decided lunatic, who from his dress appeared to be a gentleman, should be permitted to walk abroad unattended. Professors still have their crotchets like other people ; but we can scarcely conceive a professor of our day coming out like Adam Smith, and making fishwives to pass such observations on his demeanour.

Peculiarities in a people's phraseology may prove more than we are aware of, and may tend to illustrate circumstances of national *history*. Thus many words which would be included by Englishmen under the general term of Scotticisms, bear directly upon the question of a past intercourse with France, and prove how close at one time must have been the influence exercised upon general habits in Scotland by that intercourse. Scoto-Gallic words were quite differently situated from French words and phrases adopted in England. With us they proceeded from a real admixture of the two *peoples*. With us they form the ordinary common language of the country, and that was from a distant period moulded by French. In England, the educated and upper classes of late years *adopted* French words and phrases. With us, some of our French derivatives are growing obsolete as vulgar, and nearly all are passing from fashionable society. In England, we find the French-adopted words rather receiving accessions than going out of use.

Examples of words such as we have referred to, as showing a French influence and admixture, are familiar to many of my readers. I recollect some of them in constant use amongst old-fashioned Scottish people, and those terms, let it be remembered, are unknown in England.

A leg of mutton was always, with old-fashioned Scotch people, a gigot (Fr. gigot).

The crystal jug or decanter in which water is placed upon the table, was a caraff (Fr. carafe).

Gooseberries were groserts, or grossarts (Fr. groseille).

Partridges were pertricks — a word much more formed upon the French perdrix than the English partridge.

The plate on which a joint or side-dish was placed upon the table was an ashet (Fr. assiette).

In the old streets of Edinburgh, where the houses are very high, and where the inhabitants all live in flats, before the introduction of soil-pipes there was no method of disposing of the foul water of the household, except by throwing it out of the window into the street. This operation, dangerous to those outside, was limited to certain hours, and the well-known cry, which preceded the missile and warned the passenger, was gardeloo! or, as Smollett writes it, gardy loo (Fr. garge de l'eau).

Anything troublesome or irksome used to be called, Scotticè, fashious (Fr. facheux, facheuse); to fash one's-self (Fr. se facher).

The small cherry, both black and red, common in

gardens, is in Scotland, never in England, termed gean (Fr. guigne), from Guigne, in Picardy.

The term *dambrod*, which has already supplied materials for a good story, arises from adopting French terms into Scottish language, as dams were the pieces with which the game of draughts was played (Fr. dammes). Brod is board.

A bedgown, or loose female upper garment, is still in many parts of Scotland termed a jupe (Fr. jupe).

In Kincardineshire the ashes of a blacksmith's furnace had the peculiar name of smiddy-coom (Fr. écume, *i.e.*, dross).

Oil, in common Scotch, used always to be ule—as the uley pot, or uley cruse (Fr. huile).

Many of my readers are no doubt familiar with the notice taken of these words by Lord Cockburn, and with the account which he gives of these Scottish words derived from the French, probably during the time of Queen Mary's minority, when French troops were quartered in Scotland. I subjoin a more full list, for which I am indebted to a correspondent, because the words still lingering amongst us are in themselves the best REMINISCENCES of former days.

Scotch.	English.		French.
Serviter	Napkin	From	Serviette.
Gigot (of mutton)	—	,,	Gigot.
Reeforts	Radishes	,,	Raiforts.
Grosserts	Gooseberries	,,	Groseilles.
Gardyveen	Case for holding wine	,,	Garde-vin.
Jupe	Part of a woman's dress	,,	Jupe.
Bonnaille	A parting glass with a friend going on a journey	,,	Bon aller.
Gysard	Person in a fancy dress	,,	Guise.
Dambrod	Draught-board	,,	Dammes.
Pantufles	Slippers.	,,	Pantoufles.
Haggis	Hashed meat	,,	Hachis.
Gou	Taste, smell	,,	Gout.
Hogue	Tainted	,,	Haut gout.
Grange	Granary	,,	Grange.

Mouter	Miller's perquisite	,,	Mouture.
Dour	Obstinate	,,	Dur.
Douce	Mild	,,	Doux.
Dorty	Sulky	,,	Dureté.
Braw	Fine	,,	Brave.
Kimmer	Gossip	,,	Commère.
Jalouse	Suspect	,,	Jalouser.
Vizzy	To aim at, to examine	,,	Viser.
Ruckle	Heap (of stones)	,,	Recueil.
Gardy-loo	(Notice well known in Edinburgh)	,,	Gardez-l'eau.
Dementit	Out of patience, deranged	,,	Dementir.
On my verity	Assertion of truth	,,	Verité.
By my certy	Assertion of truth	,,	Certes.
Aumrie	Cupboard	,,	Almoire, in old French.
Walise	Portmanteau	,,	Valise.
Sucker	Sugar	,,	Sucre.

Edinburgh Street Cry :—" Neeps like sucker. Whae'll buy neeps ? " (turnips).

Petticoat-tails	Cakes of triangular shape	*From*	Petits gatelles (gateaux).
Ashet	Meat-dish	,,	Assiette.
Fashious	Troublesome	,,	Facheux.
Prush, Madame [1]	Call to a cow to come forward.	,,	Approchez, Madame.

[1] This expression was adopted apparently in ridicule of the French applying the word " Madame " to a cow.

I dwell the more minutely on this question of Scottish words, from the conviction of their being so characteristic of Scottish humour, and being so distinctive a feature of the older Scottish race. Take away our Scottish phraseology, and we lose what is our specific distinction from England. In these expressions, too, there is often a tenderness and beauty as remarkable as the wit and humour. I have already spoken of the phrase " Auld lang syne," and of other expressions of sentiment, which may be compared in their Anglican and Scotch form.

CONCLUSION

I AM very anxious to bear in mind throughout these Reminiscences, and to keep in view the same feeling for my readers, viz., that such details regarding the changes which many living have themselves noticed as taking place in our customs and habits of society in Scotland, should always suggest the question to the thoughtful and serious mind, Are the changes which have been observed for *good*? Is the world a better world than that which we can remember? On some important points changes have been noticed in the upper classes of Scottish society, which unquestionably *are* improvements. For example, the greater attention paid to observance of Sunday, and to attendance upon public worship—the partial disappearance of profane swearing and of excess in drinking. But then the painful questions arise, Are such beneficial changes *general* through the whole body of our countrymen? May not the vices and follies of one grade of society have found a refuge in those that are of a lower class? May not new faults have taken their place where older faults have been abandoned? Of this we are quite sure—no lover of his country can fail to entertain the anxious wish, that the change we noticed in regard to drinking and swearing were universal, and that we had some evidence of its being extended through all classes of society. We ought certainly to feel grateful when we reflect that, in many instances which we have noticed, the ways and customs of society are much improved in common sense, in decency, in delicacy, and refinement. There are certain modes of life, certain expressions, eccentricity of conduct, coarseness of speech, books, and plays, which were in vogue amongst us, even fifty or sixty years ago, which would not be tolerated in society at the present time. We cannot illustrate this in a more satisfactory manner than by reference to the acknowledgment of a very interesting and charming old lady, who died so lately as 1823. In 1821, Mrs Keith of Ravelston, grandaunt of Sir Walter Scott, thus writes in returning to him the work of a female novelist which she had borrowed from him out of curiosity, and to remind her of " auld lang syne " :—" Is it not a very odd thing that I, an old woman of eighty and upwards, sitting alone, feel myself ashamed to read a book which, sixty years ago, I have heard read aloud for the amusement of large circles, consisting of the first and most creditable society in London? " There can be no doubt that at the time referred to by Mrs Keith, Tristram Shandy,[1] Tom Jones, Humphrey Clinker, etc., were on the drawing-room tables of ladies whose grandmothers or great-grandchildren never saw them, or would not acknowledge it if they *had* seen them. But authors not inferior to Sterne, Fielding, or Smollett, are now popular, who, with Charles Dickens, can describe scenes of human life with as much force and humour, and yet in whose pages nothing will be found which need offend the taste of the most refined, or shock the feelings of the most pure. This is a change where there is also great improvement. It indicates not merely a better moral

---

[1] Sterne, in one of his letters, describes his reading *Tristram Shandy* to his wife and daughter—his daughter copying from his dictation, and Mrs Sterne sitting by and listening whilst she worked. In the life of Sterne, it is recorded that he used to carry about in his pocket a volume of this same work, and read it aloud when he went into company. Admirable reading for the church dignitary, the prebendary of York! How well adapted to the hours of social intercourse with friends! How fitted for domestic seclusion with his family!

perception in authors themselves, but it is itself a homage to the improved spirit of the age. We will hope that, with an improved exterior, there is improvement in society *within*. If the feelings shrink from what is coarse in expression, we may hope that vice has, in some sort, lost attraction. At any rate, from what we discern around us we hope favourably for the general improvement of mankind, and of our own beloved country in particular. If Scotland, in parting with her rich and racy dialect, her odd and eccentric characters, is to lose something in quaint humour and good stories, we will hope she may grow and strengthen in *better* things—good as those are which she loses. However this may be, I feel quite assured that the examples which I have now given, of Scottish expressions, Scottish modes and habits of life, and Scottish anecdotes, which belong in a great measure to the past, and yet which are remembered as having a place in the present century, must carry conviction that great changes have taken place in the Scottish social circle. There were some things belonging to our country which we must all have desired should be changed. There were others which we could only see changed with regret and sorrow. The hardy and simple habits of Scotsmen of many past generations; their industry, economy, and integrity, which made them take so high a place in the estimation and the confidence of the people amongst whom they dwelt in all countries of the world; the intelligence and superior education of her mechanics and her peasantry, combined with a strict moral and religious demeanour, fully justified the praise of Burns when he described the humble though sublime piety of the " Cottar's Saturday Night," and we can well appreciate the testimony which he bore to the hallowed power and sacred influences of

the devotional exercises of his boyhood's home, when
he penned the immortal words :—

" From scenes like these old Scotia's grandeur springs,
That makes her loved at home, revered abroad."

On comparing Scotland past with Scotland present,
we cannot evade the question : Are " scenes like these "
—devotional domestic scenes like these—become less
frequent than they were ? Do they still hold their
place by the cottar's fireside, or are they becoming
only a reminiscence of what was *once* a national distinction ? Whatever be our religious opinions, or
whatever be our views on questions of ecclesiastical
polity and church order, no Scotsman who desires
the happiness and honour of his country could avoid
a deep regret at the very idea of Burns' " Cottar's
Saturday Night " having become a thing of the past ;
and yet we must not shrink from inquiry into the true
state of the case. I have asked the opinions of friends
both of the Established and the Free Church, who have
met my inquiries in a fair and candid spirit, and, from
the answers I have received, have come to something
like the following conclusion :—I believe such scenes
as Burns' " Cottar's Saturday Night " are still to be
met with in all their freshness and all their fervour in
the dwellings of a good religious peasantry ; but in
some places the cottar population *itself* has undergone
a great change. Two causes have combined to produce
this effect :—An extensive system of emigration has
thinned the older families of the soil, whilst the practice of bringing in mere labourers in many districts has
made the old family domestic firesides less numerous.
Then, alas ! alas ! we fear cottar MORALITY has not
been such as to keep up the practice. Reports made
to both the General Assemblies of 1871 on this ques-

343

tion were far from being satisfactory. Dr Begg, too, in his striking and able pamphlet on the " Ecclesiastical and Social Evils of Scotland," refers to " symptoms of a nation's degeneracy which seem multiplying in Scotland " ; also to a " growing amount of heathenism and drunkenness."

With such representations before us regarding a decline of domestic morality, we cannot expect to see much increase of domestic piety. Burns, after he had become lowered in moral feelings by those licentious habits and scenes into which he unfortunately fell after he had left his father's house, was not hypocrite enough to profess the same love and interest for the scenes of his innocent and early days. The country clergy of Scotland have their many difficulties against which they are to contend ; and many obstacles which they have to meet. But let not the domestic piety of the lowest cottages of the land be lost sight of. The results of such worship are so blessed upon the inmates, that the practice should everywhere be urged upon their flocks by the clergy, and encouraged by all means in their power ; and in that view it would, I think, be desirable to circulate short forms of prayer for family use. Many such have lately been published ; and, whatever difference of opinion may be entertained as to the comparative merits of extempore or liturgical prayer for the public worship of the church, there can be no question that in many instances a form must be very useful, and often essential at the commencement, at least, of cottage worship. I have known cases where it has been declined on the plea of inability to conduct the service.

There are numerous indications that, *on the whole*, a regard for religion and religious ordinances is not losing ground in Scotland. The great number of

churches—and of handsome churches—that are springing up, indicate, by their attendance, how much hold
the subject has upon the people. The ample funds
raised for charitable and for missionary objects give
good testimony in the cause; and, in regard to the
immediate question before us, one favourable result
may be reported on this subject—the practice and
feelings of domestic piety and family worship have,
at any rate, extended in Scotland in an *upward* direction of its social life. Beyond all doubt, we may say
family worship is more frequent, as a general practice,
in houses of the rich, and also in the houses of farmers
and of superior operatives, than it was some years ago.
The Montrose anecdote about family prayers, told at
page 64, could hardly have place now, and indeed
many persons could not understand the point.

I hope I am not blinded to the defects of my own
countrymen, nor am I determined to resist evidence
of any deterioration which may be proved. But I
feel confident that Scotland still stands pre-eminent
amongst the nations for moral and religious qualities.
The nucleus of her character will bear comparison
with any. We will cherish hope for the mental tone
of our countrymen being still in the ascendant, and
still imbued with those qualities that make a moral
and religious people. We have reason to know that
in many departments of business, Scottish intelligence,
Scottish character, and Scottish services are still
decidedly at a premium in the market.

But now, before concluding, I am desirous of recording some Reminiscences upon a phase of Scottish
RELIGIOUS history which involves very important
consequences, and which I would not attempt to dis-
cuss without serious consideration. Indeed I have
sometimes shrunk from the discussion at all, as lead-

ing to questions of so delicate a nature, and as involving matters on which there are so many differences of opinion. I refer to the state of our divisions and alienations of spirit *on account* of religion.

The great Disruption, which nearly equally divided the National Church, and which took place in 1843, is now become a matter of *reminiscence*. Of those nearly connected with that movement, some were relatives of my own, and many were friends. Unlike similar religious revolutions, that which caused the Free Church of Scotland did not turn upon any difference of opinion on matters either of doctrine or of ecclesiastical polity. It arose entirely from differences regarding the relation subsisting between the Church and the State, by which the Church was established and endowed. The great evil of all such divisions, and the real cause for regret, lie in the injury they inflict on the cause of Christian unity and Christian love, and the separation they too often make between those who ought to be united in spirit, and who hitherto have been not infrequently actually joined for years as companions and friends. The tone which is adopted by publications, which are the organs of various party opinions amongst us, show how keenly disputants, once excited, will deal with each other. The differences consequent upon the Disruption in the Scottish Church called forth great bitterness of spirit and much mutual recrimination at the time. But it seems to me that there are indications of a better spirit, and that there is more tolerance and more forbearance on religious differences amongst Scottish people generally. I cannot help thinking, however, that at no period of our ecclesiastical annals was such language made use of, and even against those of the highest place and authority in the Church, as we have lately met with in the organs of the extreme Anglican Church party. It is much to be regretted that earnest and zealous men should have adopted such a style of discussing religious differences. I cannot help thinking it is injurious to Christian feelings of love and Christian kindness. It is really sometimes quite appalling. From the same quarter I must expect myself severe handling for some of these pages, should they fall into their way. We cannot but lament, however, when we find such language used towards each other by those who are believers in a common Bible, and who are followers and disciples of the same lowly Saviour, and indeed frequently members of the same Church. Bigotry and intolerance are not confined to one side or another. They break out often where least expected. Differences, no doubt, will always exist on many contested subjects, but I would earnestly pray that all SUCH differences, amongst ourselves at least, as those which injure the forbearance and gentleness of the Christian character, should become " Scottish Reminiscences," whether they are called forth by the opposition subsisting between Presbyterianism and Episcopacy, or whether they arise amongst Presbyterians or amongst Episcopalians themselves.

To my apprehension Scotland has recently seen a most painful indication of the absence of that charity which, according to St Paul, should " never fail " amongst a Christian people. The act of two English Prelates officiating in one of the Established churches has called forth a storm of indignation as loud and vehement as if in a heathen land they had fallen down before the image of a heathen deity, and worshipped in a heathen temple. Then the explanation which has been given by apologists for these services is not the least remarkable feature of the transaction. These ministrations have been called " Mission Services," and, in so far as I enter into the meaning of the phrase, I would solemnly and seriously protest against its being made use of in such a case. " *Mission Service* " can only be applied to the case of a missionary raising his voice " *in partibus infidelium*," or, to say the least of it, in a land where no Christian church was already planted. When I think of the piety, the Christian worth, and high character of so many friends in the Established and other Presbyterian churches in Scotland, I would again repeat my solemn protestation against such religious intolerance, and again declare my conviction, that Englishmen and Scotsmen, so far from looking out for points of difference and grounds for separation on account of the principles on which their Churches are established, should endeavour to make the bonds of religious union as *close* as possible. I can scarcely express the gratification I felt on learning from the *Scotsman*, November 20, that such were the sentiments called forth by this event in the mind of one of the ablest and most distinguished Prelates of our day. In reference to the Glengarry services, the Bishop of St Andrews (Wordsworth) has declared his opinion, that the " subsequent explanations of those services seemed to mar the good work by introducing questions of etiquette, where nothing should have been thought of but the simple performance of Christian duty by Christian ministers for the benefit of Christian people." [1]

Such is the judgment expressed by the honoured and learned Bishop of St Andrews, whose noble and patriotic exertions to draw the Episcopalians and the Presbyterians of Scotland closer together in bonds of religious feelings and religious worship have been

[1] *Scottish Guardian*, vol. ii., No. ix., p. 305.

spoken of in such terms, and such words have been applied to his labours in that cause, and to the administration generally of his own diocese, by one of the very high English Church papers, as have been to me a cause of deep sorrow and poignant regret.

As a Scotsman by descent from Presbyterians of high moral and religious character, and as an Episcopalian by conscientious preference, I would fain see more of harmony and of confidence between all Scotsmen, not only as fellow-countrymen, but as fellow-Christians. When I first joined the Episcopal Church the Edinburgh Episcopal clergy were on most friendly terms with the leading clergy of the Established Church. Every consideration was shown to them by such men as Bishop Sandford, Dr Morehead, Rev. Archibald Alison, Rev. Mr Shannon, and others. There was always service in the Episcopal chapels on the National Church communion fast-days. No opposition or dislike to Episcopalian clergymen occupying Presbyterian pulpits was ever avowed as a great principle. Charles Simeon of Cambridge, and others of the Churches of England and Ireland, frequently so officiated, and it was considered as natural and suitable. The learning and high qualities of the Church of England's hierarchy, were, with few exceptions, held in profound respect. Indeed, during the last hundred years, and since the days when Episcopacy was attacked under the term of " black prelacy," I can truly say, the Episcopal order has received far more severe handling in Episcopal England than it has received in Presbyterian Scotland. I must think, that in the case of two churches where the grounds of *resemblance* are on points of spiritual importance affecting great truths and doctrines of salvation, and where the points of *difference* affect questions more of government and external order than of salvation, there ought to be on both parts the desire at least to draw as closely as they can the bonds of Christian charity and mutual confidence.

I believe it to be very painful to Scotsmen generally, whether of the Established or the Episcopal Church, that the Presbyterian Church of Scotland should be spoken of in such terms as have lately been made use of. Scotsmen feel towards it as to the Church of the country established by law, just as the Anglican Church is established in England. They feel towards it as the Church whose ministrations are attended by our gracious Sovereign when she resides in the northern portion of her dominions, and in which public thanksgiving was offered to God in the royal presence for her Majesty's recovery. But more important still, they feel towards it as a church of which the members are behind no other communion in the tone and standard of their moral principle and integrity of conduct. They feel towards it as a church which has nobly retained her adherence to the principles of the Reformation, and which has been spared the humiliation of exhibiting any of her clergy nominally members of a reformed church, and, at the same time, virtually and at heart adherents to the opinions and practices of the Church of Rome. English people, in speaking of the Established Church of Scotland, seem to forget how much Episcopalians are mixed up with their Presbyterian fellow-countrymen in promoting common charitable and religious objects. For example, take my own experience: the administration of a very valuable charitable institution called the Paterson and Pape Fund, is vested jointly in the incumbent of St John's, Edinburgh (Episcopalian), and the two clergymen of St Cuthbert's (Established) Church. Even in matters affecting the interests of our own Church we may find ourselves closely connected. Take the administration of the late Miss Walker's will, and the carrying out her munificent bequest to our Church, of which I am a trustee. Of the nine trustees, two are Episcopalians residing in Scotland, one an Episcopalian residing in England, and six are Presbyterians residing in Scotland. The primary object of Miss Walker's settlement is to build and endow, for divine service, a cathedral church in Edinburgh; the edifice to cost not less than £40,000. The income arising from the remainder of her property is to be expended for the benefit of the Scottish Episcopal Church generally. A meeting of trustees was held, November 25, 1871, and one of the first steps unanimously agreed upon was to appoint the Bishop-Coadjutor of Edinburgh, who is a trustee, to be chairman of the meeting. There is no doubt or question of mutual good feeling in the work, and that our Church feels full and entire confidence in the fair, honourable, candid, and courteous conduct of the trustees to whom in this case will be committed weighty matters connected with her interests.

At one of the congresses of the English Church it has been said, and well said, by Mr B. Hope, that he and his friends of the High Church party would join as closely as they could with the members of the Romish Church who have taken common cause with Dr Dollinger, "looking more to points where they agree, and not to points where they differ." Why should not the same rule be adopted towards brethern who differ from ourselves so little on points that are vital and eternal? The principle which I would apply to the circumstances, I think, may be thus stated: I would join with fellow-Christians in any good works or offices, either of charity or religion, where I could do so without compromise of my own principles. On such ground I do not see why we should not realise the idea already suggested, viz., that of having an interchange between our pulpits and the pulpits of the Established and other Presbyterian or Independent Churches. Such ministerial interchange need not affect the question of *orders*, nor need it, in fact, touch many other questions on which differences are concerned.

Of course this should be arranged under due regulation, and with full precaution taken that the questions discussed shall be confined to points where there is agreement, and that points of difference should be left quite in abeyance. Why should we, under proper arrangements, fail to realise so graceful an exercise of Christian charity? Why should we lose the many benefits favourable to the advancement of Christian unity amongst us? An opportunity for practically putting this idea into a tangible form has occurred from the circumstance of the new chapel in the University of Glasgow being opened for service, to be conducted by clergymen of various churches. I gladly avail myself of the opportunity of testifying my grateful acknowledgments for the courteous and generous conduct of Dr Caird, in his efforts to put forward members of our Church to conduct the services of the College chapel, and also of expressing my admiration of the power and beauty of his remarks on Christian unity and on brotherly love.[1]

This is with me no new idea; no crude experiment proposed for the occasion. I have before me a paper which I wrote some years since, and which I had put

---

[1] "What is Religion?" a sermon by Rev. John Caird, D.D., Professor of Divinity in the University of Glasgow, and one of Her Majesty's Chaplains for Scotland. See especially concluding remarks.

into the shape of " An Address to the Bishops," to sanction such exchange of pulpits, hoping to get some of my clerical brethern to join in the object of the address. I feel assured much good would, under God, be the result of such spiritual union. If congregations would only unite in exchange of such friendly offices of religious instruction with each other, how often would persons, now strangers, become better acquainted! I wish the experiment could be tried, were it only to show how prejudices would be removed; how misunderstandings would be cleared away; how many better and kinder feelings would grow out of the closer union on religious questions! Nay, I would go further, and express my full conviction, that my own Church would *gain* rather than lose in her interests under such a system. Men would be more disposed to listen with attention, and examine with candour the arguments we make use of in favour of our Church views. We should gain more of the sympathy of our countrymen who differ from us, by a calm expostulation than by bitter invective. Beautifully and wisely was it written by a sacred pen nearly three thousand years ago, " A soft answer turneth away wrath."

I have such confidence in the excellence of my own Church, that I believe to bring persons into closer and kinder connection with our system would be the more likely way to gain their approval and their favourable judgment. In nothing do we lose more of the confidence and estimation of our fellow-countrymen than in the feeling of our being intolerant and exclusive in our religious opinions. It is curious people should not see that the arguments addressed in a friendly spirit must tell more powerfully than the arguments of one who shows his hostile feeling.

With these feelings on the subject, it may be easily

understood with what pleasure I read, in the *Edinburgh Courant* of November 10, a report of what our Primus (Bishop Eden) said, at the entertainment which was given on the occasion of the consecration of St Mary's Church, Glasgow. In speaking on the question of Union, the Primus said :—

"I think I may speak for my Episcopal brethren, when I say that if the heads, especially of the Established Church of Scotland—for that is the body that has most power and influence—if a proposal were made by the leading men in that Church, in concurrence with those who hold views similar to themselves—a conference of the representative men of the different Churches—to consider in a Christian spirit what our differences are, and what are the points on which we are agreed, we would be most happy to take part in it. Such a conference might, in the providence of God, lead to our being drawn nearer to each other. I believe that then the prayer which the Bishop of St Andrews offered up would be the earlier accomplished, namely, that the Episcopal Churches might become Reformed, and the Reformed Churches become Episcopal. If any proposal of this kind could be made, I believe we would be most ready to accept any invitation to consider whether the various Churches might not be drawn nearer to each other." (Great applause.)

The Coadjutor Bishop of Edinburgh in his address, after briefly referring to some proposals that had been made for union among the churches in South Africa, went on to say :—

"I do say, as one of the Bishops of the Scottish Episcopal Church now, and in reference to what fell from the Primus, that I most heartily concur in what he said, and I cannot but feel that, without the slightest breach of the great fundamental principles of the Church of Christ, there are many points on which we may be at one with Christians who are not part of our organic body.

" I believe the proposal made by the Primus would have the effect of drawing them nearer to us, and be a step forward to that consummation which we all desire, and which our blessed Lord prayed—with his last breath—' That we may all be one.' " (Great applause.)

That two honoured Fathers of our Church, our Primus and my own Bishop, should have made use of such terms, and that their views should have been received by *such* an audience with so much applause, I could have offered a grateful acknowledgment upon my knees.

But after all, perhaps, it may be said this is an utopian idea, which, in the present state of religious feelings and ecclesiastical differences, never can be realised. It were a sufficient answer to the charge of *utopianism* brought against such a proposal, to plead that it was no more than what was sanctioned by the teaching of God's word. In this case it does not seem to go beyond the requirements of holy Scripture as set forth in St Paul's description of charity, and in other passages which clearly enjoin Christians to act towards each other in love, and to cultivate, so far as they can, a spirit of mutual forbearance and of joint action in the sacred cause of preaching the truth as it is in Jesus. I cannot believe that, were St Paul on earth, he would sanction the present state of jealous separation amongst Christians. Take such separation in connection with the beautiful sentiment, which we read in Phil. i., 18 :—" What then ? notwithstanding every way, whether in pretence, or in truth, Christ is preached; and I therein do rejoice, yea, and will rejoice."

The determination to exclude preaching that is not strictly according to our own forms seems to me quite inconsistent with the general teaching of Scripture, more particularly with this apostolic declaration. But I would bring this question to a practical issue, and we shall find enough in our own experience to confirm the view I have taken, and to sanction the arrangement I propose. To bring forward co-operation in the great and vitally important work of preaching God's word, which has been already effected between persons holding on some points opinions different from each other, take first the case of revision of the English translation of the Old and New Testament Scriptures, as it has been resolved upon by the authorities of the great Anglican Communion. They have had no difficulty in finding Nonconformist scholars and divines whose fitness to be associated with Anglican Churchmen in the great work of arranging and correcting an authorised version has been admitted by all. Thus we have Nonconformists and English and Scottish Episcopalians united in adjusting the terms of the sacred text — the text from which all preaching in the English tongue shall in future derive its authority, and by which all its teaching shall in future be guided and directed. There is *already*, however, a closer and a more practical blending of minds on great religious questions much differing from each other on lesser points. In the field of religious and devotional literature, many of our church differences are lost sight of. Episcopalian congregations are constantly in the habit of joining with much cordiality and earnestness in singing hymns composed by authors, nonconformists with our Church—in fact, of adopting them into their church service. These compositions form a portion of their worship, and are employed to illustrate and enforce their own most earnest doctrinal views and opinions themselves. How entirely are such compositions as the sacramental hymn, " My God, and is Thy table spread," by Doddridge; the hymn, "When I behold the wondrous cross," by Isaac Watts, associated with our Church services! Nor are such feelings of adoption confined to poetical compositions. How many prose productions by non-Episcopalian authors might be introduced for the delight and benefit of Christian congregations! How eagerly many such compositions are read by members of our Church! With what delight would many discourses of this class have been listened to had they been delivered to Episcopalian congregations! Where such hymns and such discourses are admissible, the *authors* of them might take a part in conducting psalmody and in occupying the pulpit for preaching to a congregation. If the spirits of such writers as Doddridge, Watts, and Hall, have been felt to permeate and to influence the hearts of others who have heard or read their words of holiness and peace, we may well suppose that God would sanction their making like impressions, in his own house, upon the hearts of those whom they meet there face to face. Might they not communicate personally what they communicate through the press? For example, why should not Robert Hall have preached his sermons on Infidelity and on the Death of the Princess of Wales, perhaps the two most magnificent discourses in the language, in an English Cathedral? Why should not the beautiful astronomical discourses of Thomas Chalmers have been delivered in St Paul's or in St John's, Edinburgh? For many years, in want of better materials, the sermons of Dr Blair were more used in the Church of England, and more read in private, than any similar compositions. It has been for years a growing persuasion in my own mind that principles of Christian love and mutual harmony are too often sacrificed to the desire of pre-

357

serving the exact and formal marks of church order, as the Bishop of St Andrews so happily expressed it to preserve *etiquette*. Surely the great law of Christian love would suggest and enforce a union at least of spirit amongst Christian believers, who cannot join in the unity of the same organisation. Inability to join in the same form of church polity and church order need not shut the door to religious sympathies and religious communion, where there are so many points of agreement and of mutual interest. The experience of the past will tend to produce the conviction that there has too often been in our religious disputes a strong tendency in all Christian denominations to make the great principle of love, which is a principle to rule in Heaven and for eternity, actually subservient and subordinate to a system of ecclesiastical order, which, important as it is for its own purposes and objects, never can be more than a guide to the ministration of the Church on earth, and an organisation which must be in its nature confined to time.

Wherever or whenever this feeling may be called forth, it is a grievous error—it is a very serious subject for our reflection, how far such want of sympathy and of union with those who do not belong immediately to our own church, must generate a feeling hostile to a due reception of an important article of our faith, termed in the Apostles' Creed the COMMUNION OF SAINTS. According to the description given by the judicious and learned Bishop Pearson, this communion or spiritual union belongs to all who are in New Testament language denominated SAINTS; by which he means all who, having been baptized in the faith, have this name by being called and baptized. Then he states all Christian believers to have communion and fellowship with these, whether living or dead. We should feel towards such persons (evidently, as the good Bishop implies, without reference to any particular church order) all sympathy and kindness as members of the same great spiritual family on earth, expectants of meeting in heaven in the presence of God and of the Lamb, and of joining in the worship of saints and angels round the throne. I have no hesitation in declaring my full conviction that such expectations of future communion should supply a very powerful and sacred motive for our cultivating all spiritual union in our power with all fellow-Christians, all for whom Christ died. It becomes a very serious subject for examination of our own hearts, how, by *refusing* any spiritual intercourse with Christians who are not strictly members of our own Church, we may contravene this noble doctrine of the Communion of Saints; for does not the bitterness with which sometimes we find all union with certain fellow-Christians in the Church on earth chill or check the feeling of a desire for union with the same in the Church above? Nay, is there not matter for men's earnest thought, how far the violent animosity displayed against the smallest approach to anything like spiritual communion with all Christians of a different Church from their own may chill the DESIRE itself for " meeting in the Church above? " Can hatred to meeting on earth be in any sense a right preliminary or preparation for desire to meet in Heaven? Nay, more, should we not carefully guard lest the bitter displays we see of religious hostility may even tend to bring men's minds towards a *disinclination* to meet in Heaven, of which the most terrible condition was thus expressed by Southey:—" Earth could not hold us both, nor can one heaven." [1]

[1] See Southey's *Roderick*, book xxi.

One mark of any particular Church being a portion of Christ's Church on earth seems to be overlooked by some of our English friends, and that is a mark pointed out by our Lord himself when he said, " By their FRUITS ye shall know them." By this announcement I would understand that besides and beyond a profession of the great articles of the Christian faith, I would, as a further criterion of a Christian church, inquire if there were many of its members who have been distinguished for their Christian piety, Christian learning, and Christian benevolence. Is all external communion to be interdicted with a church which has produced such men as we might name amongst the children of our Established and other Churches in Scotland? Look back upon half-a-century, and ask if a similar act with that of the Archbishop of York and Bishop of Winchester would then have created a like feeling. I can remember well the interest and admiration called forth by the eloquence, the philanthropy, and the moral fervour of Dr Chalmers, amongst the High Church school of the day too— the good Archbishop Howley, Bishop Blomfield, Rev. Mr Norris of Hackney, Mr Joshua Watson, etc. I remember, too, the perfect ovation he received in the attendance of Archbishops, Bishops, Clergy, Peers, Princes, etc., of the great London world, at his lectures on Establishments. We can hardly imagine any one saying then, " This is all very well, but the Church that produced this man is no part of the true Church of Christ, and no English prelate or clergyman could possibly take service in it."

No one, I believe, who is acquainted with my own views and opinions on religious subjects would say that I look with indifference on those points wherein we differ from the great body of our fellow-countrymen. I am confident that I should not gain in the estimation of Presbyterians themselves by showing a cold indifference, or a lukewarm attachment, to the principles and practice of my own Church. They would see that my own convictions in favour of Episcopal government in the Church, and of liturgical services in her worship, were quite compatible with the fullest exercise of candour and forbearance towards the opinions of others—I mean on questions not essential to salvation.

I believe that there are persons amongst us coming round to this opinion, and who are ready to believe that it is quite possible for Christians to exercise very friendly mutual relations in spiritual matters which constitute the essential articles of a common faith, whilst they are in practice separated on points of ecclesiastical order and of church government. I am old, and shall not see it; but I venture to hope that, under the Divine blessing, the day will come when to Scotsmen it will be a matter of reminiscence that Episcopalians, or that Presbyterians of any denomination, should set the interests of their own communion above the exercise of that charity that for a brother's faith "hopeth all things and believeth all things." Zeal in promoting our own Church views, and a determination to advance her interests and efficiency, need be no impediment to cultivating the most friendly feelings towards those who agree with us in matters which are essential to salvation, and who, in their differences from us, are, I am bound to believe, as conscientious as myself. Such days will come.

But now, to close my remarks on national peculiarities, with what I may term a *practical* and *personal* application. We have in our later pages adopted a more solemn and serious view of past reminiscences

as they bear upon questions connected with a profession of religion. It is quite suitable then to recall
the fact which applies individually to all our readers.
We shall ourselves each of us one day become subject
to a " reminiscence " of others. Indeed, the whole
question at issue throughout the work takes for
granted what we must all have observed to be a very
favourite object with survivors, viz., that the characters of various persons, as they pass away, will be
always spoken of, and freely discussed, by those who
survive them. We recall the eccentric, and we are
amused with a remembrance of their eccentricities. We
admire the wise and dignified of the past. There are
some who are recollected only to be detested for their
vices—some to be pitied for their weaknesses and
follies—some to be scorned for mean and selfish conduct. But there are others whose memory is embalmed
in tears of grateful recollection. There are those whose
generosity and whose kindness, whose winning
sympathy and noble disinterested virtues are never
thought upon or ever spoken of without calling forth
a blessing. Might it not, therefore, be good for us
often to ask ourselves how *we* are likely to be spoken
of when the grave has closed upon the intercourse
between us and the friends whom we leave behind?
The thought might, at any rate, be useful as an additional motive for kind and generous conduct to each
other. And then the inquiry would come home to
each one in some such form as this : " Within the
circle of my family and friends—within the hearts of
those who have known me, and were connected with
me in various social relations—what will be the
estimate formed of me when I am gone? What will
be the spontaneous impression produced by looking
back on bygone intercourses in life. Will past thought

of me furnish the memory of those who survive me with recollections that will be fond and pleasing?" In one word, let each one ask himself (I speak to countrymen and countrywomen), "Will *my* name be associated with gentle and happy 'REMINISCENCES OF SCOTTISH LIFE AND CHARACTER?'"

THE END

OF

THE SCOTTISH CLASSICS EDITION

OF

REMINISCENCES OF

SCOTTISH LIFE AND CHARACTER

BY

DEAN RAMSAY

INDEX

'Aaple,' bottle of beer strong o', 242.

Abercairney, Laird of, prevented from *going out* in '15, 319.

Aberdeen dialect, perfect specimens of, 204, 207.

Aberdeen elders, opinion of, 20.

Aberdeen provost, wife of, at the opera, 206.

Aberdeen, two ladies of, mutual recrimination, 206.

'A bonnie bride's sune buskit,' 220.

Accommodation, grand, for snuff, 20

'Acts o' Parliament lose their breath before they get to Aberdeenshire,' 20.

Adam, Dr., Latin translation of Scottish expressions, 167.

Advice to a minister in talking to a ploughman, 260.

'A gravesteen wad gie guid bree gin ye gied it plenty o' butter,' 259.

'A hantle o' miscellawneous eating about a pig,' 88.

Alexander, Dr W. Lindsay, 131.

'And what the devil is it to you whether I have a liver or not?' 9.

Anecdotes of quaint Scottish character, 307.

Angel-worship is not allowed in the Church of Scotland, 80.

Angler and the horse-fly, 319.

'Anither gude Sunday! I dinna ken whan I'll get thae drawers redd up,' 67.

'Anither het day, Cornal,' 173.

'An inch at the tap is worth twa at the boddam,' 114.

'An I hadna been an idiot I micht hae been sleepin' too,' 275.

Annals of the parish, extracts from, 47, 236.

Answer to stranger asking the way, 238.

Answers, dry, specimens of, 237.

'A peer o' anither tree,' 140.

Appetite, farmer's reason for minister's good appetite, 256.

Asher, minister of Inveraven, anecdote of, 272.

Athole, Duke of, and Cultoquhey, 233.

Athole, Duke of, answer of his cottar, 252.

Auction, anecdote of spoon missing, 182.

Auld lang syne, beauty of the expression, 166.

Auld, Rev. Dr, of Ayr, and Rab Hamilton, 273.

Authors, older ones indecent, 341.

'Ay, ir ye a' up an' awa?' 62.

'Ay, she may prosper, for she has baith the prayers of the good and of the bad,' 163.

Baby, a laddie or a lassie, 129.

Baird, Mrs, of Newbyth, remark of, as to her son in India, 178.

Balnamoon, laird of, carriage to *haud in*, 247.

Balnamoon, laird of, great drinker, 246.

Balnamoon, laird of, joke with his servant, 266.

Balnamoon, laird of, refuses his wig, 246.

Balnamoon, praying and drinking at, 247.

Banes, distinction of, by a beggar, 253.

Banes, Frasers weel-baned, 300.

Bannockburn, guide to, refusing an Englishman's five shillings, 268.

Bannockburn, Scottish remark upon, 267.

Baptism, minister and member of his flock, 73.

Barclay of Ury, M.P., walk to London, 146.

Bathgate, mending the ways of, 292.

Beadle, equivocal compliment to minister's sermons, 325.

Beadle or Betheral, character of, 293.

Beast, a stumbling, at least honest, 262.

'Becky and I had a rippit, for which I desire to be humble,' 303.